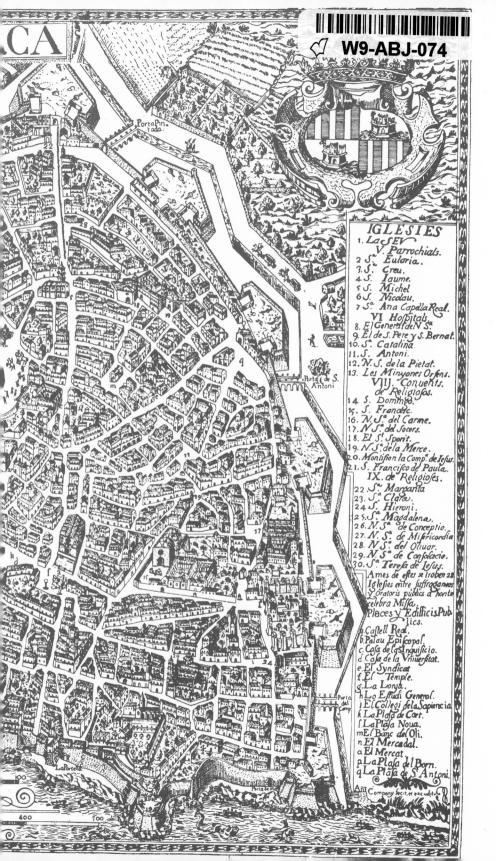

CA

IGLESIES
1. La SEV
   V. Parrochials.
2 S. Eularia.
3. S. Creu.
4 S. Iaume.
5 S. Michel
6 J. Nicolau.
7 Sa Ana Capella Real.
   VI Hospitals
8. El General de Nª Sª
9. El de S. Pere y S. Bernat.
10. S. Catalina
11. S. Antoni
12. N. S. de la Pietat.
13. Les Minyones Orfens.
   VIIJ. Conuents.
   de Religiosos.
14. S. Domingo.
15. S. Francesc.
16. N. Sª del Carme.
17. N Sª del Socors.
18. El Sª Sperit.
19. N. Sª de la Merce.
20. Montsion la Comp. de Iesus.
21. S. Francisco de Paula.
   IX. de Religioses.
22. Sª Margarita
23. Sª Clara.
24. S. Hieroni.
25. Sª Magdalena.
26. N. Sª de Conceptio.
27. N. Sª de Misericordia
28. N. Sª del Oliuar.
29. N. Sª de Consolacio.
30. Sª Teresa de Iesus.
   Ames de estes se troben 28
   Iglesies entre suffraganeas
   y Oratoris publics a hont
   se celebra Missa.
   Places y Edificis Pub-
   lics.
a. Castell Real.
b Palau Episcopal.
c. Casa de la Inquisicio.
d. Casa de la Vniuersitat.
e. El Syndicat
f El Temple.
g. La Lonja.
h. Lo Estudi General.
i. El Collegi de la Sapiencia
k La Plasa de Cort.
l La Plasa Noua.
m El Banc del Oli.
n El Mercadal.
o El Mercat.
p La Plasa del Born.
q La Plasa de S. Antoni.

Company fecit, et exc udit.

*Those of the Street*

# Those Of
# The Street

## The Catholic-Jews of Mallorca

### KENNETH MOORE

A STUDY IN URBAN CULTURAL CHANGE

**UNIVERSITY OF NOTRE DAME PRESS**
**Notre Dame** **London**

Endsheets: A map of seventeenth-century Palma
Frontispiece: Calle de Platería—Street of the Silver Shops—Palma

**Library of Congress Cataloging in Publication Data**

Moore, Kenneth, 1930–
　Those of the street.

　Bibliography: p.
　1. Chuetas. 2. Majorca—Social conditions.
I. Title.
DS135.S75M35　　　946'.75'004924　　　76-636
ISBN 0-268—01830-8

Manufactured in the United States of America

# Contents

# Acknowledgments

In some crafts an individual working alone and unaided can be productive. Anthropology is not one of them. As is evident in the reading, this book comes largely from Mallorcans who guided me through their society and confided in me their reflections on it. Among them there were a few with whom I shared the serious problems of research, and they were in effect fellow ethnographers. Bartomeu Barcelo Pons, a fellow social scientist, was helpful beyond words. Cristóbal Serra, novelist, mystic and critic, gave me a glimpse of Mallorca's soul. Antonio Aguiló Taronji tested my hypotheses against his extraordinary understanding of his own society. For help, guidance and insight I owe much thanks to José Homar Bauza, Luis Alemany Vich, Cayetano Martí Valls, Antonio Pons, Juan Crespi Pons, Juan Zúñiga, Stanley and Elaine Amdurer, Juan Miró Miró, Betty Mack, Princess Dilkusha de Rohan, Juan Carlos Martorell, and finally I could not forget the many booksellers, librarians and bibliophiles who were helpful throughout. I am especially thankful to have known and talked with Miguel Forteza before his death.

In Israel I owe thanks to many kind families in the housing projects of Haifa and Tel Aviv who welcomed me into their homes. I am grateful to Umsal Saarilan of Istanbul for showing me Israel from the perspective of a circus aerialist. My thanks also to the Turkish Consulate and to Dr. Israel Ben Zeev in Jerusalem for kindness, hospitality and truthfulness.

Over the long haul I am indebted to some very special scientists and educators, in particular the late Julian Steward, Milton Rokeach, Edward Bruner, Joseph Casagrande, Gregory Stone, Oscar Lewis, Raymond Scheele, David Eyde, Mary Pearson, David Plath, the late Frederic Reeve, George Hicks, Niels Braroe and Norris Lang. Colleagues at Notre Dame with whom I've discussed one or another part of this book include William D'Antonio, Arthur Rubel, Irwin Press, Carl O'Nell, Leo Despres, Fabio DaSilva, Andy Weigert, William Liu, Edward Fink and Tom Sasaki. I particularly want to thank Julian Samora for encouraging me to select the Notre Dame Press over others, a decision I have many times reaffirmed in working with Jim Langford, Emily Schossberger and Theresa Silio. For editorial assistance and guidance in style I am appreciative to Dr. Richard Faber of New Orleans. For extensive criticism I thank Dr. Edward Hansen of Queens College CUNY. For suggestions and photos, my thanks to Paul Mann, a Boston editor. For field work assistance in the early stages I recall with pleasure my association with Bruce and Cindy Blair of Yale University.

For providing me with a peaceful place to write while away from South Bend, my thanks to Elena Perone and Marlene Fernandez of the Division of Life Sciences at Niagara Community College. Also, in Key West, special thanks to Jack Leonard, Frank Fontes, Tennessee Williams and Mary Louise and Ray Manning in whose pads I did much of this work.

For financial support in this research, I am grateful to the National Institute of Mental Health, the University of Illinois and the University of Notre Dame. For moral support I recall with pleasure Patricia Davies, John C. Leonard, Barton Wimble, Muriel Rokeach, David Lane, May and Bernie Goodstein, Ruth Campbell, Bill Johnson, John Frells, Tom Smith, Karin Rasmussen, Sig Kempler, Gil Hansen, the late Phylles Howard Rubel and of course my parents, Gordon Moore and Marie Sinclair Moore.

For secretarial assistance I thank Shirley Schneck, Jean Motsinger, Carmella Rulli and the faculty steno pool at Notre Dame.

I save a final and special thanks to a pair who have helped me from beginning to end. They are Stefan Taussig and Edith Goldstein, whose insights, criticisms and investigations are an important part of this book.

# Introduction  1

On the island of Mallorca there lives today a category of people who are designated as Jewish by the local population, but who are at the same time ardent followers of Roman Catholicism. I have been engaged in a study of these people for a number of years. The study involved extensive historical research, analysis of public records, participant observation and surveys of contemporary Mallorcans. In the process of inquiry, I encountered diverse opinions and positions as to the origins, values and affiliations of these Catholic-Jews, and one of my greatest problems was in analyzing and evaluating conflicting data. Ultimately, I did not resolve all the questions people pose about the Catholic-Jews of Mallorca, but I have succeeded in comprehending them and thence explaining them in a framework that is relevant to current interests in urban anthropology.

Most of the existing discussions of Mallorca's Catholic-Jews have been presented in the context of the competing belief systems of Christianity and Judaism, or have dealt with the ensuing intolerance that this competition has evoked. Like so much of what has been written about Christian-Jewish relations in all periods of history, accounts of the relations of Catholics and Jews in Mallorca abound with discussions of prejudice and intolerance. I have tried, without complete success, to avoid these concerns. This study is not about prejudice, but about relations between distinct cultural traditions taking place in the intimacy and proximity of an island city. As an anthropologist, I try to view these traditions as only one portion of the great range of religious and cultural diversity that characterizes the human species. Our concern is not with why or how people should or should not treat each other, but with prob-

1

lems of real concern in urban anthropology, such as why some cultural segments persist for many centuries in the urban milieu, while others assimilate in a generation. With respect to this theoretical issue, the Catholic-Jews of Mallorca are important because they alone out of all the Jews who were once so important a part of Spanish national culture are the only ones to persist today as a distinct and definable urban category. The most fundamental concern of this study is to provide a better understanding of why this extraordinary group has persisted, and in so doing to contribute to an understanding of the larger problems of persistence and assimilation on a world-wide, cross-cultural scale.

While separating myself from direct concern with the issues of belief and prejudice, I am, nevertheless, constantly aware that the topic we are dealing with is one that is emotionally charged for many people, especially those living on the island of Mallorca. This being the case, it is especially important that we discuss our research in a tone of frankness and honesty, rather than of caution and deference. The goals and methods of this research are scientific, but we will not hide behind the mask of "scientific objectivity."

In concert with this approach it might be helpful to describe, as one might do in a seminar on research methods, the origins and development of this particular research. In this situation, the professor must somehow get around the verbiage and myths of science and tell students who are planning their first projects how research is actually carried out. In so doing, the complexities and dilemmas of studying a group as distinctive as our own in the seeming confusion of rapid social change becomes readily apparent. Often research begins with a long period of bewilderment, but ultimately the data fall into appropriate categories, and organization and meaning replace rumor and opinion. Initially, we will describe the process of early data acquisition. Beginning in the second chapter, the data will be organized as a descriptive process.

## THE PROBLEM

My first visit to Mallorca was as a visitor, not as a researcher. I arrived there, after spending six months traveling about Spain, with the intention of getting some paper work done in the midst of pleasant surroundings. I rented an apartment in a lower middle-class neighborhood, at the edge of the ancient heart of the city, and settled down to work, read and enjoy the company of my neighbors. In the course of eight months I grew very fond of Mallorca and, probably a testimony to the flux of contemporary change, I found that I had more ties, more friends, more familiar routines in Palma than I had ever experienced as an adult in the various cities I had lived in throughout the United States, including my home town.

During the latter part of my eight-month stay there, I arranged for an inexpensive apartment in the neighborhood for an old family friend from America who was coming to Spain to retire at the age of sixty-three. He was arriving with his widowed sister, aged sixty-eight. To my surprise the brother and sister both spoke fluent

FIGURE 1
Map of Western Mediterranean

Spanish, having learned it in Florida among friends in the Latin American colony there. They moved into the apartment two floors below and adjusted easily to the Mallorcan life. Having lived in Italy in the twenties and thirties they were very much at home with the Mediterranean pace.

One quiet evening after dinner, the sister burst into the parlor, obviously agitated, pointing to a headline in a Spanish tabloid. It read: *"Los Judíos: La Aristocracia de Espionaje Internacional."* The article told about the apparently high percentage of Jews engaged in espionage on behalf of the USA, the USSR and the United Kingdom. The sister interpreted this article as an attack on Jews, and an indication that Spain was following an anti-Jewish policy. "Why else would they allow such a thing to be printed?" she asked.

Her brother allayed her anxieties somewhat by telling her the article was simply cheap journalism, and was not at all indicative of any policy of the Spanish government. In the course of the discussion she tended to agree that her first response had been alarmist and irrational, but even with that she was uncomfortable about it. Considering that the last time she had changed countries was in response to anti-Semitic pressures, she was entitled to a few anxieties in this new setting. Edith, her family, her brothers, sisters, nieces, nephews, parents—all had lived in Rome up until 1939. They had a bakery there and brother Stefan had an important editorial position with the International Agricultural Association. In the thirties they lived with the shocking news of the repressive policies against Jews emanating from their native Austria. As the decade wore on, their friends told them that even Italy would not be safe, and the whole family pulled up roots in a city they loved and came to America.

Stefan did not take his sister's response to the newspaper article lightly. He wanted her to be comfortable and happy during her retirement years in Spain. We decided that she would be happier if she had some Jewish friends to talk to. Although Edith had never been motivated to get involved in Jewish community life, we nevertheless felt that she might feel more at ease hearing from Jewish acquaintances that the situation was good for Jews in Spain. But where were those Mallorcan Jews to be found? I inquired around, and while looking for Jewish friends for Edith I came to learn about the *Xuetas*.

The way I learned about the Xuetas in one way seems a bit absurd—even now—but the apparent absurdity is justified as one learns more about the situation. Looking back, I can see that my understanding of the Xuetas developed in three stages: first, from responses to uninformed inquiries about the existence of Jews on the island; second, from responses to questions about them when my questions indicated that I was aware of their existence, and third, from talking to the Xuetas myself. Although the explanation may seem orderly, the process of inquiry was characterized by great confusion. One would think that when one asked where is the Jewish neighborhood in this town, the answer would be simple and straightforward. But not in Mallorca, for the Jews were not really Jews, the situation was emotional, there were wide differences in opinion, and people did not care to discuss it.

In the course of conversation, I told my Mallorcan friends I had a friend from America who would like to establish contact with the Jewish community. I asked what they would suggest. I was told there were Jews in Mallorca. When I asked where, no one ever seemed to know. I told Edith this and she asked her lady friend, Rosa. Rosa agreed that there was a Jewish community in Mallorca, and added that they even had their own neighborhood. We asked where and Rosa shrugged her shoulders. That was the end of any information from Rosa. I later learned that these Jews were called *Xuetas* in Mallorquin, the native dialect. Rosa agreed: they were called Xuetas. She still would not say where they lived ... other than somewhere in the old part of the city.

I asked a young migrant worker from the peninsula if there were Jews in Mallorca. His response although confusing at times had great meaning in retrospect. But I had a lot to learn about Mallorca, its culture and its Xuetas before I would ever understand it. He said, "All the Mallorcans are Jews. They are not Spaniards. All the people who run businesses and factories are Jews. They attend the Catholic church, but they are really Jews." I asked him how he knew this. He said all the *peninsulares* (those from the peninsula—

or Spanish mainland) knew it. Mallorcans are not Spaniards, he emphasized. "Ask any *real* Spaniard."

When Edith asked Rosa if the Mallorcan Jews attended Catholic mass, Rosa replied that they did. It occurred to Edith that maybe the reason that Rosa didn't want to talk about it was because she herself was Jewish. Edith asked her. Rosa said, "Maybe not." Rosa's surname, translated literally, meant "teacher." Edith cited Jewish names in other languages which developed etymologically from the word "teacher." It turned out, however, that Rosa was not a Xueta. She knew she was not a Xueta but still did not deny being Jewish—nor confirm it. She in fact didn't know. It seems no one in Mallorca does.

In the first stage of questioning on the existence of Jews, it appears in restrospect that the responses were all of one type. Jewish existence on Mallorca was confirmed, but no Mallorcan would provide any additional information. The second stage seems to be that, once I demonstrated awareness of their existence, the same people who refused to tell me about them had a wide variety of opinions about them. One of the people I had questioned initially was Tomeu, a Mallorcan cab driver. Like the others he said there were Mallorcan Jews, but consciously avoided saying anything beyond that.

One chilly fall night in a sidewalk cafe I ran into Tomeu. I told him that I knew a lot about the Xuetas (I knew relatively little, but more than before), but wanted to get his opinion. He was silent.

I said, "I have heard that the Mallorcan Jews attend Catholic mass. Is this true? Which religion do they really practice—Catholicism or Judaism?"

He replied sternly, "Judaism, I would say."

"But why do people say they attend mass?" I asked.

"They do," he replied, "but I would say they are very Jewish."

"I hear they live in one neighborhood in the center of town," I said.

He told me he knew nothing about this.

Before I saw Tomeu again I learned about the *Calle de Platería*, the Street of the Silver Shops. It looked like any street in the center of town—shops on the ground floor and two or three floors of apartments above. The one obvious difference was that almost all the stores on the street were jewelry stores. I had never before seen a street which was made up almost totally of jewelry stores. In this sense it was quite fascinating. If this were the Jewish section, then the presence of jewelry stores was the only distinguishing factor—at least on first sight.

There were no signs, symbols, habits or patterns that would distinguish it from any other Mallorcan neighborhood. As on other streets one heard both Mallorquin and Castilian spoken, and as in other neighborhoods the symbols of Catholicism were present, especially in the contents of the window displays.

The next time I saw Tomeu I told him I had been to the Street of the Silver Shops where the Jews lived. He says, "Yes, I know they live there." This was in contradiction to what he had told me a few nights earlier—that he knew nothing about them living in the center of town. Now, he knew exactly where they lived. We discussed the Street of the Silver Shops. He of course knew the street well and confirmed the things I had seen there. Knowing that I knew about the Xuetas he became very confidential and intimate. He decided to tell me the truth about them.

"The Xuetas have bad manners," he said. "They are physically dirty and very ugly, and that is the real truth. The Xuetas are not really rich, but they live comfortably as well-to-do shopkeepers. They live on the Street of the Silver Shops, and in the neighborhood between there and the cathedral. Ancient people live in ancient parts of the city."

He continued. "They are good Catholics and have been Catholics for many centuries. [A few nights earlier he had told me they practiced Judaism.] As for their character and morals, they are typically Mallorcan. A friend of mine knows a Xueta girl and her family does not allow her to walk alone on the street with a boy. They are horrified by the thought of her going to the beach dressed only in a bathing suit, exposing most of her body to her fiancé. That attitude is getting to be old-fashioned. But most Xuetas are like that.

"The Xuetas have their own practices. In the seven or eight weeks before Easter when Mallorcans eat *sobresada* [a delicacy made of pork], the Xuetas also follow this custom, but they will not eat it on Fridays. It is the custom in Mallorca for each family to kill a pig some time between November and February, and to hang it outside their door. The Xuetas do this too. They eat pork, but they do not eat it on Fridays... especially the Friday before Easter.

"Most Xuetas marry only among themselves. If a non-Xueta girl marries a Xueta boy, she becomes a Xueta. If a Mallorcan boy married a Xueta girl, then the children are not Xuetas. They are just someone who has a Xueta mother. No one dares call them Xueta. It is not allowed."

Edith, Stefan and I discussed our varying information on the existence of the Jewish community in Mallorca—a Jewish community that was or was not Jewish, depending on who you asked. We never found the Jewish friends for Edith that we thought would have made her more comfortable in a country unfamiliar to her. She was a seasoned traveler and spoke five languages fluently. Having lived in Spain a few months she realized that official anti-Semitism in Spain was a dead issue, but because of the Inquisition and the expulsion of Jews from Spain in the fifteenth century, it would forever be a sensitive issue. No longer feeling any threat of anti-Semitism, Edith had no particular desire to come into contact with a Jewish community. She and her brother eventually decided to leave Mallorca and return to their native Austria where they still had many friends.

In late 1962, I returned to the United States, never thinking much about the Xuetas until one day in the library I came across a Columbia University history dissertation on the subject, done in 1936 by Baruch Braunstein. Braunstein was primarily interested in one aspect of Xueta history, the Inquisition. Braunstein dealt with the primary sources almost exclusively, and uncovered evidence that has since been of great interest to Mallorcans themselves. I also found an essay by Robert Graves (1958: 275–289) on the subject. It turned out that a number of people had written about various aspects of the topic, but I had fortunately come upon two of the best sources—Braunstein the best historical source and Graves the best literary source. It was clear from these reports that the Xueta phenomenon was still an issue in contemporary Mallorcan society, something which my limited inquiries in Mallorca had led me to conclude.

I was at that time engaged in a study of urban ethnic groups, my data coming primarily from American Indians who had moved to the city. The Xuetas, like the Indians, were extremely interesting as regards the power of traditional culture to survive the assimilationist pressures of the city. Personal values, or prejudices, led me to admire those who were proud of their heritage as opposed to those who were so eager to conform to dominant values that they hid their ethnic grandparents in the kitchen when company came. Apart from these personal values, there was the problem, very prominent in urban anthropology, of learning why some groups persisted in the urban milieu and others assimilated easily. What were the variables as regards the culture and internal structure of the group? What were the variables in the city? Another problem was the setting up of a typology of urban groups or categories. The Xuetas were particularly interesting in this respect since they did not fit well anywhere in the classificatory scheme. The Xuetas seemed almost unique.

In anthropology there is still a great interest in what is unique and different, but the reasons for this interest are different now than they were in the early days of the profession. Early fieldwork focused on the bizarre and exotic, but the concern then was to explore the total range of human behavior. Then as now people found it difficult to comprehend values and practices that contradicted or varied from patterns that were familiar. What was familiar was frequently defined as only human nature. In its early days, anthropology studied the range of variation and demonstrated that it was indeed immense. In contemporary studies that is no longer a problem: the range is a given, and we proceed from there.

One of the contemporary problems of anthropology is the classification or categorization of types of societies and cultures. In this context the unique is still important, but for entirely different reasons. Now what seems to be unique can be a challenge to the underlying principles of classification. If these principles are basic and fundamental there should be no exceptions, for in a good typology, there are no unexplainable leftovers. In this respect the Xuetas were a challenge.

As a group, set apart from others, in different ways both Catholic and Jewish, and as well a distinct endogamous group for over five hundred years, the Xuetas of Mallorca were indeed unique. They were unique historically, but they were not unique structurally, or at least they would prove not to be once we learned more about them. The problem was to learn more about the basis of Xueta persistence, within the group and within the city of Palma de Mallorca. Superficially, they seemed to resemble some other groups, the most interesting being the Eta of Japan, (Donoghue 1959: 1000–1017) a pariah subculture, occupationally distinct and endogamous. There were also the endogamous, commercial, urban ethnic groups, such as Hindu Indians in Africa and Latin America, Chinese communities in Southeast Asia, Armenians, Copts, and so on. But before the comparison could be made, more data had to be gathered on the Xuetas.

I returned to Mallorca in the summer of 1965 to learn what I could about the contemporary Xuetas and to see if a long-term research project was feasible. I spent six weeks there and talked with many Xuetas. As before, I received a wide range of responses to my questions. In fact the range was so great there was almost no pattern whatever. I was told that the Xuetas were still a strong and viable community, that they were proud of their distinctiveness, and that they did not want to intermarry with other Mallorcans. Other Xuetas told me that the distinction was ridiculous, that it meant nothing at all; "It is only a figment of the imagination," one man insisted.

However, my own observations confirmed the existence of a continuing Xueta community. On the first visit I had seen only a street composed almost entirely of jewelry stores. During the second I had learned about the fifteen Xueta names, and it was clear that the jewelry stores were owned by people with these names. The occupational and ethnic concentration was a sociological fact, and not a figment of anyone's imagination.

One of the people I talked to in 1965 was Miguel Forteza. This was an extremely fortunate choice for he more than any other Xueta has explained the meaning of being Xueta to non-Xueta Mallorcans. I was told that Sr. Forteza was a leader in the Xueta community (the community which, according to some, did not exist). Sr. Forteza was writing an account of his own experiences from childhood and through a long adult career in civil service. He was then, I believe, in his late sixties. He expressed a peculiar attitude which reflected a great pride in being a Xueta, concomitant with obvious satisfaction that the more overt signs of the Xueta community were disappearing. He talked about the Street of the Silver Shops, a street he had lived on as a child, and pointed out that it was not entirely a street of Xueta businesses anymore. It was true, he said, that non-Xuetas did indeed have businesses on the street. From his point of view this was a radical change from what had existed before. He saw this as assimilation. From my point of view it was still an obvious ethnic concentration. Four-fifths of the businesses were jewelry stores. All of these except one were owned by Xuetas. The apartments upstairs were also occupied primarily by Xuetas. Sr. Forteza was involved in the dilemma which confronts members of urban ethnic groups: the choice between retention of rewarding ethnic traditions as against acceptance in the larger society which necessitates denying one's traditions publicly.

In the course of our discussion, Sr. Forteza would from time to time consult on answers to my questions with a third party in the room, speaking Mallorquin. In these conversations he referred to particular Xuetas as Jews (*Jueus* in Mallorquin). In speaking of Xuetas to me he continually used the pronoun *nosotros* or we. (The conversation moved back and forth between Spanish and English, with side comments to a third party in Mallorquin.) Thus while Forteza was using *we* and *us* incessantly and referring to this group as Jews, he was saying that the group was not Jewish, and he spoke with great satisfaction about its alleged nonexistence. Sr. Forteza was not lying, nor was he practicing duplicity. I later learned that his attitude was not at all unusual. Xuetas do have great pride in their origins. They are very defensive and protective of their own. At the same time they want to see the designation Xueta disappear in Mallorcan society.

I talked with many non-Xuetas that summer and found that among them there also existed a wide range of opinions and observations about the group. I was told that the Xuetas were very well organized, that they practiced Judaism still and that their alleged Catholicism was only a front. Contrary to this I was told that they

were merely Mallorcan Catholics of Jewish ancestry who by tradition married among themselves. No non-Xueta that I talked to at
that time was of the opinion that they were assimilating. The following are examples of the extremes of responses that I recorded in 1965
from non-Xuetas on the topic of Xuetas.

> The Xueta situation is getting better, that is to say prejudice is on
> the decline. When I was a child and it was discovered that I was
> playing with a Xueta child, my grandmother called me in the house
> and sent me upstairs.
>
> "You can't play with him," she said. "He is a Xueta, a Jew, and
> they are traitors."
>
> I hope such things don't happen now. I know of cases where
> Xuetas marry non-Xuetas. However, the marriage is usually with a
> person from the mainland, not a Mallorcan. This refusal to inter-
> marry is absurd. Sometimes it's the Xuetas who won't intermarry;
> sometimes it's the others who won't marry Xuetas. In my many close
> friendships with Xuetas, people who share similar interests, we ig-
> nore all this. It's absurd, isn't that true?

Some people said the Xuetas were really Catholic. Others said
they were really Jewish. I asked another informant what he thought.

> They are Catholics, but to be a true Christian you have to be
> concerned about something besides money, you have to be some-
> thing of a romantic. There is nothing romantic about the Xuetas.
> They are all business like any other Jews. True, they go to church
> and are good Catholics in that sense; but they have a Jewish psychol-
> ogy, a Jewish way of looking at life. They are dull, unimaginative
> and stupid. They are very Jewish looking, too, and their women age
> rapidly. They are really a rather revolting group.
>
> But these Xuetas are of no consequence. They are only a small
> group who are victims of prejudice. Actually, all the people on this
> island are Jews. There is nothing Spanish about them. Many of the
> people here who are the worst critics of Jews are themselves Jews, and
> they know it.

I will not comment on these remarks now, but will refer back to
them later when further data will provide a basis for analyzing them.
At the time they were uttered, I could only partially understand
their meaning.

In the course of a six-week visit, I could only hope to define the problem more clearly. I could not confirm very much. One thing I was very curious about was the degree of endogamy still existing among the Xuetas. I could not do a survey at that time, but the Spanish naming system itself provided a great deal of evidence on endogamy that would not be available from our own system. In our society the child's surname is taken from the father, and the mother's maiden name is not used. In the Spanish naming system the child uses both the mother's and the father's names, resulting in appellations such as Juan García de Pérez, the first surname coming from the father and the second from the mother. When a female, María García de Pérez gets married, she substitutes for the surname of her mother that of her husband's father. So if her husband is named Arturo Rodríguez de Guzmán, she becomes María García de Rodríguez upon marriage and her husband stays Arturo Rodríguez de Guzmán. Hence husband and wife have different names. The husband's name reveals both his father's and his mother's surname and the wife's name is made up of her father's and her husband's father's surnames.

Among the Xuetas there are fifteen names which are known as Xueta names. From one's combination of names it is easy to tell if one's mother and father were both Xueta. When I saw these names in the telephone directory they were frequently found in combination, an indicator that there was still a great deal of endogamy. The 1965 phone directory showed evidence of approximately 70 percent endogamy. This could only be an indicator, as a telephone directory is not an entirely reliable source. Clearly, not all people have phones, and those who did might well not be an accurate representation of the whole segment of the population called Xueta. Nevertheless, this indication of 70 percent endogamy was impressive, a remarkably high degree for any urban group. One wondered whether the rule of endogamy was still enforced among the Xuetas. Asking questions got one nowhere. Some said yes, some said no, and most refused to discuss the subject.

Figure 2 is a sample of names from one page of the 1968 telephone directory. The name Forteza is a Xueta name. The following are also Xueta names: Aguiló, Bonnín, Cortés, Fuster, Martí,

Miró, Picó, Piña, Pomar, Segura, Taronji, Valenti, Valleriola and Valls. The combinations marked with a triangle ▲ are names that represent endogamous unions. Those with a circle ● are exogamous unions. Those with a square ■ indicate neither, which means there is not enough information provided, such as in the cases where the listing is the widow of M. Forteza or the surname Forteza stands alone.

From this page of the Palma directory we see that of those names which provide the surname of both parents 86 are names which indicate an endogamous marriage and 37 are names which indicate an exogamous marriage. Seven names marked with a ■ indicate neither. Endogamous name combinations represent 69.9 percent of the total. Again I must say that this was used only as an indicator, but it was sufficient evidence for assuming that a rule of endogamy was responsible for the high percentage of name combinations in which both surnames were Xueta.

My conclusions about the Xuetas from that summer's work were that the Xuetas were a pariah subcultural segment whose persistence and endogamy was a product of both their own values combined with external pressures from other segments in the city. They were involved in a process of change that no one seemed really to understand. If one were to study the Xuetas one had to see them in the context of Mallorcan society. The cultural traditions involved were Spanish as well as Mallorcan, Jewish as well as Christian. They were a product of a long process of culture change, one that involved a period of at least five hundred years, probably more. We will attempt to describe this change in a theoretically meaningful way. This necessitates some clarification of approaches.

The study of the Xuetas is a problem in urban culture change. Like other types of culture change, it is concerned with the values, worldview and structural arrangements of a particular people as they are influenced by a changing relationship with their environment, technological advance, the influence of other cultures, as well as alterations in internal values and structure. Studies in urban change such as this one are somewhat hampered by the absence of a conception of culture specifically applicable to the urban level. As we use the term culture in this study, we will ordinarily have in mind

FIGURE 2
## Directory Data

■Forteza Laboratorio
■Forteza Miguel
■Forteza Vda de
■Forteza Vda de
▲Forteza Aguiló F
▲Forteza Aguiló F
▲Forteza Aguiló L
▲Forteza Aguiló L
▲Forteza Aguiló L
▲Forteza Aguiló L
▲Forteza Aguiló M
▲Forteza Aguiló M
▲Forteza Aguiló M
▲Forteza Aguiló M
▲Forteza Aguiló M
▲Forteza Aguiló M
▲Forteza Aguiló M
▲Forteza Aguiló N
▲Forteza Aguiló P
▲Forteza Aguiló R
●Forteza Alemany A
●Forteza Arrecio M
●Forteza Barceló J
●Forteza Barceló M
●Forteza Bauzá J
●Forteza Bennasar J
●Forteza Bennasar J
▲Forteza Bonnín J
▲Forteza Bonnín J
▲Forteza Bonnín M
▲Forteza Bonnín M
▲Forteza Bonnín M
●Forteza Cambra L
▲Forteza Cortés F
▲Forteza Cortés G
▲Forteza Cortés J
▲Forteza Cortés M
▲Forteza Cortés M
▲Forteza Cortés M

●Forteza Font J A
●Forteza Fornés F
▲Forteza Forteza A
▲Forteza Forteza F
▲Forteza Forteza I
▲Forteza Forteza I
▲Forteza Forteza I
▲Forteza Forteza J
▲Forteza Forteza J
▲Forteza Forteza J
▲Forteza Forteza J
▲Forteza Forteza J
▲Forteza Forteza J
▲Forteza Forteza J A
▲Forteza Forteza J M
▲Forteza Forteza L
▲Forteza Forteza L
▲Forteza Forteza M
▲Forteza Forteza M
▲Forteza Forteza N
▲Forteza Forteza N
▲Forteza Forteza S
▲Forteza Forteza S
▲Forteza Fuster A
▲Forteza Fuster A
▲Forteza Fuster F
▲Forteza Fuster F
▲Forteza Fuster J
▲Forteza Fuster L
▲Forteza Fuster L
▲Forteza Fuster L
▲Forteza Fuster M
●Forteza Garí M
●Forteza Marcet A
●Forteza Marcet A
●Forteza Marcet L
●Forteza Marcet M
●Forteza Marcet M
●Forteza Marcet M

●Forteza Marcet M
●Forteza Marcet M
▲Forteza Martí J
▲Forteza Martí J L
▲Forteza Martí P
●Forteza Mas A
●Forteza Mas M
●Forteza Mas M
●Forteza Mas M
●Forteza Mas R
●Forteza Mesana F
▲Forteza Miró A
▲Forteza Miró A
▲Forteza Miró F
▲Forteza Miró F
▲Forteza Miró F
▲Forteza Miró J
▲Forteza Miró J
●Forteza Moll F
●Forteza Morro B
●Forteza Pascual R
▲Forteza Picó F
▲Forteza Picó J
▲Forteza Piña A
▲Forteza Piña A
▲Forteza Piña G

▲Forteza Piña M
▲Forteza Piña M
▲Forteza Pomar A
▲Forteza Pomar M
▲Forteza-Rey Forteza I
▲Forteza-Rey Forteza J
▲Forteza Rey Forteza J
■Forteza-Rey N
●Forteza Ríbas E
●Forteza Roca J
●Forteza Roca P
●Forteza Salamanca R
●Forteza Sancho M
▲Forteza Segura D
▲Forteza Segura J
▲Forteza Segura M J
●Forteza Serra J
■Forteza Teodoro S
■Forteza Tomás M
▲Forteza Valleriola J
▲Forteza Valls J
▲Forteza Valls J
▲Forteza Valls J María
●Forteza Vich A
●Forteza Vich P
●Forteza Vich R

the traditional conception of culture—adaptive modes of behavior that are passed on from generation to generation. However, in the urban context the conception of culture as shared cognition is especially useful. In this study we will make reference to both the cognitive and behavioral aspects of culture; that is, the values, conception of self and estimation of others that people "carry around in their head" as criteria for interaction, as well as distinctive patterns of observable behavior.

Our study of urban culture change focuses on two levels, the segment and the urban whole, two distinct entities formed and affected by different cultural traditions. The Xuetas as an urban segment are a product of Judaic culture which in its long history existed first as a tribal confederation, then as a nationally organized political state, and later as a nation without territory, composed of communities dispersed throughout the Christian and Muslim sectors of the Mediterranean littoral. The City of Mallorca, later called Palma, is on the other hand a product of the Catalan-speaking culture of the northwest Mediterranean, with its history closely intertwined with the formation and continuity of the nation of Spain. Given these outside influences, emanating from both ends of the Mediterranean, it is unrealistic to talk about change using only Mallorcan data. Instead, we see change in the Xueta community occurring with various degrees of influence from the city and the island, which are themselves provincial units in the Catalan linguistic area and the Spanish nation, with the Xueta community itself seen as a product of the shared culture of the network of Jewish communities that extend throughout the Mediterranean.

There are theoretical as well as empirical reasons for studying change at two levels. As we have seen, the Xuetas and the city they live in are products of and responsive to two entirely different cultural traditions. This is not an extraordinary situation, even in the marked contrast between segment and city that the Xuetas and Palma present. But when the segment and the city represent two different cultures, by their very nature they play two entirely different roles with respect to their distinctive cultural traditions.

As Robert Redfield has pointed out, the cultural role of cities is either that of the apex of a unified great tradition, or of the meeting place and power center of diverse traditions—the orthogenetic and heterogenetic roles (Redfield 1954). The cultural role of the segment is the opposite of that of the city. Instead of being the center of a tradition, it is almost always an offshoot; instead of being a center of power it is frequently powerless; and its presence in the city has usually come about as a result of a search for improved subsistence or survival.

## EVOLUTION OF A SEGMENT

An understanding of the role of a segment within a city is inevitably enhanced by a study of the historical processes that brought its members into the city. Where particular people come from, the circumstances of their survival, and the nature of their culture before their arrival are of critical importance in understanding how they function within the urban social system. The city as an environment is rewarding to some pre-migration types of adaptation while destructive of others. This is best explained in an analysis of the breaking-down, building-up process.

Migrants to the city bring with them well-entrenched values and patterns of social interaction which have in most cases served them well in their previous setting, whatever that may have been. Frequently, in fact all but exceptional cases, these rural-based organizational principles are no longer viable in the city, and we recognize as part of the urbanization process the dissolution of extended kinship ties and other rural-based patterns. In this respect, urbanization is a breaking-down process. However, in the city we also see a building-up process, the creation of new forms of association more suitable to the principles that govern interaction in the urban environment. Contrasted with the food-gathering and food-producing activities of the country, the city survives on trade, manufacture and the rewards of domination. In the city we see the creation of new institutional arrangements that serve these purposes. This is the building-up aspect of the urbanization process.

As stated earlier, our theoretical focus in the study of the Xuetas is on the axis of persistence/assimilation. Why do some ethnic categories disappear in the city and others persist? If we are to find an answer for any particular ethnic group, we inquire as to how it survived the breaking-down, building-up process. We analyze what it is that a particular rural culture brings with it that is viable in the city, and what is not. Those aspects of rural social organization which have no utility in an urban setting tend to disappear. If interdependence is the key element of group cohesion, then those whose organizations are not viable in the new setting will assimilate more rapidly than others. But assimilation-persistence is not entirely a structural-functional matter. Those who bring with them a strong ideological principle as the basis of group cohesion will persist even when their traditional social organization is dysfunctional in the city. They will, of course, reorganize, creating a new system of relationships which provide for both ideological purity and functional utility in an urban environment.

That part of the urbanization process that has to do with the integration and adjustment of migrants in the city has been one of the primary foci of urban anthropological research. In addition to the questions on identity, reorganization and ideology posed above, researchers have also asked other important questions such as those having to do with the point at which the migrant becomes urban, the kinds of value and attitude changes that are required for urban living, the cultural categories that make up cities, and the perceptions migrants have of their urban development.

If we ask these questions about the Jews of Mallorca, we encounter one of the most basic differences between Jews and other migrants to Spanish cities. All through its early history Mallorca received Jewish migrants from diverse points in the Mediterranean. But the urban adjustment and integration was minimal; that is to say, there was no breaking-down, building-up process. There were few changes in values and attitudes, and the new arrival encountered little difficulty in relating to the city. The reason, of course, was that the migrants came almost entirely from other cities, and the new community of co-religionists in Mallorca was almost a duplicate of the former. Robert Park (1928) saw change of residence from community to like community, even across national and cultural borders, as merely *movement* rather than *migration*. Migration involves the breaking-down of old ways, the secularization of "relations which were formerly sacred" (Park 1928). Movement, he emphasized, does not involved the breaking-down of old ways to adjust to new social situations. In avoiding the reorganization that is involved in migration, the Jewish community's relation to the city is in Park's words "symbiotic, rather than social."

So, unlike migrants to the city from tribal or village settings, the residents of the Mediterranean Jewish community did not endure the breaking-down, building-up process. They were of another type. In fact, those who move from urban setting to urban setting represent one distinct process in urban culture change, just as those who move from food-gathering to the city represent another, and those moving from food-producing to the urban setting, still another. The origins of a group outside a particular city must inevitably influence the role that group can play within it for many years to come. So in examining the integration and adjustment of Jews in the city of Mallorca, we begin by emphasizing that their origins are urban rather than rural, and many of the questions we ask about their integration into the city will relate to this condition. But our inquiry cannot end there, for Jews were certainly not always urban. Like all urban communties the Jewish community had rural antecedents at one time in its past, and its social system was a product of the restructuring that moving and adjusting to the city requires. To understand the Xueta adjustment/integration we must go back to the long and difficult adjustment to urban life that precedes the formation of the first Jewish communities. To do this, we will examine in a later chapter the breaking-down, building-up process that rural Jewish migrants to Babylon experienced following the exile of 586 B.C. Examining this early urban reorganization enhances our understanding of the fundamental principles of Jewish community life and the integration of these communities in a particular foreign culture. Many non-Jews find the integration-adjustment of Jews in foreign cities difficult to comprehend. Looking back at the adjustment that Jewish shepherds and peasants made to Babylon and comparing that to the urbanization of contemporary folk cultures does much to improve that comprehension.

## THE CITY

As stated earlier, we separate our analyses of the city and the segment, for each operates on different principles and frequently relates to different cultural traditions. We said that, typically, the city is a center of power and authority, while the segment is often an offshoot of some distant center of power and authority. That distant center may be a powerful nation or merely a religious leader or a village chief who commands nothing more than the respect of tradition. The ethnic segment in successive stages of assimilation or persistence is always responding in a varying degree to two sets of values, those of its origins and the dominant values of the city. The culture of the city has different kinds of roots.

When we refer to the culture of the city, we are actually talking about an urban level of sociocultural integration (Steward 1955). Steward himself did not discuss an urban level of sociocultural integration but he anticipated its utility. (Moore 1975). The urban level of analysis is further clarified by the work of Redfield on the role of cities. He said that cities are either the centers of diverse cultures—"heterogenetic"—or the focal point of a great tradition— "orthogenetic." Another way of perceiving this is to see the culture of the city as being made up either of the relations between the diverse peoples who have come together in it or of the shared traditions of people in one cultural area, such as a nation, where the common culture is qualitatively altered in the complexity, intensity and frequency of urban interaction.

In the first case the culture of the city is made up primarily by those patterns of interaction formed within the city, in the process of people of diverse origin arriving at accommodations of interaction on economic, social and political matters.

This kind of city may contrast vividly with the territory that surrounds it. An example would be New Orleans, a port city with French, Spanish, Italian, Irish, German, Creole, African and Anglo-Saxon traditions surrounded by an area where the Anglo values of the Confederacy remain supreme. The culture of this heterogenetic city is mostly a product of diverse traditions within. On the other hand, the city playing the orthogenetic role, for example Holland, Michigan, is more influenced by the input of surrounding little traditions. The culture of the city, that is to say, the urban level of analysis, is by the very nature of what is urban the product of many inputs, but particular cities may be differentiated by the source of value and traditions that guide urban interactions.

Looking at the city of Mallorca in this respect, we see the city playing various cultural roles, and the changes in these roles are reflected in changes in the urban culture. In the period of the Christian conquest, from 1229 on, the city of Mallorca was a frontier outpost for the kingdom of Aragon and, as such, people of diverse origins were invited to inhabit it. Aragonese values were predominant, but its unique culture was a product of the Saracens, Jews and Catalans that made it up. By the fourteenth century the city of Mallorca was the leading trade center of the Kingdom of Mallorca and in its heterogenetic role it flourished and reached its height. In following periods the city changed as its role changed from international to local to international center, and as the values of diverse or local cultures predominated. We will look at its role and contrast it with the role of the segment of Xuetas. In studying this changing relationship, we will understand both better.

Our procedure in this study of urban culture change will be to analyze and describe the segment and the city in the major stages of change. We will look at the Xueta community as it has existed up until the more recent years, viewing it as the only community that remained from a period when almost every town in Spain had its own Jewish quarter. Examining this unique form, we will recognize much that is Jewish and much that is not. Its basic structure stems from Jewish communal forms, but five hundred years of a Christian overlay have done much to modify even the most ingrained of Jewish customs. After examining the Xueta community of modern times, we will go back to examine its origins in thirteenth-century Mallorca. Then we will probe the origins of Jewish communities in the history of ancient Judah, where the ideological basis of persistence has its roots. First, then, the Xueta community.

# The Xueta Community

We should begin our description of the Xueta community by first distinguishing it from the earlier form, the community of *Conversos*, (converted ones). The Converso community was made up of Jews who had legally converted to Christianity but were in many respects still Jewish. In Mallorca the Converso community members secretly practiced Judaism while publicly practicing Catholicism, and are referred to as Crypto-Jews. The period of the Conversos lasted from 1435 until the end of the seventeenth century. The Xueta stage lasting from 1700 to the present was not crypto-Jewish, it was Catholic. It was characterized, however, by principles of Jewish social organization; and traditional Jewish values were predominant. Its ideology, that is, those values and ideas which directed activity towards the maintenance of the existing social order and which governed its relationships with the rest of Mallorcan society (Mannheim 1936), was syncretic, a combination of Jewish and Catholic elements—a unique creation.

The Xueta community as it once was, prior to the influences of recent years, remains vivid in the memory of adult Mallorcans. As Jews living in upper Manhattan or Queens recall with nostalgia the rich community life of the lower east side in its heyday, so do Xuetas recall life on the Street of the Silver Shops. There were intense family ties, neighborhood unity, a strong sense of place, and there was also degradation. A study of the Xuetas must begin with an understanding of this community life which changed little over the centuries. Although the jewelry shops are all there, still owned by Xuetas, and Xueta families still live upstairs, the community has nevertheless been influenced by recent industrializing trends. Before we can talk about these changes, we must describe the base period of community organization that persisted from 1700 until the 1950s. To describe the base community we have obtained data from the recollections of adult Mallorcans and those of their parents. We have not used data that were not provided or verifiable by living sources. Although limited written sources confirm that the community has changed little over the centuries, information on social organization from them is inadequate for a description of the whole. The community is described under headings familiar to anthropologists in order to provide bases of comparison with other urban communties.

## THE NAME, RESIDENCE AND POPULATION

The term Xueta is at least 280 years old, and probably older. Given its antiquity there is some dispute as to its origin. It is a Mallorquin word, not Spanish. The X in Mallorquin is pronounced as a sound that is not equivalent to either the *ch* or *sh* in English, but rather something in between. The term is probably derived from an old Mallorquin word for Jew *(Xuhita)* which changed to the diminutive (Xueta) could be translated into English as *Jew-ette.* Some say it comes from *Xua,* the Mallorquin word for porkchop, for converted Jews were known to eat pork in front of their shops to demonstrate their non-adherence to Jewish dietary regulations. Whatever its origins, its meaning is now rather explicit as a designation for a relatively small group of people who are descendants of Conversos, converted Jews, and who are easily identified by their family names.

The importance of location is emphasized by the second most popular designation for the Xuetas—*d'es carrer, those of the street.* It is not necessary to say which street: that everybody knows. The term is popular among Xuetas themselves who seem to prefer it to Xueta. In talking to Xueta informants the conversation frequently arrives at a point where we talk about *"los de la calle"* (those of the street)* and

---

*Documentation from the eighteenth century (for example, Perdigó, Informe Del Año 1773) reveals that the full designation was either *"los habitantes del Barrio de la Calle"* or *"los individuos de la Calle."*

Street of the Silver Shops on a Sunday afternoon. The church
Santa Eulalia is in the background.

Entrance to Santa Eulalia—
the Xueta church

Formal gardens near the
Cathedral, Palma

"*los que no son de la calle*" (those not of the street). Ultimately this shortens to "*los que son*" (those who are) and "*los que no son*" (those who are not).

The street, as I have already indicated, is called Calle de Platería, Street of the Silver Shops. The residences of Xuetas extend out from this street, occupying an area of at least three blocks and parts of others. The ethnic neighborhood touches on Calle Jaime I, traditionally the main business section, so that the jewelry and silver stores are a specialty section, almost immediately attached to the main shopping center. Xuetas also had a variety of types of shops on Calle Jaime I, and still do, even though a number of other business districts in other parts of the city have developed over the years.

The ancestors of the Xuetas have lived in the heart of the city for centuries. A concentration on what is now called Calle de Platería probably extends back to shortly after the 1435 conversion of Mallorcan Jews. Prior to that time the official Jewish quarter was along the sea wall, only a few minutes' walk from the present residence. A sense of place in the winding narrow streets of the old city has always been a strong factor in Jewish and Xueta identity. The history of streets and buildings are part of the general knowledge of any moderately informed Mallorcan. The Church of *Montesión* (Mount Zion), in the heart of the old city and still very much in use, was once the great synagogue of Mallorcan Jews. A smaller building, the Church of Santa Fe, very old and no longer used, was also a synagogue. The square that was the official residence of the Inquisition is only steps from Calle de Platería. It is not romanticism to say that the old city of Mallorca reeks with history. And when one sector of the population has occupied the same street for half a millennium, then a designation such as "those of the street" can be used without fear of confusion.

The population of Xuetas is of necessity an approximation, for there are no official records using this designation. According to Quadrado (1887) there were over eleven hundred Jews in Mallorca in 1391. The Inquisition records speak of 300 families of converted Jews in 1691, providing population estimates as high as 1500 for that period. A German writer visiting the island in the nineteenth century (Lewin 1883) provides an estimate for that time of 600

Xueta families, possibly 3,000 people. Forteza (1966) provides an estimate from the year 1933 of 3,300 persons and a count by name for 1955 of 4,718 persons and 1,445 families. The Xueta percentage of the total urban population of Palma has ranged between three and four percent in modern times.

## KINSHIP

Among the Xuetas everyone is related to everyone else. The interlocking of families through marriage enables any one person to trace ties of blood or marriage to almost any other member of the community. With a population that has been endogamous and that has numbered around three thousand for the last century the amount of inbreeding is of course high. One inevitably marries a relative. Kin ties which extend out through the community provide one of the most enduring supports of its persistence. It enables the community to be cohesive with relatively few formal community organizations. The importance of kinship is emphasized in the answer to a question on community organization by an informant. He said, "We really don't have a community, but we feel like one group because we are all more or less related to one another."

There was probably no single time when all or even a large percentage of the entire Xueta community assembled in one place for a meeting. There has not been and are not now any community leaders holding posts of leadership, but only more prestigious and well-liked members of the community who may at times act on behalf of the whole. The only community-wide organization was one devoted to charity, and that has not functioned as a formal structure for many years.

The endogamous condition of the Xuetas has been supported by values of the group as well as pressures from the outside. Prior to 1691, in the Converso era, there was strong sentiment against exogamous alliances, and the reasons were traditionally Jewish. These are no longer in effect. I have never found a Xueta who supported Xueta endogamy because of the mission, survival or chosen status of the Jewish people. But many do support the rule of endogamy on the ground that mixed marriages simply will not work.

Older people have warned their children that on the occasion of the first argument in a mixed marriage, the outsider would relate the dispute to the spouse being a Xueta. Every Xueta knows the term "*Ya la has hecho*" (now you have done it), the charge the non-Xueta spouse will eventually make "now you have behaved like a Xueta."

Some say the Xueta attitude towards endogamy is merely a "sour grapes" response to the refusal of members of other groups to consider the Xuetas as marriage partners. The pariah status of the Xueta makes the consideration of marriage alliances next to impossible for some groups. This has been a topic of a number of novels published in Castilian throughout Spain. In one of these, *Los Muertos Mandan* (The dead command), Blasco Ibáñez (1919) describes the dilemma of a debt-ridden aristocrat, Jaume Fabrer, who was tempted by the possibility of ending his financial problems by marrying the niece of a wealthy Xueta. Although the uncle was his friend, and the niece desirable, the social pressures against such a match were insurmountable. Such were the elements of a Mallorcan novel of class and manners in the early twentieth century. Other restrictions on marriage arrangements, in addition to those having to do with the Xuetas, were customary at the time. They reflect occupational and class alignments that date from the days of estates and guilds. One informant, a rural town dweller, recalled for me a rebuff suffered in the twenties when he tried to talk to an attractive Xueta girl on a public square. She said, "Please go away, you are not of my *gremio* [guild]."

The power of parents in arranging marriages, though weakening, is still highly influential in determining mate selection. In the past, the young met each other quite freely through flirtations on the promenade, but before the relationship ever reached the hand-holding stage the parents intervened. Although the parents had a choice of sanctions which could be used against a noncomplying offspring, the strength of custom was such that they rarely had to be used.

Many courtship institutions such as dances and neighborhood festivals served to enforce the endogamy rules. A non-Xueta would be careful to avoid a predominantly Xueta dance at the Church of Santa Eulalia, and the entrance of a Xueta in a non-Xueta dance could be a source of such embarrassment that the transgressor of the rules would be unlikely to repeat it.

Restrictions against marriages with Xuetas have existed only on the island of Mallorca. To a mainlander a Xueta is just another Mallorcan Catholic, and he is unlikely to deem the Xueta, non-Xueta distinction important, even when told about it. The only problem a Xueta encounters on the mainland is that of being a stranger from Mallorca. If he were to marry in his new home, it is likely that an exchange of references would be necessary, as this is still very much the custom in Spain. There are bitter accounts by Xuetas who tell of local priests answering the inquiries of the parents of a fiancée on the mainland with information to the effect that the prospective son-in-law is a member of a traditionally Jewish group. This kind of fanatic anti-Semitism has not been tolerated among the clergy in the last thirty years, although prior to that time it was not rare. Among the clergy there have always been those allied to the Xuetas and those who obviously despised them. A Xueta informant in his forties told me that when he first began to go out with girls he was advised by the priest in the confessional to marry a non-Xueta even if it meant marrying beneath his station. As with most other groups the Xuetas were willing to marry outside if it was a move upward in status. They were more than eager to marry with aristocrats, and against marrying with those of the working class. With recent in-migration from the peninsula, the Xuetas have found marriage partners outside their group of indeterminate status.

## OCCUPATIONS

Xuetas have been and are in almost as many different occupations as any other segment of the population, from comedian to butcher, but their concentration in some occupations is notable. The figures on business ownership from the *Boletín de la Camara de Comercio* reflect a situation that all merchants and professionals are aware of and consider the norm for Mallorcan society. The figures, which data from 1922, represent a general situation and are not guaranteed to be totally accurate as criteria for classification of a business or a type of business have changed with the years, and we obviously cannot check with the sources who gathered the data fifty years ago.

In 1922, there were twenty-seven silversmiths (*plateros*) listed in the Boletín and three businesses listed as repairers of silver (and gold) objects. Out of a total of thirty businesses involved in the manufacture and repair of silver and gold objects, all thirty were Xuetas. Seven out of ten manufacturers of gold and silver coins and three of the manufacturers and wholesalers of zinc objects were Xuetas, as were sixteen out of twenty businesses listed under the heading *tinsmith*. Thus we see in the area of metal working involving both rare and utilitarian metals that fifty-six out of sixty-three or 89 percent were Xuetas in the year 1922.

The same concentration existed in wholesale and retail sales of jewelry, and in watch repair. Out of four wholesalers of dry goods listed in 1922, four were Xuetas; and among retailers, the figure is twelve out of forty-five. Five out of eight furniture stores were Xueta owned. From these figures we see again almost a monopoly in the area of dry goods and furniture. That only twelve out of forty-five dry goods retailers were Xueta is explained by the fact that this is a neighborhood business, frequently run by a housewife at her place of residence. In other types of businesses we see no Xuetas whatsoever. Out of twenty-six clothing manufactuers, not one was Xueta. The same holds true for the twenty-four leather manufacturers, one of the leading industries of Mallorca. Six out of thirty-seven clothing retailers were Xueta and only four of sixty-one businesses engaged in construction had Xueta owners. Two drugstores of seventeen listed were run by Xuetas. In random selections of businesses not considered as Xueta specialties we see a Xueta representation of about 7.5 percent, about double their percentage in the total population.

These percentages also hold true for 1935, but again we emphasize that exact comparisons are not possible because occupational categories are not entirely equivalent. Technological change is reflected in the shift away from manufacture and to the sale of metal objects, that is, from metal working to stores listed under the title *hardware*. Of twenty-four hardware stores in 1935, twenty-two were

Xueta owned. In the area of businesses not known as Xueta specialties the percentage of Xueta ownership varies from two to three
times their percentage in the population as a whole. By 1950 we see
the number of businesses listed as silversmith dropping and the
number listed as jewelry stores increasing. The concentration of
Xuetas in stores listed as jewelry or jewelry and watch repair is 87
percent. The move away from metal manufacture to metal sales
continues with twenty-six out of thirty-one hardware stores and nine
out of twenty plumbing businesses now Xueta owned. This overall
trend continues into the sixties, that being that there is a heavy
concentration of Xuetas in metal and jewelry businesses with a shift
from small business manufacture to sales. The percentage in businesses not considered as Xueta specialties runs about 8 to 10 percent.

In the small towns in the countryside the Xuetas frequently represent the entire merchant class. The term for merchant in Mallorquin is *marxando* (the *x* pronounced as *sh*) and this is used as a
synonym for Xueta in rural areas. There are no Xuetas involved
directly in agriculture. More explicitly we should say no Xuetas are
involved in the tilling of the soil and the harvesting of crops. In
some cases there have been Xuetas connected with agriculture re-
motely such as with the merchandising of agricultural products.
Occupational distinction contributes to group endogamy in the small
towns. Rural residents say that it is economically impractical for an
agriculturalist to marry a Xueta. In the rural areas female agricultural labor is for all practical purposes equivalent to the male and a
young agriculturalist who found a Xueta girl attractive and person-
ally desirable in every respect would reject her as a wife for her
inability to do farm work. The Xueta girl would interpret marriage
to an agriculturalist as downward mobility, and would have to overcome severe parental objections should she decide in favor of it.
Emphasizing the importance of occupation in endogamy, it should
be noted that should a small-town Xueta girl seek marriage with a
non-Xueta merchant, the family would very likely favor it.

Xuetas are also found in the legal, medical and teaching professions in numbers far above their percentage in the population.
Xuetas involvement in manual occupations apart from those con-

nected with metals is extremely rare. Even with the deliberate exclusion of the Xuetas from some occupations, the Xuetas are well represented or over represented in all high status occupations. The only sector where exclusion has been successful was in the church where up until recently the Xuetas have been prevented from obtaining religious posts. This has decreased significantly since the twenties and there is now a high percentage of Xueta nuns, brothers and priests.

## XUETA CHARITY

Being a member of an extended family has always been the best defense against poverty in Spain, in Mallorca, and certainly among the Xuetas of Mallorca. But in addition to help within the family, neighbor helped neighbor in times of personal misfortune. There has undoubtedly been organized charity with the Xueta community back through the centuries, but it was of necessity mostly *sub rosa*. The best data we have on formal charitable organizations are from the period just prior to the turn of the century. At that time the society of St. Vincent de Paul was the most effective agent for the collection of funds and distribution of aid in the city of Palma. Xuetas who asked to join were refused membership. The response of the community was the formation of their own St. Vincent de Paul society, a close copy of the one in the larger society. Two well-known and wealthy Xuetas were the principal organizers and contributors. All the officers were Xueta as were all the recipients of aid. The very poor were assisted in the day-to-day problems of survival, but much of the aid was devoted to the advancement of the community. For example, a number of young men who had been forced by circumstances to take jobs of the lowest rank, this being in Mallorca those crafts connected with slaughtering, were given funds to train for better positions. The society assisted them while they learned carpentry, masonry, bread baking and various other trades of higher prestige (Forteza 1966).

The goal of the society was to emulate the St. Vincent de Paul society of the city, and to provide equivalent services to Xuetas, but operating on a smaller scale and within the framework of an ethnic tradition it was much more personal and neighborly. The members of the society visited the poor once a week, providing them with food and counseling them on their problems. They were able to provide this aid through monthly contributions that were expected from all in the community, in addition to a special Christmas offering. This private and neighborhood organization was so successful that even after the city-wide society invited the Xuetas to come in, many of the officers continued their work within the community. There is no organized system of charities today; however, I have spoken to Xuetas who told me that in times of distress they were aided by funds from wealthy Xuetas whose identity was not revealed to them. I asked them if they knew the high moral value of *anonymous* charity in Jewish tradition. They said they did not.

Numerous informal systems of aid characterized the Xueta barrio. The poor did not go to the hospital when they were ill, but were cared for in their homes through funds collected by neighbors in door-to-door solicitations. The funds paid for the doctor, the medicine and the maintenance of the household. Neighborhood solicitation was also used in cases where a particular family fell on hard times due to the loss of a job or business failure. On many occasions when a promising but poor member of the community got married, various Xuetas would contribute funds towards the purchase of a business and merchandise to set the couple off to a good start. Whether a particular charity was organized on a community level or more or less informally developed among friends and neighbors, the effort was motivated by a strong sense of responsibility towards other Xuetas, supported by the belief that Xuetas must help each other, for help could not be expected from outside the community.

## DISPUTES

A great distinction was made between legal disputes which involved Xueta with Xueta, and those which involved Xuetas with outsiders. It was a common belief that one's class or ethnic identity had a great deal to do with how a dispute would be settled in the courts. In the case of those disputes severe enough to reach the courts, Xuetas would use non-Xueta attorneys whether their dispute was with another Xueta or an outsider. In either case it was thought that having a non-Xueta attorney was an advantage. Xuetas did not believe that they could get a fair hearing in the courts, so they used them only as a last resort. Most disputes could be settled within the community through neighbors and friends intervening. When this did not work the disputants could appeal to an *hombre recto,* a man recognized for his fairness and knowledge. The hombre recto has been compared to a rabbi, and in the broadest sense the comparison is valid. He was a community leader who embodied the highest ideals of the group and could be appealed to as the final arbiter before going to outside courts. Officially, the hombre recto held no office. He was more than likely a well-educated businessman whose reputation for honesty and fairness had been affirmed over the years and had served him in his own success. Such a man would be motivated to make the fairest of judgments.

The policy of settling disputes within the community is a good example of pressures towards persistence coming from the outside. If the Xuetas had felt that they could have gotten a fair hearing in the provincial courts, they would have used them much more than they did. But lacking this confidence they were compelled to rely on an informal internal system of justice, which was based upon traditional Jewish and Mallorcan notions of fairness. Hence we see an increase in the complexity of internal organization, in this case coming more from pressures from the outside than from a desire to continue traditional practices.

## SOCIALIZATION

As has been stated earlier, there is no answer to the question, "Is the Xueta really a Jew?" For he is surely Catholic. The same kind of dilemma is posed in asking about a Mallorcan, who is also a citizen of Spain, as to how and in what ways he is each. Some Mallorcans are very Castilianized. Others consider their attachment to Spain a misfortune. This generally is the attitude of Xuetas, who for the most part are fiercely Mallorcan. They show great pride in their island and language, and among themselves Mallorquin is spoken almost to the exclusion of Castilian, the national language. Their pride in being Mallorcan exists in spite of the fact, obvious to all, that Mallorca is the only place in Spain where they still encounter prejudice. As a Spanish citizen, a Xueta can travel to or live in any part of Spain, and no matter where he goes he will find himself treated as just another Mallorcan Spaniard. Nevertheless, there is no indication that Xuetas have migrated from the island in any greater numbers than have other Mallorcans.

The Xueta child grows up in this ambience of Mallorcan provincialism, learning pride in his Jewish ancestry and acquiring a sincere belief in Jesus Christ, the sacraments, and the authority of the Roman Catholic Church. He learns a profound attachment to Mallorcan society along with some resentment about his position in it. Xuetas believe that there are no better citizens in Mallorca than themselves, and they affirm this belief by taking any steps necessary to see that Xuetas are not disgraced and do not disgrace themselves. The behavior of any Xueta is a reflection on all; thus one has more than his own personal reputation to worry about.

Neighborly intimacy and defensiveness in their relations with other Mallorcans are among the most distinctive traits of the Xueta social milieu. The Xueta child learns early to distinguish between *we* and *they*, before really knowing who we and they are. A Xueta informant told me that he was sure he had learned a distrust for people outside of his immediate neighborhood that was qualitatively different from attitudes towards outsiders that other Mallorcans learned in their formative years. This is affirmed by the conversation of Xuetas in which the usage of terms such as *un dels nostres* (one of ours), *de nosaltres* (of ourselves), *els nostres* (those of us) is continuous and unceasing. The term Xueta is hardly ever used within the group, simply the well understood *we* and *us*. The degree of group consciousness evident in conversation is phenomenal. A child maturing in this environment learns a certain fear of and a hostility towards those on the outside. But while he is learning this, he is also learning a profound pride for the island of Mallorca and a child's faith in the ideals of Christianity.

Prior to the turn of the century, children's formal education was carried out in privately arranged classes, when it occurred at all. Most children had no opportunity for acquiring a formal education, but instead learned some trade or skill from a parent or a relative, along with some writing and arithmetic skills. Private formal education was very prestigious, and most reputable schools forbade the entrance of Xueta children, even though in many cases their parents could well afford the fees. So the Xuetas had to form their own classes with their own teachers. Because of this situation, prior to the period of World War I a Xueta child had little chance to encounter a non-Xueta age-mate during the primary school years. When state supported education programs were developed in the twenties, all children attended schools on an equal basis. For most children, though, secondary education was the apprenticing of a craft, and this was done back in the environment of the family and the neighborhood.

In the pre-puberty and puberty years, the Xueta boy would inevitably encounter many age-mates who were not Xuetas. The free and open attitude that exists between Spanish males stands in vivid contrast to the numerous restrictions placed on females from the earliest age. Mallorca is a very secure place for children to grow up, the only real danger being traffic; thus the typical Mallorcan boy roamed the city at will, visiting the port, playing ball games in the narrow streets or wandering to the open fields. In this early play situation the Xueta boy inevitably learned of the hostility existent in the larger society towards Xuetas. Many Xueta men can tell of childhood experiences in which they joined their age-mates to shout anti-Xueta rhymes or make derisive remarks about Xuetas while passing a jewelry or watch-repair shop. A Xueta informant told me of a childhood experience in which he walked down the Street of the Silver Shops singing anti-Xueta songs. He said his friends did not have to persuade him; he was eager to do it. One of the childhood games was a turkey fight in which the loser was called a Jew. Xueta and non-Xueta children both played this and similar games.

During the period of courtship, the Xueta, non-Xueta distinction was re-emphasized. Although a Xueta boy might stop and talk with a non-Xueta girl on the promenade, by the time they exchanged names, and thus identities, the flirtation was understood by both to have little chance of going any further. Xueta, non-Xueta friend-ships and evaluations in sexual terms occurred rather freely, but the problems of an engagement and marriage were so formidable that attachments rarely passed the superficial state. The only realistic thing to do was to seek a fiancé in one's own circle. The Xueta girl's socialization occurred very close to her mother and was lacking in the informal encounters with outsiders that young boys experi-enced. They were especially warned against alliances with non-Xueta boys by their parents lest something unpleasant should de-velop.

The Xuetas' pariah status did not prevent them from looking down at other members of the society. Children were especially warned against associating with the children of the poor or taking any interest in an occupation of low status. Although being Jewish had a negative value in this provincial society, the Xuetas em-phasized among themselves the Jewishness of Christ, Mary, Joseph and Paul. The hostility they bore was, they told each other, nothing compared to the trials of the first Jews who chose Christianity; so they could take pride in both their Jewish ancestry and Christian beliefs, and could endure the hostility of other Mallorcans. This peculiar socialization process produced an adult Mallorcan as pro-vincial as any other, who had many of the ghetto experiences of Jews in other parts of the world along with the belief in salvation and redemption through Christianity.

## STATUS

The data on occupations shows quite clearly that the Xuetas are for the most part an entrepreneurial, middle-class group. A few have become quite rich, but the Xuetas are not as a group a financially powerful part of the Mallorcan economy. Community lending ar-rangements and self-help program have set the Xuetas apart as the group with the smallest number of poor in their midst. Those who are poor are for the most part in that condition because of age, illness, inherited deficiencies or some other circumstance that makes the individual unemployable.

For centuries there has been an internal two-class system in

which the terms *orella alta* (high-eared) and *orella baixa* (low-eared)
were used to distinugish the wealthy and the common. Xuetas say
they do not use these terms any more. However, they were in use
from as long ago as the thirteenth century up until the 1940s.
Regardless of the terms used, there is still a high awareness of status
within the community. The present condition seems to be more of a
three-strata set-up than two, even though the top and bottom
categories are quite small.

The Xuetas, like the Mallorcan peasants, do not consider hard
work demeaning. In this respect they are unlike the nobility of
Spain or those of the poor who emulate them. The values of nobility, to be discussed later, place high value on bravery and daring and
low value on day-to-day labor. A large number of Xuetas are involved in laboring tasks, but they are unlike other laborers in that
their effort is for a family business rather than a non-kin proprietor.
In spite of the non-noble character of their work values, there is a
historical case of Xuetas trying to emulate the aristocracy, and this
ended feebly.

In the eighteenth century the nobility began to assume greater
importance in Mallorcan society than they ever had previously. The
values of nobility became very fashionable and a number of Xuetas
who were quite rich set out to secure titles for themselves. In 1773
they appealed to Charles III, King of Spain, explaining their case,
and the king looked favorably upon their request. They were assigned noble titles and became known in Mallorca as the *perucas* or
wigs.

The wigs lived in a style beyond their means, supporting opulent
summer homes well staffed with servants and decorated with valuable paintings and furniture. As they were Xuetas, the non-Xueta
aristocracy would not marry with them, and as they were noble,
they would not marry with non-noble Xuetas. So for eighty years
they aspired to a rule of aristocratic endogamy. Each family had its
own coat of arms and these they displayed with great pride. They
continued as an indentifiable segment of Xueta society up until the
period of World War I, and then through intermarriage blended in
with the rest of Xueta society.

The substitution of the ethics of the aristocracy for those of the

Xueta community are apparent in a letter from King Charles III to Don Bruno Cortes, one of the original committee of six who went to the king seeking noble status. In the letter the king pointed out that Cortes came from a family of high distinction with a reputation for propriety and honesty; that this family dealt in business only at the wholesale level, and that Sr. Cortes himself had never worked with his hands. The king also recognized that he had been kind to the poor, and because of this honored him with the responsibility of taking care of the feeding of the prisoners in the royal jail, and of those who were imprisoned in galleons as oarsmen. In response to the king's letter, Cortes and his friends gave the king a large and modern sea vessel, and in return the king gave Cortes the right to build a public chapel in his home, a truly singular award.

The local Christian nobility was impressed by these royal favors and treated the wigs with appropriate demeanor. The final touch was provided when the Queen, María Teresa de Villabriga, came to Mallorca and stayed in the summer home of a Xueta noble. The downfall of the *perucas* parallels the downfall of many other noble families. Decreasing incomes and the expenses of supporting the appurtenances of aristocratic living ended in financial disgrace (Forteza 1966).

This episode is interesting for a number of reasons. Jewish communal values and customs have survived among the Xuetas long after knowledge of Jewish law and religious beliefs had been forgotten. The Xueta nobles having acquired their wealth with these values began to lose their fortunes as they emulated the ways of Christian aristocracy. Downward mobile, anti-work and anti-commerce nobles particularly resented the industry and acquisitiveness of the Xuetas. In a short commentary written in the first decade of this century, the Catalan artist Santiago Rusiñol, in "Another Street" (1905), describes his impressions of the Street of the Silver Shops, and in this essay a kind of tolerant disdain towards the industry of Xuetas felt by a deteriorating aristocracy is very apparent. Sr. Rusiñol's own dedication to leisure is revealed in a recent book by Luis Fabregas y Cuxart (1965), in which he states that the author spent thirty-seven months sitting in the same cafe writing the little pieces for the short book *Isla de la Calma* from which the following excerpts are taken. In the introduction to this essay, Rusiñol talks about the quiet and restful streets of old Palma, but notes that on the Street of the Silver Shops there is only the clamor of business. Then he asks:

> What can they be doing here, so many people gathered together in these boxes; poking their noses out of the little windows and furtively watching the passers-by; amusing themselves with their lacemaking; working on little wheels with pincers; pulling out drawers full of precious stones and putting them in the presses? Anyone would think they are playing at keeping shop or something of that sort; that they are watching the souls of the clocks to see what makes them move; making samplers with hair, or embroidering with gold or silver thread. But, they must have some other occupations, because with so many children that to find room for them in their houses they have to put them on the shelves, they cannot spend their lives in amusement only. There must be some secret here that the stranger is unable to discover.

Later on, Rusiñol describes the Xuetas, and comments on their relations with the noble families of the island.

> They are active, restless, amiable and communicative, and as nearly all are related, the whole street is like one great family. Sometimes, the women and children, chattering like magpies, set out with a box which means they are off to play at buying and selling. They go to the villages and farmhouses, running hither and thither sniffing about and examining everything. Here they change a new ring for six old and two new ones besides. There they regulate a clock, and a little further on they break another and buy it too; and up and down, going and coming, they eventually get to the nobelmen's houses where they find the best collections. The porter's cat, inflated with sleep, does not even give them a glance, as they come towards the house; so if the door is open they go straight in. The old servants, because they are old, and no longer have any use for jewels or jewelry, let them select what they like. The majordomo, resting comfortably in an armchair, is scarcely conscious of what is happening and continues his nap which he began two generations back. His master has gone out . . . to the place where the ancestral estates used to be, and the people with the little box poke their noses into all the cupboards, search in every writing-desk, force the secrets of the family chests and, selecting this,

replacing that, at last they come to something glittering, make an offer, and buy it.

Sometimes it is a memorial medal; at others the cross of a rosary which has been hanging there ever since the days when these same people with the box committed those offences that are alleged against them; occasionally it is a relic, the ring of an old countess, or the seal of a barony. As long as it glitters or is an antique they buy it; there is nothing which does not amuse or serve to distract them. They would and do buy, if they can, the very parchments, carpets, bridal-chests, jewel-cases; the stones of the capitals and the windows of the facades.

They carry everything away, and their doing so is watched with indifference by the inhabitants of the palaces. The cat, the porter, the servants all see it; the master too knows, but considers the arrival of someone with a box to buy things of so little importance (moreover, one who asks so courteously) that he is quite content to let the things go; such absurd things too, so rusty and out-of-date. So, too proud to haggle, or too lazy to refuse, he lets them carry the things away, shrugging his shoulders and smiling as if to say "Poor things, go back to your street and amuse yourselves."

And certainly they do return to their street and quickly too. They gather all the family round them, husband, little ones and big ones; they show them what they have bought and spend all the week arranging and altering; taking away the coat of arms from some jewel, adding an inscription to another, mending, pulling to pieces, and remounting, with every pair of scissors in action.

Such activity and clamor; this disturbing the waters of the pond of tranquillity; this aptitude for amusing one's self with old things and making them into new; the spreading of clipped wings even in a country of repose; making money and not spending it, are not these greater evils than those old offences against the Christians? Too much activity is not in harmony with these calm islands.

## PERCEIVED DISTINCTIVENESS

We see in city life the problem of both too little and too much identification with a particular segment. In the midst of complexity and diversity some people lose the customs and identities of their ancestors and find themselves coping to survive in a system they do not really understand with little or no awareness of who they themselves are or how they fit into all that is around them. And others find, in this same milieu, that their identity is so vivid, and their enculturation so distinct, that their every action is perceived in terms of their segment membership. They spend their lives denying, avoiding, apologizing, justifying and rationalizing this identity, and their very existence in the city can be seen as ways and means of coping with the problem of too precise identification.

The Xuetas, to be sure, fit the latter extreme. So much of what they do is commented on in terms of their being Xueta that the individual must overcome widespread preconceptions to provide an identity for himself. There is an old saying in Mallorca "*Es Xueta, fa Xuetadas*," which can be translated "he is a Xueta, he does Xueta things" or "he is a Xueta, so he acts like one." With Xueta distinctiveness being affirmed in a positive way from within the group and negatively from without, the individual's conception of self is inevitably strongly associated with segment membership.

The conception of self as a Xueta includes an awareness of physical distinctiveness as well as cultural and social difference. In 1936, Baruch Braunstein wrote "For the most part the Chuetas intermarry among themselves, their offspring revealing, after so many generations of inbreeding, the outstanding Semitic characteristics, almost to a point of caricature."

Miguel Forteza (1966) describes his group as having "large curved noses with a sack at the bottom, curved spines with caved in chests, bald in the center of the head with lots of hair on the sides. The hair is typically dark with small curls. Women use wigs because they don't have much hair on the top of their heads. Eyes are small and vague and the voice has a particular timbre or quality." Xueta informants have said to me, "I know I look like a Jew. Why shouldn't I. I am one." Many Mallorcans are convinced they can recognize a Xueta on sight just by physical features. Obviously the belief that Xuetas are morphologically distinctive is general. Nevertheless, I think it is more myth than reality.

Xueta endogamy has resulted in a distinctive urban gene pool, but the physical features to not *contrast* with the surrounding population. Both the Xuetas and the non-Xuetas are products of similar combinations which occurred at different periods in history. Both are mixtures of so-called Semitic, Mediterranean and Alpine sub-racial types. Centuries of Islamic domination have resulted in a strong semitic infusion into the larger population. From the thirteenth to the seventeenth century Mallorcan Jews were intermarrying with Christians, such that more than fifty percent of the overall population has some Jewish ancestry. If the Xuetas "look Jewish" so does such a large part of the Mallorcan population that it is absurd to make a distinction. Almost any Mallorcan would "look Jewish" if he stood in front of a jewelry shop in the Street of the Silver Shops, and almost any Xueta would easily blend into the range of variation characteristic of the Mallorcan population and in no way appear distinctive. So given the endogamy and inbreeding, I am still convinced that the morphological distinctiveness of the Xuetas is more myth than reality. But in his conception of self, the individual Xueta is very conscious about the ways in which he does or does not appear as Jewish.

The Xuetas feel they are culturally different than the larger population. This is usually stated in defensive terms, such as "we have our own life here, but it's a very good life." Forteza not only points out that the voice quiality of Xuetas is different, but he describes them as exceptionally oral and talkative while at the same time reacting in a defensive manner, inspired by feelings of inferiority. Many Mallorcans who praise the Xuetas as fine Mallorcan citizens and undeserving of popular criticism nevertheless maintain that the Xuetas are sub-culturally different. One well educated informant said, "If you were to come into a room of people talking and one were a Xueta, you could pick him out from his attitude and demeanor. One can't say why exactly, but you can recognize a Xueta by his behavior." This sub-cultural variation, if it exists, and many people say it does, is not apparent to an outsider. It is not apparent to mainland Spaniards who have lived on the island for ten years nor to an anthropologist who has lived there for three. It is nevertheless true that Mallorcans perceive Xuetas, and Xuetas perceive themselves, as culturally distinctive, a variation of the Mallorcan mainstream.

If an individual is not perceived as Xueta by other indicators, revelation of his surname clearly identifies him as Xueta to even the most innocent Mallorcan. As pointed out in the first chapter, there are fifteen surnames known as Xueta names. Away from Mallorca these names have no connection with Jewish identity, and as far as origin is concerned, some are Castilian, some Catalan, and some Italian. But in Mallorca they are the clearest markers of all of Xueta origins.

All Mallorcans, and even some foreigners, are aware of the fifteen names, even today. One man with six children said, "I have never discussed Xuetas with my children nor pointed out the names, yet all my children know them. They learn them in school and from their friends." I asked his ten-year-old son if he could tell me the fifteen Xueta names. With little difficulty he game me ten of them. The five he could not provide he could identify immediately when he heard them.

The apparent Jewishness of Xueta names is in direct contradiction to their historical origins. Cortés is a common Spanish name, the origin of which is probably Andalusia. In Mallorca it is Xueta. Fuster is a Catalan name meaning carpenter. Carpentry was never a Jewish occupation in Mallorca, yet Fuster is a Xueta name. The same applies to the rest of the Xueta names: Aguiló, Bonnín, Forteza, Martí, Miró, Picó, Piña, Pomar, Segura, Taronji, Valenti, Valleriola and Valls.

At the same time other names which are unquestionably of Jewish origin are not identified as such in Mallorca. One of the most notable figures in Jewish history is Moses Maimonides. He is known in English by this Greek spelling of his name. The name he used was Moses ben Maymo. The name Maymo is quite common in Mallorca and its possessors are quite surprised to be told that it is of Jewish origin. Some of the names common in Mallorca which are etymologically Jewish, but which are not in contemporary times identified as such, are: Abraham, Daviu, Elias, Jordá, Sansó, and Solom.

The Xueta names are identified as Jewish as they are the names of those people who were punished for relapsing into Judaism in the late seventeenth century. Books, documents and memorabilia from the *autos de fé* of this period have served to remind the populace as to who the heretics were. Jewish names of those who assimilated such as Maymo and Daviu, names that were not associated with seventeenth century *autos de fé*, have come to be thought of as just ordinary Mallorcan names.


RELIGION

As stated earlier I will not try to answer the question of whether the Xuetas are really Catholic or really Jewish because such a question is unanswerable. One can look at church affiliation, and see that in that respect the Xuetas are quite Catholic. Those who declare adherence to Catholicism are inevitably ardent followers of the faith. Some might even be described as fanatic. Overall, the variation in adherence to Catholicism parallels the larger population. There is a Spanish saying that goes, "Everyone in Spain follows the Church, some with a cross and some with a stick." That some Xuetas are anti-church does not make them Jewish, it merely reflects the range of responses of all Spaniards to Catholicism. The church has been a participant in various political struggles throughout the history of Spain, gaining strong allegiance from some and antipathy from others.

In discussing this topic it must be remembered that religion comprehends more than affiliation, ritual and ceremony. It includes values, morals and a theory about the meaning of life and those aspects of our existence that are beyond rational explanation. As regards ritual, the Xuetas are almost exclusively Roman Catholic. Yet traces of Jewish ritual survive, in many cases without the practitioner being aware of their origin. However, in percentages that most think are higher than in the population as a whole, the Xuetas attend mass, receive communion, go to confession and adhere generally to all the requirements of the seven sacraments of the Catholic Church.

Participation in ritual has been, according to a variety of informants, characterized by great ostentation. Miguel Forteza says that Xuetas are religious exhibitionists, but their fervor is none the less real. They pray with great passion and gesturing and some have been known to climb upon the pew in a kneeling position so that the extent of their passion could be seen by all. Xueta women are generally thought to be more ostentatious than non-Xueta women, and this propensity plus religious fervor and Xueta control of the jewelry business accounts for the enormous religious pendants, broaches, crucifixes and madonna-bearing medallions that they display in their dress. There is little doubt that this religious exhibitionism, and concomitant defensiveness, is a product of religous persecution in earlier times.

But with Catholic commitments, Jewish identity nevertheless remains strong, even in these days when there is reason to believe that it is getting weaker. It must have been much stronger at the turn of the century or even in the thirties and forties. Jewish sympathies were strong during the six-day war, and the admiration for Moishe Dayan was effusive if not public. A Xueta man, curious about his Jewishness, travelled to Barcelona to attend services at the synagogue there. Certainly this is not an isolated incident. However, upon returning he confided his experience to and discussed it with a close friend in the Catholic clergy. One particularly anti-Catholic Xueta has a sign on his door in which he identifies himself as a Protestant and Sephardic Jew. He says his Protestant affiliation is a step in the direction to eventual Judaism—when he understands it better. I could list various other manifestations of Jewish consciousness and feelings, but such remarks serve only to upset the majority of piously Catholic Xuetas and infuriate the minority whose commitment to Catholicism might be described as pathological. Encountering members of this latter category, I have been rebuked for suggesting that they might not be two hundred percent Roman Catholic, even after I made it clear that my inquiries were only academic. In contrast, it is the opinion of many thoughtful Xueta informants that feelings of Jewish identity or retention of Jewish customs are no barrier to one being a good Catholic. Many of the clergy share this opinion. We will discuss the syncretic quality of Xueta beliefs further in another chapter.

## BARRIO SOLIDARITY

Kinship, occupation, proximity and patterns of mutual assistance form the backbone of Xueta social organization. They are supported by a feeling of unity derived from common ancestry and a Jewish communal tradition. Overlaying this are Mallorcan and Spanish traditions of community, such as those of the neighborhood, or *barrio*. We will now look at the community as a whole and compare it with other barrios in the city of Palma. Like other barrios, the neighborhood whose nucleus is the Street of the Silver Shops has its own stores and bars which are neighborhood gathering places. The women gather in the grocery stores, in no hurry to select their purchases, and much involved in gossip in the interim. This is the pattern in any neighborhood. The men gather at the bar at the end of the street during the day and at night, passing hours amidst conversation, games and social drinking that stops far short of drunkenness. This is common in most barrios, but the degree of affinity between the bar and the residents in this neighborhood is somewhat unusual. Not only is the clientele almost exclusively from the street, but the street is in fact an extension of the bar. One sees this in the form of a waiter running up and down the street carrying a tray of soft drinks, coffee and alcoholic beverages to the jewelers in their stores. One can get service in one's shop as easily as from a table in the bar.

Another important institution is an old Spanish tradition with antecedents from cosmopolitan centers known as the *tertulia*. A tertulia is a circle of friends, usually meeting at one cafe, whose coming together is devoted almost entirely to conversation. Some tertulias are devoted to special topics sush as philosophy, science and art, and most typically to literature. A famous literary tertulia in Madrid is said to have lasted fifty years. One of the more famous tertulias in Mallorca, devoted to literary and political topics, and a critical center of city life in the early 1900s, was held in the Café Oriente in the heart of Palma. The best remembered Xueta tertulia which was also of that period and continued for many years was held in a drugstore. It was neither literary nor scientific, but merely a center of gossip, politics and camaraderie, with the most important topic being the jewelry business and the meaning of local politics for Xuetas. We know about this tertulia from Miguel Forteza whose uncle owned the pharmacy, C'an Querol, and who remembers it well. This was only one of many tertulias, for they come and go. In contemporary times the Bar Plata is not the only important center of conversation. In a drugstore just around the corner another group of Xuetas gather each morning. This is not a tertulia of jewelers, but is rather made up mostly of men who have moved to other parts of the city and who come back regularly to partake in an ongoing conversation. Only the most enduring become well known, but as an institution the tertulia represents a recurring pattern of male association and an important network of neighborhood and segment communication.

Another center of male activity was organized sixty years ago so that Xuetas could partake, as other Mallorcans do, in the ceremonial processions of holy week. Holy week, including Easter, is by far the most important ceremonial date on the Spanish calandar, far exceeding Christmas in importance. The processions of holy week, held in the major cities of Spain, are among the most moving and spectacular commemorative events held on the continent. The procession takes place on the evening of Holy Thursday, and is made up of floats depicting scenes from the life of Christ, especially the events leading up to the crucifixion, and these floats are borne on the backs of men who do the labor as penance. In order to have their own float, a group of Xueta men formed a brotherhood called the *Cofradía de la Cruz de Calatrava*, the Brotherhood of the Cross of Calvary. The name was common for brotherhoods in other cities, but none so named had existed in Palma. To insure its authenticity, the founders travelled to Seville to study the costumes, traditions, and regulations of the Seville chapter, for Seville has the most authentic and well-known holy week procession in all Spain.

The penitents who carry the floats wear a hooded costume that closely resembles the ceremonial dress of the Ku Klux Klan in America—great peaked hoods and long robes. Mallorcans had long worn these robes for the procession, but colors varied. In their exuberance for correctness and authenticity, the Xuetas had all their penitents wear robes of the same color, a practice that was quickly copied by all the other brotherhoods. The Cofradía de la Cruz de Calatrava continues till this day. It has various community functions but its major activity is preparation for the events of holy week.

Little has been mentioned about the church of Santa Eulalia, a gigantic and ancient structure at the end of the main street of the "ghetto." This is a center of Xueta religious ritual, and this was the first church where Xueta men were admitted to holy orders, delivered sermons and said mass. Santa Eulalia is not the church that was formerly a great synagogue. That is Montesión only a few minutes' walking distance away. But the church of Santa Eulalia has been jokingly referred to as the synagogue of the Xuetas, and no one in Mallorca ever found it very strange that the descendants of Jews should all worship together in one Catholic church. So this particular church served to unite the neighborhood, with its boys' clubs, teenage dances, men's clubs and ladies' sodalities. It is generally agreed that church-imposed boundaries, as much as anything else, served to keep the Xuetas apart from the rest of the city.

As already stated, a Xueta priest was likely to be assigned to Santa Eulalia, although certainly not all the priests of this parish were Xuetas. Their acceptance in other parishes was tenuous, and for years Xueta priests were not allowed to preach in the great Cathedral of Palma. The occasion of the first sermon by a Xueta priest in the Cathedral was an event of great importance in the community. It occurred in the time of the Spanish Republic (1930s), and although an enthusiastic throng came to hear him, Padre Bartomeu Cortés, the Xueta priest, gave an ordinary sermon, as if preaching in the Cathedral were something he was very much accustomed to (Forteza 1966).

The Street of the Silver Shops is not like it used to be, especially as regards the informality of interaction. Today the shops have expensive plate glass windows, and shopkeepers wear suits. This came with the shift from jewelry manufacture to jewelry sales. Not so long ago the craftsmen worked at tables on the street in front of their stores with hammers, forceps and gas torches. Families sat at open windows talking across the street, which is at most about twenty feet wide, a distance which allowed for much sharing of household activities for those apartments that were opposite each other. A child practicing an accordian or a guitar could be heard throughout the neighborhood, as could a family fight or a party. The apartments go up three to four flights over the stores and consist on the average of about five rooms. Usually the only windows are the two facing the street, with the bedrooms in the back totally enclosed, and in darkness even during the day. For those who lived in the back of shops there were no windows in their apartments, only the light that came from the store, the meeting place for visitors, and actually part of the home.

The streets that made up the Xueta neighborhood were a world so cut off from the rest of the city that outsiders on the street were seen as tourists. In business hours the traffic was heavy and outsiders passing through the neighborhood were known to hurl traditional insults quite freely at those residing on the street. Being a Xueta, in one sense, meant becoming accustomed to aspersions on your identity, and accepting them without outward response.

The community and its internal organization have long shown a high degree of solidarity and unity. It is a community where even today the actions of one reflect on all, and where cooperation far outweighs competition. While shopping for jewelry on the street, which I did frequently as part of this study, I told shopkeepers that I wanted to look in other stores before making a decision. Although sorry at not having made a sale, the owner would never criticize the merchandize or selection of his competition. The competitive feeling was there, for Xueta merchants are known for the enthusiasm for which they meet customers at the front of the shop and guide them into the store, but it is never expressed in deprecating remarks about the competition.

To the degree that one Xueta's disgrace is a disgrace to all, and one Xueta's success an achievement for all, the Xueta community is qualitatively different from other barrios in Palma. Nowhere else, even among the artistocracy in their two neighborhoods or among the transient gypsies, is the individual so closely linked to his group. The cohesion of this community is clearly based on the tradition of the religious community of Jews who are the ancestors of today's Xuetas. The persistence of this community through a period of openly organized Judaism, then a period of crypto-Judaism, and a Xueta period of Catholic-Jewish syncretism is a product of both internal organization and the isolating pressures imposed by the larger society.

The Xueta community we have looked at has direct continuity back to Muslim dominated Mallorca and the Christian reconquest of the island. There have been Jewish communities in Mallorca as far back as Roman times, but continuity to the present cannot be established historically. For our purposes, we are only interested in the Christian era, the last 742 years, for with reconquest, a whole new culture displaced the Muslims, and a newly organized capital city dominated the island. We will now proceed to search out the foundation of the contemporary Xueta community. The roots of this community are to be found in the forms of the medieval *aljama* in thirteenth century Mallorca, the subject of the next chapter.

# Medieval Jewish
# Community of Mallorca

In the middle of the thirteenth century, during the reigns of James I of Aragon and his sons, Jews and Christians lived together as two very distinct and different cultures in a relationship of close contact. The contact was highly formalized by tradition and the laws of the state, characterized by economic symbiosis, ritualistic isolation and endogamy. Although the Christian society was by far the larger and more powerful, the smaller Jewish society was notably more advanced in technology, and more sophisticated in the intricacies of international and regional commerce. The Jews retained a distinctive Hebraic culture preserved within the community by religious conservatism, but were at this time in their history largely under the influence of Islamic culture and the Arabic language. They had been an integral part of the great Islamic empire which in its zenith extended from the Atlantic to the Indus valley, an empire which though diminishing in size in the thirteenth century had been from the eighth century to the twelfth the most powerful and advanced in the world.

At the time of the Christian conquest of Mallorca in 1229, the cities in the Mediterranean north had matured to a point where they were comparable to the great centers of trade in the Islamic world. Genoa and Pisa, as major trading centers in the Christian world, dominated trade in the western segment of the Mediterranean. But this trade was harassed and stunted by the threat of Saracen pirates operating out of Barbary coast ports and from the southern shores of

Spain. Mallorca, located in the center of the western Mediterranean, was a strategic base of operation for whoever sought to dominate the area. The conquest of Mallorca by James I is usually seen
as a major step in the reconquest of the peninsula by the Christian
north, but represents in the larger scope of history the achievement
by the north of developed urban trading economies to a level which
the Muslims had maintained for five hundred years.

The Jews, as an easily controllable segment which possessed the
mercantile and technological achievements of the great Islamic
civilization, were seen by James as part of the booty of conquest.
Mallorca was worth more with a Jewish community than without.
The king told his Christian subjects to leave the Jews in peace,
because they were the concern only of the royal house. James might
be compared to the leaders of developing countries today who are
militarily antagonistic to colonial overlords, but seek to emulate
their technology and sophistication. As a Christian warrior, James
was in large part motivated by religious ideals; but this did not
prevent him from recognizing the clear superiority of Islamic culture in technology and commerce. Aragon was at that time in the
process of escaping the restraints of feudal tradition, and the reign of
James I was a conscious effort to minimize royal dependence on the
vassalage obligations of nobles, and to increase royal power through
emulating the successes of urban trading economies in the Islamic
south and the Italian cities of the north. Keeping the Jews as part of
the booty of conquest while driving out Islamic military power can
be seen as an attempt to conquer and at the same time emulate one's
enemy. All historical evidence indicates that the Conqueror's plan
for Mallorca was to encourage its growth as a free, unfettered urban
trading community, and retaining the Jewish community in Mallorca was an important part of that plan.

James I was more than successful in his venture in Mallorca. He
lived to see Mallorca become a center of Mediterranean trade that
was the equal of Barcelona. During the reign of his son, James II,
Mallorca, as a port, was the rival of the great Italian trade centers,
Venice, Pisa and Genoa. At its peak, the city of Mallorca housed
30,000 seamen in the western section of the port which extended
out past the city walls to Porto Pi. It had at least 360 large trading

vessels and probably more. The products of its agriculture and craftsmanship were distributed to the most remote ends of the Black Sea, to Ethiopia, Constantinople and Alexandria. In return, they received slaves, or "heads" as they were then called, primarily of Slavic, Tartar and Circassian origin. The island held a monopoly on trade with the Barbary Coast where they exchanged oil and cloth for a fine quality of gold. Mallorcan merchants had consuls and contract houses in all the principal cities of North Africa, and had less frequent though regular exchanges with other trading centers, going northward as far as Flanders (Sevillano Colom 1968).

Both Jews and Christians grew rich on this trade. Neither monopolized it, but with their contacts abroad and with a long tradition of commerce within the community, the Jews were, in the word of Álvaro Santa María, "the propelling nerve of Mallorcan commerce" (Santa María 1956). Along with this trade came the development of the interior of the island. As a result of the conquest, the Saracens had either been driven out or ended up as indentured servants in agriculture. The countryside was an underpopulated, low-producing, agricultural region. It was not until the reign of James II that we see the settlement of the countryside and the creation of agricultural towns, whose political boundaries remain in effect today.

This period of Mallorcan history is worthy of detailed examination for it stands out as a "Camelot" in the history of Jewish-Christian relations. It is a period in which the most advanced thinking on symbiotic relationships between diverse cultural groups was given legal form by one of the most progressive leaders of the era. The rights of minorities were guaranteed, not because of the idealistic motives of the king, but because it was necessary in a culturally pluralistic society devoted to commerce. The rules that governed the relationships between Christians and Jews may seem crude to us now, but they dealt realistically with the situation, and were for the most part just. Rules such as those that responded to an obsessive concern with the protection of Christian women from the advances of Jewish men, and of Jewish women from male Christians, seem undemocratic and unfair to some. But they dealt with a cultural norm still common in the Mediterranean, where the honor of a

Calle del Sol, Palma

religious ethnic group was believed to reside in the untarnished
purity of its females. We see in thirteenth-century Mallorca an
urban system of values that effectively governed a new, growing and
culturally pluralistic city.

The historical description of Jews in Spain is frequently presented
in a tolerance-intolerance frame of reference, or is seen as a struggle
between competing ideas and belief systems. Although a great deal
of valuable historical data has been organized under these approaches, they are, as we asserted at the beginning, inadequate for
dealing with the complex problems that were involved in the survival of a Jewish community in a Christian society. One wonders
what the word tolerance meant to those who lived in this period, or
what it could have meant amplified to the limits of comprehension
within the framework of the culture. In what ways and to what
degree were the doctrines of Christianity and Judaism in competition, if at all. That the two systems had great difficulty living together does not mean that they were competing with each other. In
most periods the relationship seems better described as symbiotic
rather than competitive, or symbiotic with at least some segments of
Christian society while competitive with others. As we look back
over the centuries of Jewish-Christian relations in Spain, and more
specifically in Mallorca, one wonders whether the Jewish community as it was could have lived together with the thirteenth and
fourteenth-century Christian community, with neither assimilation
of one by the other, nor serious confrontations in periods of stress.
The historical evidence allows for a great deal of discussion pro and
con.

The question is answered in the affirmative in Mallorca, at least
in the good years lasting from 1229 to 1391. For 162 years the
Jewish community of Mallorca was one of the most peaceful and
productive in the Mediterranean. The larger Christian society,
made up primarily of Catalan migrants of bourgeois and peasant
origin, certainly benefitted from the community of cosmopolitan
traders who vastly improved commerce and contributed heavily to
the cultural advances that were concomitant with a flourishing sea
trade.

The question is answered in the negative by the evidence from the final years of the Mallorcan Camelot, a period that ended with the sacking and plunder of the Jewish quarter in 1391. Given the underlying patterns of relationships between the major segments of the society—the alliances, the struggles, the competition for limited resources, the doctrinal severity of both belief systems, and the inability of each to comprehend the other—it seems that the outcome was beyond the control of any group in the society. One can seriously question whether the outcome would have been very much different, had the greatest tolerance and diplomacy been exercised. It is not the kind of question we are prepared to answer now. We can look at the historical record of the Mallorcan Jewish community, examine it in the context of its relationships with the various segments of Christian society as well as the larger trends of the period, ponder the question, and hopefully reach some conclusions in the final chapter.

## THE JEWISH COMMUNITY

The thirteenth-century Jewish community in Mallorca was a state within a state, with its own assemblies, ordinances and magistrates. It was a legal body officially recognized and protected by the king. It levied its own taxes, set penalties for offenses and wrote and administered its laws in conformity with Hebraic tradition. It was not as some imagine medieval Jewish communities to have been, a group of persecuted people forced to live in segregation in one part of the city. To the contrary, it was a proud, wealthy and independent community whose members *chose* to exclude themselves from the rest of the population to practice their own religion, live by their own laws and customs, profit by their traditionally productive skills in trade and manufacture, and protect themselves from the contamination of foreign ideas and from the assimilationist pressures of the dominant culture. During the years from 1229 to 1391, the generations that lived out their lives in the Jewish community of Mallorca did all these things with great success. The community grew in size and wealth, kept the law, and retained its independence and cultural distinctiveness.

There is a tendency when discussing events that transpire over centuries to minimize the values of time and to think of centuries as if they were something much less than they are. The 162 years of the good life in Mallorca must be thought of as eight generations, or three or four full life cycles. The society that persisted through those years was in many ways quite sound and functional. The people who were born in that period lived out their lives in fulfillment and tranquility. It is from this base that we must account for what happened later, something which happens with tragic regularity in the history of the Jews. The chapter closed with violence, and with the persecution and slaughter of the innocent; and for those that survived there remained the choice between submission and denial of faith, and escape to a new life as refugees to a Jewish community in some little known and distant land.

Examining this community and comparing it with others, we see that there was only a small range of variation in the internal organization of Jewish communities in the area of the western Mediterranean, or for that matter throughout the entire Mediterranean littoral. Nevertheless, there were always local variations in its relation with the host society. There were also very basic structural differences in the way the community articulated into the Muslim society as compared with the Christian, and there was wide variation within each. However, there was one characteristic of the relationship which typified the community's ties in all Mediterranean cultures, and that was a carefully spelled out alliance with the center of power which served to guarantee the position and survival of the community within the system. In Aragon-Catalonia, in Castile, in Muslim Andalusia, and in other Christian and Muslim states, the Jewish ties with the larger society rested firmly on a contract with the ruling head of state: sultan, emir, king, or noble. Because the Jews were beholden to the ruler for their safety, he was able to rely on their whole-hearted allegiance, and in times of need he could make excessive demands on their material resources. Although Jews in Christian countries were not supposed to hold official posts, many did, and in some cases provided the backbone and manpower for state administration. For a king who was interested in doing away with feudal forms and encouraging the growth of commerce, Jewish administrators were clearly more helpful than were those from the noble class. Also, Jews were less likely to be involved in political intrigues in court society than were the nobles. For these and other reasons, their influence in the kingdoms of Mallorca and Aragon were great. Abraham Neuman, referring to the entire Iberian peninsula, writes: "Undoubtedly, Jewish power and influence in the court reached their zenith in the brilliant reign of James I . . ." (Neuman 1948: vol. 2, p. 230).

Under James I, the pattern of relationships between Christians and Jews was defined for many years to come. James I, king of Aragon and Catalonia and Christian conqueror of Mallorca, had established good relations with the Jewish communities of Aragon prior to his conquest of Mallorca. When his armies approached the walls of *Medina Mayurka* in 1229, the Jews ran from the Saracen-controlled city to protection behind the lines of the Christians. Although in most cases Jewish communities were better off in Islamic states than Christian, the Mallorcan state was at this time under the tyranny of the *Almohades*, fanatical Berber tribesmen who were provincial and intolerant zealots in contrast with prior Islamic dynasties. The Jews of Mallorca had learned from their co-religionists in other western Mediterranean communities of the brilliant and tolerant leadership of the Christian king of Aragon. With the conquest of the island, James became known as the Conqueror (*Jaime el Conquistador*) and added the title King of Mallorca to his many others. From the very beginning of this new reign, he provided the Jews with a central role in the organization of governance and commerce on the island. The year of the conquest, 1229, is for the Mallorcans comparable to the year 1776 for Americans. It is the year of their society's beginning, certified by a founding document, the *Repartimiento*, which formally divided the land of the island among those who had participated in the conquest. The participation of the Jews was officially recognized in this document. They were given sizeable lands, proportionate to their contribution to the conquest. However, the major concern of the Mallorcan Jews was the location of their community within the capital city, and their rights, duties and obligations under the new leader.

## INTERNAL ORGANIZATION

The Jewish *aljama* (from Arabic, meaning "meeting of men"), *call* (in Catalan), *Judería* (in Castilian) or *Kahal* (in Hebrew) was situated next to the royal palace, which was indicative of its special relationship with the king. Unlike the image of the ghetto we have from other times and places, the aljama of Mallorca was located on the most desirable property and ventilated by breezes from the sea. It contained within it a variety of dwelling types, the largest of which were equal to the palaces of nobles. The wealthiest of Jews were in many ways treated on a par with nobles, in light of their position with the king as his most trusted allies and the financiers of his military adventures. With their connections with Jews in other ports they provided an additional network for commerce as well as an alternative source of valuable news from other countries. What they wanted most from the king was safety, independence and the freedom to practice their religion and the skills that had become tradition in the aljama. With protection from the royal house, they had little to fear from the animosity of other elements of the society, who frequently perceived them as foreign intruders voraciously in pursuit of wealth.

Inside the aljama we find a highly structured society, regulated in minute detail by Hebraic custom and law. This was the level of government that Mallorcan Jews related to first. Their relationship to the larger state was almost totally through the offical representatives made up from the community's legislative body made up of twenty-four councilors and its administrative arm of five secretaries who were responsible for executing the decisions of the council and organizing the tax system (Pons 1957, 1960). There was also an executive secretary who maintained the archives and of course the rabbi functioned as ceremonial leader. This government had extensive powers granted to it by the king, but the ultimate sanction, ostracism from the community, emanated from the community's own tradition and was out of the jurisdiction of regal authority. The king recognized various sets of laws for the different estates in his kingdom; laws for nobles, clergy, city dwellers, the military and peasants. By the same logic there were separate laws for Jews and

Christians. Jews who looked to their own community for order and proper conduct found it perfectly reasonable that they should not be subject to the laws of Christians on the outside.

Among the rights belonging to the community were the apportionment of taxes and the organization of social services. The residents paid taxes in proportion to their wealth. Taxes on personal property and real estate were assessed regularly. Taxes for maintenance of the synagogue and the public baths and for tributes to the king could be assessed at any time with little advance notice. In recognition of the solidarity of their community, the king assigned taxes to the Jews as a group, while taxing Christians as individuals. This meant that the decision of who would contribute what toward payment of the tax bill was entirely an internal matter of the aljama. Apportioning the tax was a source of lively debate, especially the payment of irregular assessments. Taxes paid to each king varied with his needs and the general conditions of the economy. As the crown was almost continually at war, the pressures for increased taxation were great.

The tax officials within the aljama were usually from the official governing board. Their power was formidable. In their tax apportioning sessions they discussed each man's known wealth and any information that had been obtained on secret possessions. From this they arrived at the amount due by each citizen. There were many disputes, but the commissioners were armed with the authority of the secular government as well as that of Jewish law. The tax bill had to be paid. When the king demanded a specific amount, the community paid it, even if the rich had to pay for the poor. If someone refused to pay their assessment, threat of the ban of excommunication, or *herem*, could be used to obtain compliance. No one could leave the city without a certificate of clearance on tax debts. The king kept careful track of income in the aljama, frequently resorting to a secret census or the reports of informers.

The medieval Jewish community was not only a state within a state, but a culture within a culture. The foundation of cultural continuity as well as the bulwark of resistance against relentless assimilationist pressures was sacred law and revered tradition, which governed relations between Jews within the community and each member's relations with the outside world. Inside the community the law regulated every facet of aljama life through extraordinarily complex regulations on food, as well as detailed ordinances on sexual, fraternal, business and governmental matters. The law limited Jewish participation in extra-communal organizations, and imposed restrictions on the consumption of food that made personal alliances outside the community next to impossible. Refusing to eat with someone was a serious matter. As Max Weber has observed, "... in the Middle Ages commensality was the indispensable foundation for any kind of integration..." (Weber 1963, p. 154).

The primary function of education in the aljama was the learning of sacred law, a law which according to religious beliefs had its beginnings in a covenant with God. Since obeying the law was seen as nothing less than compliance with the terms of an agreement with the Almighty Himself, the motivation for correct learning was intense. Formal education, an important part of aljama life, was organized around two school, one for the children and one for the adults. Both met in the synagogue where education in law and participation in formal prayer were recognized as equally hallowed activities in the good Jewish life. Through the study of law, as well as by example, the Jewish child learned the rigidly ordered conduct expected of an aljama member. Beyond this socializing function, formal education included supplementary study in grammar and mathematics. Restrictions were imposed on inquiry as they were on personal contact with outsiders. Not only Christian but also Greek learning was considered suspect, especially the latter from whence it was feared the child might become tainted by the sins of Sodom and Gomorrah (Pons 1957). Expectations for female learning were considerably less than for the male, the young woman spending most of her day apprenticing in the management of a household.

The Jewish child started his education by learning in Hebrew, "Moses commanded us the Law as an inheritance of the congregation of Jacob. Hear, O Israel: The Lord our God, the Lord is One." If a young man's family could afford the payment of a tutor, he studied the Torah and Hebrew during the years six to eight. Following that he studied the *Mishnah* and from tradition and law he learned discipline and ritual. Few Jews in medieval Mallorca had training beyond this basic study. Having completed it, the young person apprenticed a trade or profession. For a person devoted to scholarship, however, the pinnacle of Hebrew learning was the Yeshiva, but this course necessitated a long sea voyage and financial support for years of study. The teacher-scholar produced by Yeshiva training returned to a crucial role in aljama life, for the simple people of the community, frequently the most religious, could not hope to understand the law alone, and they looked to the scholar for advice and assistance. Here we see the roles of scholar and holy man converging in one person, paralleling the synagogue's function as center of education as well as ritual.

The central role of the synagogue in Mallorcan aljama life can hardly be exaggerated, as it was the center of all community-wide activities, religious or secular. It was the largest building in the community and was located within easy access to all. It was usually of Moorish design and formed a complex with the schoolhouse, the public assembly hall, and any edifice specifically built for charitable purposes. The size was restricted by state regulations which stated that it could not compete in size and beauty with the Christian church.

We have seen the synagogue's important role in worship and education, but for many aljama members an even more important function was its decisive role in measuring status in the community. Nothing except possibly tax assessments was more important to a man than his position in the seating arrangements of the synagogue. Places were allotted in accordance with social standing; hence great disputes arose over this public recognition of status, especially where distinctions were not clear cut. Pons's work (1957, 1960) reveals that the class terms the Xuetas used—*orella alta* and *orella baixa* as well as *del fas*, the ignorant—were in use as far back as the fourteenth century. Although these three terms defined broad categories, there was competition over smaller increments of status, and this lead to an active traffic in synagogue seats. An investment in a synagogue seat was not entirely for vanity, for when alll else was lost a once rich man could sell his space, or a dying man could bequeath it to his son. The synagogue seating arrangement was not only a manifestation of status, but also reflected the high degree of individuality in the community. Where some men might bring chairs into the synagogue, others would use only a bench. The more ostentatious could and did bring in ornate divans. This all took place in the men's section, while the women, according to custom, were segregated in a special compartment in the rear (Pons 1957, 1960).

As the community grew the number of synagogues increased. Mallorca had two in the fourteenth century. This division into two synagogues has been speculated upon as revealing some division within the community, but more than likely it was the product of normal growth, or the product of occupational rather than doctrinal divisions. In larger aljamas there might be twenty or twenty-five synagogues. The majority of these would be occupational synagogues attached to particular guilds or brotherhoods.

The synagogue, unlike the church, was a center of all aspects of life, not just religious worship. The court met there, oaths were administered, and *herem* was pronounced there. Resolutions of the council were submitted to worshippers during the religious service (Neuman 1948), and visitors from other aljamas were housed there when necessary. It was the lost and found, the school and the center of charity. Going to the synagogue was not seen as an obligation, any more than going to the *bodega* to play cards was an obligation for the Christian Spaniard. If it was sometimes lacking in the reverence displayed in Christian churches, it was because an essential difference between Jewish and Christian attitudes was the way in which they distinguished the sacred from the profane.

This was a community bound to and regulated by a sacred tradition, but more prosaically it was an association of jewellers, tailors, cloth merchants, shoemakers, bookbinders, dyers, butchers, etc., working closely with each other and involved in mutually productive though regulated contact with Christians on the outside. It was a community in which the possession of a specific skill was almost a religious matter, for the Talmud taught that the man who did not provide his child with a profession prepared him for a life of misery. Emphasizing industry over idle piety, communal values insured that no Jewish boy would mature without training in some useful skill. Ideally he would be a doctor, for this was the most important of learned occupations, and medicine was an area in which Jewish superiority was undisputed. It was also a profession in which the practitioner could greatly benefit his community by the influence that came with treating heads of state and religious leaders.

In the area of communal social services we see the medieval foundations of the nineteenth- and twentieth-century Xueta's distinctive institutions of charity. In the early community there was meticulous concern for the sick, the poor and the dead. The sick were provided with nursing care and medicine without charge. Those too poor to attend to their own needs were provided food and lodging by the community. To attend to the dead there was an association for the washing of bodies and the supervision of funeral ritual. Also the community provided and cared for three cemeteries for its members. In light of these traditions Antonio Pons (1957, 1960) has observed that if to the Christians on the outside "the Jews appeared avaricious, usurious and self-seeking, to each other they were kind, compassionate and considerate."

Finally, we come to the subject of marital arrangements, the key element in the social order of any community. In accord with the times, marriages were arranged in both Jewish and Christian sectors. However, if anything, the Jewish concern with marital arrangements exceeded those of the Christians. Anxiety for a good arrangement provoked numerous child marriages among the Jews. Spiritual rather than physical attraction was the ideal in marital relationships, and it was assumed that a secure relationship would develop in time simply through proximity. The personal preferences of the marriage partners was of secondary importance. When a young person reached maturity at thirteen, he or she might express strong feelings for an age-mate, but any display of emotion was frowned upon. In short, the Jewish marriage was ideally an arrangement which satisfied the status concerns of the parents, and which in the course of time produced an almost idyllic spiritual love between the spouses. In the end, however, it should also result in healthy progeny.

Although Jews and Christians tended to make much of each others alleged immorality, we find in this period many similarities in moral ideals. Sexual norms were very similar. For example, marital unfaithfulness was merely denounced when it occurred among males, but was condemned and severely punished when the transgressor was a woman. Even the suspicion of infidelity was sufficient for a man to break up his marriage. If a rumor was rampant, the victims of the gossip were forced to find its origin and prove it false, for a marriage could not survive with even the taint of distrust.

Marriage was a communal affair in more than the usual ways. As stated, community gossip by itself could break up a marriage, even if it were not true. It had to be exposed and proven false. If a marriage were secret, which in effect meant that it took place without the consent of the community, then it could be nullified on those grounds. Only a public ceremony was valid. When a bride lacked a dowry, the community treasury provided one, and when she married, a throng of people escorted her from the house of her father to that of the groom (Pons 1957, 1960).

The Jewish custom of betrothal was quite different from that of Christians. The law said that a woman was betrothed to a man when she accepted a gift from him, accompanied by the statement, "I betroth thee." Under the circumstances a girl could accept no gift from any man, lest she be tricked into a betrothal, for the law was very strict on this point. Jewish law protected the woman through a contract which spelled out the terms of the marriage, called the *ketubeh*. Most important of all, it included a list of the wife's dowered property. The list was frequently inflated in value at the bride's insistence and made divorce for a poor man all but impossible. If the husband should die, the wife was automatically wed to a surviving brother. This tradition of levirate marriage was usually a burden to the widow rather than a protection, for she could become subject to the power of a man with whom she might share little and who, if he so desired, could legally confiscate the family wealth for his own use rather than that of the widow and children.

We see in the medieval Jewish community a highly organized, formal and cooperative realtionship between all its members. It was an order, we have emphasized, that rested on adherence to sacred law. Although the law was meticulous and rather strictly enforced, it was not unchanging. Adapting the law to changing times and situations was the focus of scholarship in Jewish jurisprudence. The carefully measured change agreed to by legal scholars throughout the Diaspora was accepted with few reservations by particular communities, while the pressures for other kinds of change emanating from the host society encountered the full force of Jewish tradition.

## OUTSIDE THE WALLS

A mark of distinction for the aljama was its own gate through the city wall to the port area. This allowed merchants to reach the harbor quickly without passing through Christian sections of the city. As the port was the center of commerce, easy access to it was of the utmost importance. It was there that agreements and contracts were made, usually on an oral basis, requiring a minimum of two witnesses, with the number increasing in proportion to the importance of the exchange. The port was also the source of important trading news from ships coming in from Valenica, Sardinia, Genoa, Marseilles, Barcelona, Sicily, Tuscany, the Barbary Coast of North Africa, and at times, points far beyond that (Piferrer and Quadrado 1968, 1888).

In addition to foreign commerce, Jews were involved in numerous businesses throughout the city and the countryside. Although commerce took them to every corner of the city and the island, their own laws and those of the state required them to return to the aljama for meals and sleeping. Many gained their livelihood as street merchants in wool and cotton. Wealthy residents of the aljama had considerable land holdings on the island and in Aragon, but in no case were Mallorcan Jews known to have been directly engaged in agriculture. The only important restriction on the ownership of land by Jews was that they were not to use it as a basis for seigniorial rights in competition with nobles. But agriculturally based privilege and wealth was not in the mainstream of tradition with the Jews, and at this time in their history there was little interest in noble titles. Their connection with agriculture was almost exclusively limited to the sale of produce, the lending of money, the

Calle de la Portella, Palma

collecting of taxes and rents, and the sale of their tradesmen's goods and foreign imports to those who worked the land.

In many areas of day-to-day interaction, Jews and Christians got along cordially, if not affectionately, but there were a number of centers of repeated trouble. One of these was the market place. The Christians accused the Jews of defying custom and arriving at the market place before sunrise to purchase the best fruits, vegetables and animals. The custom of the agriculturally based Christians was to get up with the sun, but by the time they reached the market they found only the less desirable goods remained. They petitioned the king on the matter and a statute was put into effect which forbade Jews from entering the plaza until three hours after sunrise (Pons 1957, 1960).

Another center of conflict was the meat market where the Jews were guaranteed, in perpetuity by royal decree, the right to slaughter animals in their customary way. The rabbi was responsible for the correctness of the ritual; and for the concession of supplying the meat, he paid a tribute to the king of twenty morabatines a year, a considerable sum for the time. For reasons that can only be surmised, the meat market was a center of perpetual bickering between Jews and Christians and no matter what the king did to stop it, it persisted. This site of continual hostility confirmed the belief held by most people of the period that it was impossible for Jews and Christians to live in proximity without conflict.

The Christians were not prepared to understand the basis of Jewish slaughtering ritual, which to them appeared strange, mysterious and foreign. Also, failure to comprehend their business practices and medicine, which were a fusion of Hebraic and Arabic tradition, contributed to the cultural gap between Christians and Jews. This had not been the problem in Muslim countries. The Muslims thoroughly understood the dietary laws; and values having to do with conduct in the market place were a product of shared tradition (Goitein 1971).

As is typical of most minorities, the Jews understood the ways of the larger society better than the Christians understood them. The Christians followed a religious calendar highlighted by saints' days and holy days, and in doing business with the Christians, Jews signed contracts dated the day of St. John, James, or Peter and Paul. Inside the aljama, however, they followed another calendar which ordered religious duties, ceremonies and their relations with each other. In some cases Jews spoke the same language in and out of the aljama. In Mallorca Catalan was spoken by all. However, Jewish contracts, books, and records were frequently in Hebrew or Arabic, but never in the detested Latin of the church (Pons 1957, 1960).

The most fundamental distinction in the everyday activity of Jews was the profound awareness of difference between themselves and the outsiders that surrounded them. If the Christians viewed the Jews as killers of Christ who were compelled to live in suffering as a witness to the world for their dastardly act, the view the Jews had of Christians was equally devoid of admiration. Although there was beneath this contempt some pervading regard for all humanity as good and noble, each religious body ensured that the other was sufficiently well defined in semi-human terms to make any close relationship impossible. Continuous daily contact fostered a degree of tolerance and friendship, but in spite of this the Jews found the personal habits of Christians intolerable by their own standards. Their food was inedible, their women were impure, having never been cleansed of menstrual pollution, and their belief in a false messiah made them pitiable. In Mallorca, there was no visible barrier in the commercial sphere between Christian, Jewish, and Saracen merchant, but it was with a great sense of relief that the wandering peddler returned to the comfort of the aljama where he found a satisfying social order, which even though it was excessively rigid functioned in harmony with the word of God.

## INTERNATIONAL RELATIONS

The Jewish community of Mallorca can be seen as a small and isolated group surrounded by a Christian society, but it can also be seen as one of a network of societies that covered the Mediterranean from one end to the other. Therefore, the Mallorcan aljama cannot be fully understood if studied in isolation. The outside ties of the Jews of Mallorca were strongest with communities in Barcelona, Montpelier, Narbonne and Perpignan. There were also strong ties with communities living under Muslim rule in the areas that we now call Morocco and Algeria. But there was in addition continuous communication with numerous other communities throughout the Mediterranean on a regular basis.

The foundations of these relationships were banking and commerce. We know that Mallorcan Jews had continuing financial arrangements with Alexandria (Pons 1968). This of course is not surprising; only the distance involved is. But the regularity with which merchants traveled throughout the Roman sea is nothing less than amazing, considering the dangers and the means of transportation. S. D. Goitein, commenting on travel in the eleventh century, writes:

> A journey from Spain to Egypt or from Marseilles to the Levant was a humdrum experience, about which a seasoned traveler would not waste a word. Commuting regularly between Tunisia or Sicily or even Spain and the eastern shores of the Mediterranean was nothing exceptional. [Goitein 1971]

But even though merchants found sea voyages "humdrum experiences," the dangers and risks connected with them were real and serious. Also risky were the business alliances one made in foreign countries. One frequently traded with merchants of other religions: Jews in Tunisia with Christians in Italy, Muslims in Berberia with Christians in Spain, and Muslims with Jews throughout North Africa. If the agreement was to be fulfilled and not reinterpreted to the convenience of one or the other party, it was useful to have a co-religionist there to protect your interest. Thus, the value of ties between Jewish communities throughout the Mediterranean was based on the trust that existed between them. One looked out for the interest of Jewish foreigners in one's own port, knowing that reciprocal concern would protect one's interest in foreign ports.

The bonds between communities were in part based on law and tradition, but they were reinforced by exchange of personnel through migration and marriage alliances. The important heads of large commercial houses were predisposed to arrange diplomatic marriages with important families in other countries (Goitein 1971).

Also, when a good marriage was not available in one's own community, a traveling friend could arrange one in another. If a young man wanted to establish himself in a foreign country, the safest way for him to secure a reputation and position in the community there was through a good marriage. Marriage arrangements between communities set up a kin network that extended through national boundaries and for all practical purposes ignored the difference between Christian and Muslim states.

Craftsmen were mobile, too, as proven by the dispersion of trademarks throughout the Mediterranean. Although much less likely to travel than a merchant, a craftsman frequently found a change of location attractive, especially if he practiced a trade in which the people of his region excelled. In the new location he could profit from the reputation of his skill and his origin and assume a leading position practicing his craft. Of course, the craftsman was just as likely to move for reasons of economic decline, family problems, war and persecution.

Jewish scholars, like those of Islam and Christianity, were prone to wander merely to learn. Travel by itself was an asset to a learned man, but frequently the travel had some goal such as pursuing special studies with a scholar of reputation, or enrolling at one of the famous academies in the east. Among the Jews, the centers of learning were well known to all. They changed with the times, Cordoba, Jerusalem and Baghdad each being the most reputable during a particular period of history. Scholars travelled to these centers of learning to resolve legal disputes or to clarify leadership conflicts within their communitites. The leaders of Jewish communities were routinely approved by regional centers or by the religious authorities in Baghdad or Jerusalem. Submission to regional centers of outside authority was not automatic, however, as indicated by the agreement between Mallorcan Jews and King James, that the Mallorcan community would not be under the jurisdiction of the community of Barcelona.

Hebraic culture in the medieval Mediterrenean did not manifest itself in the empires or nations, such as those which characterized Latin Christian or Arabic traditions, but the organized and systema-

tic network of communities was nevertheless an intergral part of the
mechanisms of power and change in the region. Lacking armies, the
Jews made themselves known, respected, hated and feared through
their power in the market place. This power rested firmly on a then
incomparable network of communication and conditions of mutual
trust. In the Mediterranean cultural area, the scene of piracy, ship-
wreck and warring armadas, the ties between communities were
stable and unvarying. Based on kinship, reciprocity, a common law,
a central ideology, a shared language, specialized skills, and a zeal to
demonstrate that they were indeed the chosen of God, the Mediterranean Jews of the middle ages were at least as united and probably
more powerful than they could have been as a nation organized
under one government in a defined territory.

Unlike a territorially based nation, the Jewish network of communities could not fall with the loss of an army, or the willingness
of a leader to surrender or compromise. It was an ever-functioning
refugee organization, each community ready to pay the ransom of
pirates for the safety of unknown co-religionist, or to temporarily give
aid to victims of oppression. For those who would violate the relations of trust by betrayal, informing or dishonest dealings with fellow
Jews, ostracism was the ultimate penalty. Although a refugee from
persecution could find help in a foreign community, an ostracized
Jew would, through an efficient communications network, be discovered not too long after his arrival at a new location, and find
himself suffering again from the decision of his native community.
The dispersion of the communities in no way made it easy for the
individual to escape the sanctions of community law.

It was through the international communications network that we
explain the rapid increase in the population of the Jews of Mallorca
following the conquest of the island in 1229 by James I. Under the
*Almohades*, the Mallorcan community dwindled to fewer than four
hundred. The *Wali* of *Mayurka* had allowed the community to
function, but only under the severest of regulations and prohibitions. Following the conquest there was a rapid increase in the
population as the news travelled throughout the Mediterranean
Diaspora that Jews were welcome in the new domain of the tolerant
Aragonese king.

## THE KING AND JEWS IN MALLORCA

We have seen that James I maintained friendly relations with Jews while conquering Mallorca, Valencia and Menorca in the name of Christianity. Before the Holy See, he defended his exceptionally indulgent policies toward Jews by emphasizing their role in the collection of taxes to support his armies. James invited Jews to Mallorca as part of a plan of expansion and conquest, and to lure them, he provided what they wanted and needed most.

First of all, the Jews were offered full citizenship as townsmen. City dwellers were protected by *fueros*, carefully documented privileges and exemptions guaranteed by the king to specific cities and provinces. Shortly after the conquest, the king proclaimed the *Carta Pobla* or people's charter (March 1, 1230), that took the form of a constitutional document (Pascual y González 1956). It was composed of thirty-seven chapters dealing with civil, criminal, judicial and political matters. It clearly favored small landholdings over large, in an attempt to halt the transplantation of feudal forms and noble power. It encouraged tolerance of both Saracens and Jews. It separated civil from ecclesiastical power. Although property could be disposed of in any way the owner cared, there were restrictions on its passing into the hands of nobles, the church, or religious orders. The Carta Pobla instituted the basic organs of government and set the judicial norms. The Conqueror left the island in the hands of a royal bureaucracy that had the power and obligation to enforce the rules and the spirit of the founding document.

To the Jews specifically James I granted the following: the permission to keep all the wealth they brought with them to Mallorca; a guarantee that the testimony of a Jew in legal and business matters would be equal to that of a Christian; and a guarantee that in disputes between Jews and Christians there had to be Jewish as well as Christian witnesses. Jews were specifically granted the right to take securities for loans, to acquire lands of all types from any person or class, and to partake in all kinds of commerce. A formal proposal of marriage in Hebrew would be recognized as legal, equivalent to one witnessed by a Christian notary. No Christian or Saracen could remove as much as a stone from a Jewish cemetery. If a Jew were

treated unjustly by a local administrator, he had the right of direct
appeal to the king. The king promised that Jews would never be
compelled to reveal the contents of documents in the archives of the
aljama. The Jews of Mallorca were guaranteed autonomy and economic independence from the aljamas of Barcelona and the rest of
the kingdom. All contracts and oaths in Hebrew witnessed by Jews
would be as valid as those witnessed by a public notary (Pons 1957,
1960).

They were also, however, subject to the following prohibitions.
Jews could not hold public office over Christians (this was violated
in practice). Jews could not keep a Christian woman in the house in
any way including employment as nursemaid or servant, nor could
a Christian woman enter the house of a Jew for reasons of business.
A baptized Jew was forbidden to maintain business relations with his
former community. Christian women could not enter the aljama
except to buy merchandise, in which case they had to be accompanied by a responsible citizen; a married woman could enter the
aljama only when accompanied by two Christian men of good
reputation, and a widow or spinster had to accompanied by one.
Whores were not allowed in the aljama, it being required of them
that they restrict their business to the public plaza. Jews could not
sell meat to Christians, invite them to meals, bathe in their presence
or administer medicine to them.

It is easy to see in the privileges the Jews obtained that they were
primarily concerned with conditions for commerce, and that the
restrictions imposed upon them reflected the Christian concern
with the purity of their women and with countermeasures to Jewish
exclusiveness, such as those regulations which prohibited Jews from
sharing food in Christian homes.

In addition to the above, the Jews secured a privilege that was
probably the most important of all—the rights to a specific territory
that would be theirs alone. This was fundamental for carrying out
the law, which was in large part composed of rituals and exercises
which supported the maintenance of cultural boundaries. Jewish
relations with the larger society demanded both interaction and
isolation, and the terms for each were specified by religious law and
tradition. Rights of independence, self segregation, and their eco-

nomic role in the larger society were anchored to their agreements with the king. To protect these rights they were obliged to pay considerable taxes. That they might fulfill these financial obligations, the king encouraged them in their commerce and moneylending. The granting to Jews of the right to charge higher interest than Christians made the king's intentions unmistakably clear.

## COMMERCE AND MONEYLENDING

We see the aljama as a community held together by a religious ideology and a common cultural tradition. These internal bonds were reinforced by economic ties that were manifest in activities of cooperative enterprise. The aljama was not, as some suggest, a primarily economic organization. This is no more true than saying that a village or a town or a family is primarily an economic unit. Maintaining that a social unit of diverse function is really or basically organized around one of these functions is useless reductionism. We can, of course, say that any of these groups is organized first for survival, but survival is as much dependent, for example, on a unifying ideology as it is on the production and distribution of economic goods. The ideology and tradition which united them set limits on the ways Jews could relate to national and regional cultures, and some degree of economic specialization was inevitable. In some areas the specialization was in crafts or professions; in others trade and civil service predominated.

In the middle ages, the traditional and still enforced religious regulations within both groups had much to do with Christian-Jewish economic relations. Jews were, for example, forbidden to lend money at interest to other Jews. In spite of its inconvenience, this regulation which had its origin in the Old Testament and which was reinforced in the Talmud and responsa was strictly enforced. Christians were forbidden to charge interest on loans, for any interest whatsoever on any kind of loan was designated as usury. Charging interest was viewed by Christians as "contrary to the course of nature, inimical to the welfare of society and opposed to the teachings of God" (Neuman 1948: vol. 2, 192). Absurd as the restriction

may seem to members of capitalist society, it made sense to those
whose world view was organized around feudal norms. Restricting
interest retarded capitalistic ventures and promoted fair exchange as
opposed to exploitative relations. Both the Jewish and Christian
restrictions on interest emphasized traditional obligations of co-
religionists to each other over the ephemeral obligations of
monetarily based contracts. Christian popes promoted the norms of
the feudal order under which Christian religious harmony had
thrived, and talmudic scholars reinforced the traditional communal
forms that had been the bedrock of survival for Judaism. In both
cases this resulted in restrictions on usury, for clearly the relationship of borrower and lender did little to reinforce the unifying bonds
within either religious order. It is not unusual then, that the developing demands of city-based capitalism would result in the
borrower-lender relationship occurring between religious bodies
rather than within them.

Much has been written on the role of Jews as moneylenders in the
middle ages. In some countries they were restricted to that single
function, serving at the same time both a vital and much despised
role. In medieval Aragon and Castile, Jews had few restrictions, and
their economic activities included commerce and manufacture as
well as moneylending. The degree to which Jews were involved in
moneylending in Mallorca is not settled. From the evidence available we shall try to approximate the extent to which this occurred
and its effect on Jewish-Christian relations.

A study of Perpignan (Emery 1959) in which moneylending is
studied in detail provides data from seventeen notarial registers,
dating from 1261 to 1287. This study is highly pertinent to an
understanding of Mallorcan Jews for the following reasons. The
regulations regarding Jews, commerce and moneylending were very
similar, as both the cities of Perpignan and Mallorca had been
under the rule of the kings of Aragon. During the period of the
study, Perpignan was part of the kingdom of Mallorca. It was in fact
its capital, for King James II of Mallorca found Perpignan con-
venient to other capitals, and a better place for his court than the
island. Although Perpignan is today French, in that period it was
very much in the Catalan speaking community of the western

Mediterranean and, though two hundred miles of sea separated them, both cities had Christian and Jewish populations that were related by economic and kin ties.

Emery approximates that the Jewish community had a population of about 400. Of the 228 males mentioned in the notarial register over 26 years from 1261 to 1287, 178 appear as lenders to Christians in one or more of 1,643 cases. This represents an 80 percent involvement of Jewish males in moneylending. Jewish women who were widowed were also involved in lending money. Emery notes that Perpignan Jews were so involved in putting their capital in loans that members of the community commonly exchanged debts rather than cash in meeting obligations with each other, and inheritances frequently took the form of collectible debts. Those holding high office in the aljama were likely to be the largest lenders, and loan contracts were the primary criterion of wealth (Emery 1959).

Everyone in the Christian community borrowed; villagers, townsmen, knights, nobles, clergy and royal officers. Loans to clergy and nobles represented a small percentage of the total, as both were inclined to borrow from Christian sources. Jews lent a large part of their money to small merchants, especially cloth dealers. Craftsmen were also heavy borrowers. The largest single group of debtors were those living in rural areas. They were in fact the largest single debtor group in the records of the registry, but recorded debts are probably only part of the total. It can be assumed that numerous small loans secured by pawns represented a large part of the total rural debt, and these would not be recorded in the registry.

The Mallorcan data conform with that of Perpignan insofar as the most frequently mentioned conflict between Jews and Christians on the matter of loans comes from the rural peasants and urban craftsmen. The Perpignan data show that Jewish lending was primarily to these two groups. Thus in the economic aspect of segmentary relationships we see the rural and urban proletariat as a debtor class owing primarily to Jews, the nobles who were commercially oriented as competitors to Jews, the clergy as having little direct economic contact with Jews, and the king as using the Jewish community as a bureaucracy for extracting wealth from the peasants

and urban poor. The king encouraged Jewish lending and high
profits, for the greater their income the larger would be the tax
assessments that he could impose on the aljama. The king's relationship to the Jews was purely opportunistic, making only the
minimum of concessions to the doctrinally-based demands of the
church and the complaints of other segments of the society.

## FORMAL RELATIONS BETWEEN THE JEWISH COMMUNITY AND THE CHRISTIAN STATE

The variable relationship of the aljama with the state is better
understood through an examination of the two legal traditions and
the jurisdictional disputes that occurred between the *Bet Din* (aljama court) and the various courts of the state. According to the
Carta Pobla, all litigation involving Jews and Gentiles was within
the domain of the regular courts, and the increasing involvement of
Jews in activities outside the aljama in the areas of commerce and
government service increased the possibility of disputes across religious lines. But the Jews avoided the regular courts whenever possible for reasons that were both religious and practical.

The Jews had a complex and well-developed system of jurisprudence that originated in the Torah, and which was clarified and
developed in the Talmud and throughout the rabbinic courts of the
dispersion. The whole tradition, from biblical and talmudic sources
to the decisions made in accordance with rabbinic jurisprudence,
represented the divine word. Jewish law was religious law and relin-
quishing authority to the law and courts of the state was tantamount
to submission to the religious beliefs of outsiders. The rabbis taught:

> God forbid that the holy people shall walk in the ways of the
> gentiles and according to their statutes. [Neumann 1948]

On the practical side, experience taught that Jews could not expect the same fair treatment in the regular courts that they could in
their own. In a small community, compromises were frequent, and
Jewish judges tended to avoid decisions where the jurisdiction of the
Bet Din was not clear cut. There was little motivation for the judicial officers of the Bet Din to be severe. They received no pay, did

not profit from fines or charges, and would probably have to live in close relations with the litigants for the rest of their lives. Judges were frequently appointed against their will. The post was both an obligation and a reward for status and piety. A man acting under these circumstances was more inclinced to relinquish authority than assert it.

As a communal organization, the Bet Din was as much a paternalistic watchdog on personal morals and spiritual correctness as it was a court of justice. In matters of personal comportment its jurisdiction was clear cut, and here it acted firmly. The most serious violation was that of informing on fellow Jews to those on the outside. The *malsin*, or informer, was considered the most dangerous of criminals for he threatened the very survival of the community. Informing could range from careless gossip and currying the favor of outside officials with bits of news, to a malicious betrayal of one's co-religionists. The penalty was always severe, ranging from monetary fines to excommunication, the amputation of a limb, or death.

It is interesting to note that appealing one's case to the jurisdiction of an outside court was within the realm of the most serious crime of all—informing. A man who was dissatisfied with the rule of the Bet Din might take his case to an outside court and win, but in doing that he was subject to the vilification of the community. It was an accepted premise in Jewish law that whenever there was a conflict between Jewish codes and the general codes, Jews were obliged to abide by their own. To accept outside jurisdiction was a betrayal of the law of God, a betrayal of the community, and was as such considered the equivalent of treason. One could in extreme cases appeal to regional rabbinic courts, if a principle of law was involved, or even to the king, who when he was forced to hear cases appealed from Jewish courts was obliged to make a decision based on Jewish law.

The tradition of a Jewish judiciary was one of the strongest in the aljama. In small communities it might consists of only one judge, but in the larger there was usually a three-man tribunal. The authority for setting up the court rested with the lay officials. They selected the judges, the recording secretary, the messenger and the public notary. All these officials followed procedures that were of Talmudic or *Gaonic* origin. The court was both a lay and a religious institution, and as such it involved the rabbi, who as teacher of the law was considered by the community as the living repository of the Torah.

The Jewish courts applied concepts of law that were altogether unknown in Christian Mallorca or Aragon. The general courts made no attempt to claim jurisdiction in matters that were clearly the internal affair of the aljama. One principle that had the widest acceptance was that matters involving only Jews were to be resolved with reference to Jewish law even when the judge was a Christian. Nevertheless, there was a wide area of unclear jurisdiction where Jewish and regular courts had to cooperate with each other or challenge each other's jurisdiction.

Jews were forced to go to the regular courts to enforce payment of loans or the terms of a business contract with Christians. They were challenged in the courts to pay taxes to the church on real property, especially that purchased from Christians, and they responded within the regular courts to summons brought by Christian plaintiffs. In such cases, utilization of regular courts was little disputed, but nevertheless Jews feared outside courts due to the differences in requisites of evidence and the nature of oaths. Prior to the fueros of James I, Jews, like Saracens and heretics, were not on a par with Christian witnesses. Their testimony was invalid against Christians in criminal matters. Though, as we have seen, this condition was alleviated in the Carta Pobla, the tradition was sometimes stronger than the law that countermanded it. The equality of Jewish and Christian oaths was one of the most basic considerations of the Jewish populace, and the guarantee of it by James I was one of the primary attractions for Jews migrating to Mallorca. One of the problems of oaths was that Jews would swear only to the Law of Moses. This was not always acceptable and at times they were asked to take oaths that were insulting or otherwise unacceptable to them. Aljama courts were preferred by the violators of the law, even though the aljama lawbreakers faced punishments that were characteristic of the age. A woman convicted of adultery had her nose cut off and her wealth confiscated. Being disfigured and poor, it was assumed that she would not likely encounter the opportunity to partake of this sin again. An informer could be put to death by the severing of veins in his arm, and one who profaned the Holy Name could have his tongue cut out.

As we have seen, the only power to which Jewish law acceded was royal power, the bulwark upon which communal survival rested. This highly stable relationship between crown and community was based on a mutual dependence so deep that the survival of one was tied to the other. Taxes from the Jews provided the king with a large and steady flow of funds to support standing and conquering armies; and without the support of the king, the Jews would surely lose their independence and rights through the proselytizing efforts of the church, and be placed at an economic disadvantage through competition with nobles.

## TRANQUILITY AND CALAMITY IN MEDIEVAL MALLORCA

We have looked at the community as it existed from 1229 to 1391, and labelled the period as a "Camelot" of Christian-Jewish relations. The relationship was, overall, a profitable one for the whole economy. Mallorca grew to unprecedented prosperity, and to some degree the new wealth was shared by all. But towards the end of this era events on the island and in Aragon, along with a series of natural disasters, led to the downfall of the island as a center of commerce. Increasing competition for diminishing resources led to open hostility and eventually to a peasant revolt and the plunder of the Jewish quarter in 1391.

In 1229 Mallorca had been a frontier, a sparsely settled and rugged terrain, open to exploitation for those who had the necessary stamina. Though urban based, the Jews were equally involved in the development of frontier areas, having to face all the risks that itinerant peddlers in the social disorder of newly settled lands must always contend with. They might be defined in Max Weber's terms as pariah capitalists—buying, selling and lending in areas where respectable capitalists chose not to go. The difficulties encountered by King James in getting people to settle the island makes it quite clear that Mallorca was not the kind of place that respectable men went to. For the most part, those who acquired land in the conquest did not settle it. Those with holdings in Aragon returned to them. However, as a newly developing area, Mallorca offered great hope for two segments of society: land-hungry peasants and mercantile Jews. Both were attracted by the extensive rights offered to all by the Conqueror, rights which left both groups free from the imprisoning restraints of manorial traditions.

In the Mallorcan countryside of 1229, there was barely a trace of manorial aristocracy. The Repartimiento had distributed much of the land into small parcels, and even those with large holdings subdivided their share. But settling the land was not easy, for there were few roads and the customs of planting, harvesting and distributing that characterized the agriculture of the Saracens had been disrupted in the conquest. Only the most unfortunate of the Saracens remained, and in a serf-like role they worked with the Catalan settlers to get a living from the land.

The class system reflected patterns prevalent in Aragon, at least in name. The designations of estates were used, but the proprieties attached to them were little respected in day-to-day interaction. A noble was one who claimed to be a noble and who could in some way support the claim. Recognition from the king was possible through a promise to defend the land, and this required nothing more in wealth than the ownership of a horse. In the countryside, the distinction between a well-to-do peasant and a rural noble was almost nonexistent. Both lived on larger than ordinary tracts of land and benefitted from the labor of Saracen serfs and slaves and both were directly engaged in the supervision of fields and the management of livestock. Either was likely a horseman, a hunter, and a devotee of the sport of falconry. A non-titled man who sought a noble title could secure one with little difficulty, through either a present to the king or the marriage of his children to financially troubled noble families. In the course of events, he who acquired prosperity also acquired titles, and "that's all that nobility in Mallorca ever meant" (Melia 1967).

Just as the rural nobles of Mallorca were more rustic than their counterparts in other Mediterranean kingdoms, so were the city nobles more plebian. Many were engaged in commerce, and those who were not might easily lose their status through dwindling personal wealth. This was a period when people grew wealthy or returned to penury with extraordinary rapidity and frequency. The documents of the period show numerous families who rise to prominence and then disappear, never to be encountered in any dealing of importance again (Quadrado 1939, 1895). As in the country, urban wealth easily secured a noble seal. Some families had members in three divisions, merchant, noble and artisan, a situation which clearly demonstrated the fluidity of the urban status system. Many of the urban rich maintained country estates, and rural nobles kept town houses. Behaving more like the bourgeoisie than inheritors of titles, the noble families vied with each other in the possession of luxury items such as cloth, tapestries and works of art imported from abroad.

Also within the city was a very important class of artisans who manufactured the basic necessities: clothing, tools, harnesses, rope, glass and metalware. The typical artisan was a humble craftsman, living and working at the same location, operating at a small profit and hiring assistants and apprentices. What later ages considered as nobler professions were also within the artisan class: notaries, doctors, lawyers and teachers of trades. At the lowest level within the city were the day laborers who hired out for the least desirable work—maintenance of the city walls and streets, gravedigging, night-soil removal, and slaughtering.

The bottom of the status ladder in the rural areas was occupied by serfs and slaves who were either Saracens from pre-conquest Mallorca or imported from the east. Their value to the Catalan land owners was great, for the Saracens retained the agricultural skills from the Almohade era. Although agriculture was in disarray in the post-conquest years, there remained a complex irrigation system, far advanced over what the Catalans possessed, and the Saracen slaves were the means by which it was put into operation again for Mallorcan agriculture. The distinction in the countryside between slave and serf was that a slave and his children could be sold, while a serf or his progeny could not. Otherwise, their lives were little different. Peasants were distinguished from serfs by their ownership of land. The ultimate disgrace for the Mallorcan peasant was to lose his land holdings. The peasants' lust for land, which was at times clearly irrational, was derived from an association of land with freedom and status. Frequently this desire for land was self-defeating. Families sacrificed to acquire more land when the means for exploitation were not available and still taxes had to be paid on it. The peasants' financial naiveté was easily exploited by urban wealth, and ultimately, as we shall see, the peasants lost everything.

The economic changes in Mallorca in the period of decline were strongly influenced by political events. The reign of James I of Aragon had been a period of expansion and growth. Mallorca was a new addition to the kingdom providing the king with an opportunity to experiment with novel ideas that had been gaining currency. Innovation ended with his death in 1276, at which time the kingdom was divided into two parts, each for one of James's two sons. To Pedro III went a reduced kingdom of Aragon, and to James II went the newly formed kingdom of Mallorca which included not only the island but a number of mainland cities in an area which is now part of southern France—Montpelier, Perpignan, Narbonne and Cerdagne.

The reign of James II was the period of great trading houses, a time when Mallorcan ships filled the harbor with a forest of masts. It was in this period that Mallorca surpassed Barcelona in importance, and the interior of the island became involved in the thriving economy. The demand for agricultural products was so great that a large market in slaves to work the land became an important part of the port trade.

Mallorca continued as an independent kingdom under two more kings, Sancho I and James III. A slow decline marked these reigns, but the real decline in Mallorcan prosperity began with its return to the kingdom of Aragon in 1343. The great period of Mallorcan economic success is concurrent with its period of independence. The Jews prospered through this period, and maintained their respected commercial position in the city. However, by the mid-fourteenth century, the island had become a scene of poverty and misery, and the Jews, though not themselves poor, were nevertheless the victims of economic decline.

The freedom of the formative period disappeared slowly as the society slipped into oligarchy with the wealthy, setting themselves apart, taking control of the city and the island. It was a series of calamitous events that enabled those with power to assume even more, until eventually they controlled both the economy and the once-just political institutions. In 1348 and 1351 the island was visited by the bubonic plague which took an enormous toll in lives. In addition, Mallorca had been returned to Aragon under the rule of Pedro IV, who taxed his new colony to the limits of its ability to pay. His attention was at this time devoted entirely to a series of wars with Castile and Sardinia, and his interest in the island did not extend past the taxes it could supply. In the course of these ruinous wars, the king confiscated the trading ships of Mallorcan merchants and lost 140 of them at sea. This resulted in a sharp decline in Mallorcan commerce. However, the taxes of the Aragonese king did not let up. In the decade of the 1360s Mallorcan trading companies were reduced from one hundred to six. In 1375 and 1384 the plagues returned. Once rich Mallorca was ruined.

In the course of disasters and the loss of trade, the urban wealthy turned their attention to the countryside where the plight of the peasants made land available at little cost. Crushed by the weight of taxes and heavily in debt, the peasants who had colonized the land had no choice but to sell their holdings. While the urban aristocrats shifted their investments from commerce to agriculture, the peasants became an impoverished rural proletariat. Along with the land, the artistocrats secured new privileges from the king which secured their political control and made their position unchallengeable. The declining conditions in the countryside led even the rural aristocracy to move to the city, resulting in a situation of an entirely urban aristocracy completely dominating the lives of landless peasants (Bisson 1969).

The Mallorcan peasantry did not accept their misery fatalistically. Through the people's charter they were free men, and living in isolation in the countryside they had developed a fierce independence. No one doubted that their land had been confiscated unfairly, and their hatred for the city dwellers knew no bounds. They and their ancestors had settled the land and worked it for a century and a half. In the last years of the kingdom of Mallorca, the land had been owned almost totally by small farmers. In the period of development, peasants had invested all their profits in new properties, and through the division of inheritance the countryside was covered with small intensely worked plots. But with the general decline in the economy the peasants were unable to cope with the increasing tax burden imposed by a council of government controlled by merchants and aristocrats in the city. With the open countryside devoid of government forces, the peasants were able to organize to discuss their plight. They decided to take their case en masse to the city.

At dawn on August 2, 1391, seven thousand peasants assembled at the eastern wall of the city. They were met there by the governor who tried to calm them. In an ensuing argument the peasants forced entry through the gate of San Antonio, and in the process wounded the governor and killed some of his aides. They roamed through the city and found that the government officials and aristocrats had fled to the castle of Bellver on a hill above the city. They left the city to attack the castle but in spite of all their efforts they were unable to break through, climb over or burn down the high, ten-foot-thick walls. Frustrated in their attempts against the castle, they returned to the city, where they were joined by the urban poor. Together the peasants and proletariat swept into the Jewish quarter where they set fire to the buildings, stole what was valuable and slaughtered the inhabitants.

Three hundred residents, men, women and children, were killed, mostly by knife. In the homes, the raiders found gold, silver and jewels which they carried off, and in the residences of the moneylenders they burned files and contracts. The seige continued for three days before the peasants could be driven back to the counside. The consequence of the attack was complete economic chaos. Huge sections of the city, including the residences of government officials, were destroyed. With records gone, commerce was brought to a standstill. The mass murder in the aljama left those Jews that remained in a state of panic ready to flee the island (Xamena Fiol 1965).

The three hundred Jews that were killed were those that had been left behind when the peasant army reached the city. The vast major-

**Castle Bellver, Palma**

ity of the Jews had found refuge in the palaces of Almudaina and Bellver, along with Christian officials and aristocrats. The evidence is insufficient for a clear understanding of why the Jews were the principal victims of the attack. There is a great deal of data available on the peasant revolt, but not enough to explain all that happened. One wonders who were those three hundred Jews who remained in the aljama. Were they the merchants and moneylenders guarding their wealth, or were they the less wealthy Jews who lacked the connections for securing safety behind the castle walls.

One reason that Jews were the victims of peasant wrath was the news of a wave of anti-Jewish riots throughout Spain had just reached Mallorca. Mobs had attacked the aljamas of other Spanish cities that same year. But it is doubtful that the peasants intended the aljama as a target before arriving at the city walls. All that can be said for sure is that they came in large numbers to demand relief from taxes and debts, and it seems that violence developed in the process. In their poverty and misery they had come to appeal to those who oppressed them, and there is no escaping the fact that the Jews were part of the oppressing establishment. But it is apparent that the Jews were a *secondary* target, an alternative to satiate the fury of the mob after they had been frustrated by the castle walls. That the mob gave full vent to its fury in the aljama may well be due to any of a number of reasons. The aljama contained much portable wealth and held the records of loans. The peasants carried off the gold, silver and jewelry and were careful to destroy loan records. Another motivation was surely the feeling that one could find moral justification in Christians attacking Jews, given all the anti-Jewish propaganda put out by the church at that time. And finally, it seems that the three hundred were the only remaining target for the fury of the mob. The artisans, sailors, and small merchants of the city were not the oppressors of the peasants and were safe from their fury. But the Jews as a group, all Jews rich and poor alike, were included by the peasants as among those who had forced them into indigence; and the three hundred who, for whatever reasons, remained in the aljama were the victims of those circumstances and conditions.

The peasant revolt continued for two months with assemblages as great as the first falling on the city repeatedly, to rob food storehouses, vineyards and orchards. Proclamations by the king and threats by the governor did little to calm the rebels. There was no alternative but to negotiate with them and this the governor finally did. An agreement was reached which relieved the peasants of some of their taxes and loan indebtedness. They specifically asked to be relieved of obligations on loans from Jews and the usurious loans of Christians, explaining that after ten years interest the capital had been repaid. The resumption of payment on loans was all but impossible in any case, for so many records had been destroyed that even those contracts supported by documentation were not really valid any more (Quadrado 1939, 1895).

With Mallorca in a state of economic chaos, with hungry peasants in a state of insurrection, with the aljama mourning the loss of three hundred victims of murder, the Camelot of Christian-Jewish relations was at an end. If we look at this period, from conquest to massacre, we see the Jewish community flourishing in periods of economic growth and remaining viable through disorder and disaster. Following 1391, many Christians who were horrified by the massacre pleaded with the Jews to convert so that this would not happen again, but few Jews did. A number of Jews left the island in despair, but those that left and those that were killed were more than replaced by new migrants to the island. The new arrivals had been lured into coming by special privileges offered by the king. So following disaster and the loss of large number of individual members through murder, conversion and emmigration, the Jewish community was as strong as ever.

It is clear that the community more than the individual members is the key to Jewish persistence; and as we have pointed out, the strength of community organization to flourish and resist assimilationist pressure is in large part based on the fact that it arrives in any particular city as an association already adapted to urban survival. It is as we have said a form which is transplanted from city to city by members who move rather than migrate. That this is the key to persistence is well demonstrated by a comparison of the experiences of Jews and Muslims in the post-conquest period.

Both Jews and Muslims found themselves as foreign segments in the conquering society of Catalans. If we compare the two insofar as their commitment to the faith is concerned, there is no difference. On the battlefield and before the stake the Muslim faith in Allah matches Jewish trust in Yahweh. Mallorcan Christians found the beliefs of the Muslims no more tolerable than those of the Jews. Like the Jews, their beliefs were not only different but also contradicted basic Christian assumptions. As Flannery (1965) has pointed out, Jewish and Christian beliefs were especially competitive as they were based on conflicting interpretations of the same historical facts. This is just as true for the Muslims, who as late arrivals to monotheism both re-invoked and contradicted basic tenets of Christianity and Judaism. Mohammed's scorn for the concept of the Trinity was every bit as offensive to Christians as the Jewish denial of the divinity of Christ. Being both as committed and as at odds with the Christian society as the Jews were, the Muslims were equally distinctive culturally. In fact Jewish and Muslim values had great overlap, both having shared in the five-hundred-year dominance of Islamic civilization and the Arabic language. However, given these similarities, each played a different role from an entirely different organizational base. It is their organization and their role in the larger society with respect to economic function and articulation, rather than religious and cultural distinctiveness, that accounts for the total assimilation of one and the persistence of the other.

The Muslims, as serfs and small landholders in the island's interior, were excluded from even the possibility of forming a community; and had they lived in the city, it is still doubtful that they would have formed one, for they had no comparable preconceived communal plan in their culture such as that of the Jews. So history shows that individual Muslims lived out their lives loyal to their native faith, and their children, having only the example of their parents, became less and less committed. Though they were assimilated, the cultural contributions of the Muslims were enormous, matching in agriculture the Jewish contribution to commerce. To this day their customs and their technology survive in rural Mallorca, but as an identifiable group the Muslims have completely disappeared.

Had the Muslims resided in the city, the comparison would have been more valid, but the outcome would have been the same, perhaps taking a generation or two longer. The Jews, on the other hand, flourished in the period of Muslim assimilation, a period in which their only ally was the king, while the rest of society, merchants, artisans, clergy, nobles and peasants, maintained an ongoing antagonism. This was, of course, the best period, and things would never be so good again. The remnants of Jewish society that survive today in the Xueta ghetto on the Street of the Silver Shops is what is left of a community that endured massacre, forced conversion, inquisition and confiscation of wealth. Before we examine Jewish persistence through the period of suffering from 1391 to the present, we will go back into history to study the origin of Jewish communal forms in the ancient city of Babylon.

# Babylonian Exile and Jewish Urbanization

From the aljama of thirteenth-century Mallorca to the Xueta community in the twentieth century, there is continuity in the persisting themes which are the core of Jewish communal life. What were they, and how did they come into being? How did they allow the Jews to persist in medieval Mallorca, in a milieu that assimilated an equally tradition-bound Muslim population? Obviously, these questions have pertinence beyond the cultural domain of our island study, for the social forms characteristic of Diaspora communities have considerable uniformity, and with them Jews have persisted in a variety of assimilationist settings.

As has been noted, Jews were not always urban, nor were they always communal. And, the movement of individuals from place to place was not always from one urban community to a homologous form somehwere else. To explain communal formation, we will use Robert Park's frame of reference (1928) and examine the creation of the community in the breaking-down, building-up process of rural to urban migration. Migrations to cities by Jews happened many times in history, but one occasion was more important than all the others, for in this urbanizing process we see the foundation laid for all future urban Jewish communities in the millennia of Diaspora survival. That most important of all migrations took place as a forced exile from the essentially rural kingdom of Judah to urban Babylon under conditions of war in 586 B.C.

In the land of Judah, prior to their exile to Babylon, the Jews of

91

the sixth century B.C. were a primarily rural people engaged in sedentary agriculture in the Jordan River plain and mountain valleys, and in nomadic stock breeding in less fertile areas. Political and military power was in the hands of a town-dwelling oligarchy of traders and landlords who dominated the countryside. Although the towns did not match in size the city of Mallorca in the thirteenth century, the domination of the peasantry by a patrician class of townsmen was, with respect to the nature of urban control of the rural sector, not unlike the Mallorcan pattern. This highly stratified rural Jewish population was organized under a loose confederation of tribes whose unity rested on their sharing of the guardianship of a common god, Yahweh.

The Jews of the sixth century B.C. lived in constant fear of conquest and extinction. They were all that was left of the twelve original tribes of Israel, the ten in the north having been conquered in 721 B.C., and since then assimilated into Assyrian society. There was among the members of the two remaining tribes of Benjamin and Judah a strong sense of mission; a concern with the survival of their society, its beliefs, values and special status with God, apart from the individuals who were members of it. In 586 B.C., the much feared invasion came and the mission of Israel seemed lost. The Jews who were taken in captivity were resigned to a fate arranged by an angry god, obviously dissatisfied with their compliance with the law he had entrusted to them.

We see in the captives who were taken to Babylon the core of what was left of a society organized around a belief in one god and the Covenant the people of Israel had with him. Yahweh had promised to deliver his people if they showed themselves worthy by obeying the commandments revealed to them through Moses on Mount Sinai. The prophets of the Jewish people had interpreted conquest and catastrophe as acts of God in which he showed his displeasure with the quality of their compliance with the law. It is with this logic that the exiled Judeans interpreted their plight. Conquest by Babylon and captivity in their capital was the will of God. The armies of Babylon were no more than agents revealing divine displeasure with the people of Israel. To appease God, to regain the hope of deliverance, the people must make an even greater effort to comply with the law. In captivity the hope of survival was sustained by the prophets who preached that the hope of deliverance lay in returning to the old ways. The prophets looked to scripture for a way out of their dilemma; and in exile in an urban setting they re-applied the old rules with greater vigor and rigidity than had even been the case before.

The threat to the exiled Jews of the loss of their religious identity and the concomitant promise of redemption should not be confused with any threat to their physical survival. As a captive people, they were treated relatively well in Babylon, being required to work as laborers on the construction of canals in the early part of their stay, and after that attaining the freedom to follow whatever trade or profession they chose. Nor was there really a threat of biological assimilation, such as that which had occurred with the northern tribes. Cities of the ancient and even contemporary Near East allow for the survival of ethnic migrants, indeed pressure towards their persistence by the nature of their structure. Endogamous occupational-religious-ethnic groupings were fundamental to the social system of urban Babylon. Recent linguistic evidence (Weisberg 1967) has confirmed the existence of guild organization in Babylon, and in this system it would have been only natural for the Jews as a cultural group to re-form in the city under the guild structure.

In Babylon it was natural for ethnic migrants to occupy a specific quarter of the city, become occupationally specialized, retain their customs and worship their own god. But this was insufficient for the special needs of the Jews. What the prophets feared was failure to comply with the will of God in the relations of Jews with other demes in the city. In the larger binding culture, each group recognized the gods of others in a kind of democratic polytheism. The god of one was as good as the god of another, and those of one sector gave homage to the gods of their neighbors as nothing more or less than a gesture of good diplomacy. The omnipotent god of Israel would not allow this. That there was but one true God was the most fundamental principle of Judaism. He was the creator of the universe and the absolute sovereign over the destinies of man and nature. In his commandments he had forbidden the recognition of other gods, and having suffered his displeasure for the previous three centuries the Jews of Babylon were not about to incur his wrath again. The Jewish right to worship Yahweh was never threatened in Babylon, but the larger society's adherence to a rather congenial polytheism conflicted with their most fundamental precepts. The complex rules and rituals of self isolation which the Jews developed in Babylon were an outcome of the fear of punishment by an angry god. It was the retention of ideology, more than concern for economic or biological survival and persistence, that impelled the development of the distinctive urban social organization of the Jews.

The total reordering of the social structure to preserve a religious ideology is far from unique. In periods of stress it is the reinvoked religious doctrines of the past which unify a people in a movement towards change (Wallace 1956). In one sense this reordering of the social structure of the Jews in Babylon was a nativistic movement, a process wherein people change in order to preserve. Most aspects of the new social order should be seen as an old rule or ritual reinterpreted for the needs of a new environment. The changes were sometimes difficult, as so many of the original rules pertained so specifically to an agricultural life. Those which had little pertinence, such as the sabbath year, the unharvested edge of the field for the poor, and gleaning, became irrelevant in the city, or were entirely reinterpreted. Also some of the new rules had no basis in scripture, but were pragmatic steps towards the overall goal. Outstanding among these was the most fundamental rule of all, the very basis of self segregation, prohibitions against mixed marriages. During the first commonwealth, Israelite peasants had married freely with outsiders. As emphasized by Max Weber, scripture provides evidence of mixed marriage in David's lineage, and this was neither condemned nor condoned (Weber 1952, 1917).

Rules of commensalism were particularly effective in ensuring the isolation and continuity of the Jews in Babylon. In the rural society, Old Testament law forbade the consumption of carcasses. In the city this was redefined to include all animals not slaughtered in accordance with a highly detailed ritual. Any mistake in the ritual resulted in the classification of the animal as carcass. A notch in the blade of a knife which resulted in a piece of torn flesh was sufficient to make the food forbidden (Weber 1952, 1917). With this new rule it became impossible for a Jewish family to live any distance from a ritually correct butcher. Although the rule developed from scripture, the end result produced something far removed from the original instruction. Prior to exile, commensalism had been readily practiced with non-Jews. At the separate meal of the Egyptians and the Hebrews in the Joseph story, the denial of commensalism is laid at the door of the Egyptians in contrast to the openness of the Israelites (Weber 1952, 1917).

The sabbath day, that is, one day of rest in seven, derived from the commandments received by Moses. Prior to exile it provided a day away from the fields for agricultural Israelites, and gave them an opportunity to take their goods to market. In Babylon this commandment was reinterpreted as a prohibition against any kind of work, including lighting fires, cooking, going to market, loud speech, and so on. The new interpretation of how the sabbath should be observed made cooperation in work or business with those of different ethnic or religious affiliation extremely difficult and made the segregated condition of the Jews highly visible to outsiders. It made service in the military next to impossible (Weber 1952, 1917).

During the agricultural period, or the first commonwealth, ritual had been conducted in the Temple by a hereditary priesthood. The focus of ritual in that period was a sacrifice of animals conducted by the priests. In Babylon, the Judeans came together to re-create as best they could the rites of the Temple. At first the elders of the community organized the new rites. Later priests and prophets shared in the creation of new rules and ritual. Where there was any hesitancy to accept the new puritanism, the role of the prophet was to remind the less sanctimonious of the destruction of the Temple and the burning of Jerusalem, which was the incontrovertible proof of the correctness of the warnings of earlier prophets that those who did not change their ways would suffer the effects of disasters and conquest at the discretion of Yahweh. So the city-dwelling Jews exiled from their homeland and residing in Babylon complied with the rules and laid the groundwork for congregational or communal Judaism.

## RETURN TO JERUSALEM

After the Jews had spent fifty years in captivity, Babylon was captured by the newly powerful Persians, and many of the captives were allowed to return to Jerusalem. Only a minority did. Life in the city had been a rewarding experience in retrospect. With almost total freedom to pursue any interest, they had learned new trades and professions in the cosmopolitan atmosphere of Babylon. Some had become wealthy and refused to leave. For those who had lived through the original captivity, returning to Jerusalem was not a pleasant prospect after having established themselves in the city. For those who had been born in Babylon, it was a return to the old country of their parents, to agricultural life and all its limitations. We have never seen in history any great migrations back to the country, except in cases of great economic decline or natural disaster. It takes tragedy or privation to reverse the process of urbanization, and even under these circumstances it rarely occurs. Those that went to Jerusalem from Babylon were supported in their trip and encouraged by leaders of the Babylonian community.

The basic idea of the urban community had been formed in Babylon, and with the return of more and more exiles the new community of purists became dominant in Jerusalem. The Persians who controlled both Babylon and Jerusalem were happy to let the Jews live where they wanted. They hoped to control the Jews through their own priests, and through the influence of the state the priests took over power in both communities. They formally defined the rules of worship and ritual for Babylon and Jerusalem and through their priestly role and the power of the Persian court their edicts overcame all opposition. Two leaders who were outstanding in this period of change were Ezra and Nehemiah. Nehemiah was a regent in the court of the Persian king and Ezra, a priest, was granted similar powers by the Persians. It was in Jerusalem that the formal proclamation against mixed marriages was made, both Ezra and Nehemiah insisting that existing marriages with non-Jewish women be dissolved. This was the most important step in the community's strong purist position, but the idea pervaded the community, and was replicated in the objection to the use of mixed seed in agriculture, mixed thread in weaving, or the use of bastard animals for transport (Weber 1952, 1917).

The urban character of the community is emphasized by the fact that it could really take hold only in Jerusalem. There the puritanical reforms were supported by the populace while the rural class of landowners vigorously opposed them. The urban community set itself apart not only from the Persians and other foreigners, but from fellow Jews who did not conform to the new rules and the new interpretation of old rules. Outstanding in opposition were the Samaritans, descendants of the conquered people of the north who now represented a mixture of Jews, Mesopotamians and Aramaic migrants. They worshipped Yahweh, but recognized other gods. They were anxious to help in the rebuilding of the Temple in Jerusalem, but their help was rejected by the purists. They were seen as *amme ha aratzath*, outsiders, ignorant country people.

The purist community was eager for new members, but only when they accepted compliance with the maze of ritualistic regulations which characterized the urban community. The Jerusalem community grew steadily with new migrants from rural areas. Some of the fundamental obligations for those who sought membership were, according to regulations imposed by Nehemiah in Jerusalem: (1) suspension of marriages with outsiders, (2) boycott of all market traffic on the sabbath, (3) remission of debts every seven years, (4) a head tax of one-third shekel every year for Temple needs, and (5) support of the Temple through supplies and tithes for priestly maintenance. In the new community the traditional role of the priestly class was recognized by their formal approval of revisions of ritual, but exemplary religious behavior ultimately gained recognition over inherited priestly rights in the long run. (Weber 1952, 1917).

One aspect of community organization apart from ritual but of fundamental importance in community structure were the developing patterns on the use of power. In the exile under Babylonians and Persians, and in the homeland under Persians, Greeks, and Romans, the community found its security in agreements and alliance with imperial military power. Although the ideal of return to Jewish nationhood and independence was ever reemphasized in worship, the day-to-day strategies of the communities' relations with the court developed forms that would prove viable and persist. The idea of a Jewish army remained important among a minority, but actual survival rested with strong religious leaders who could demonstrate their own powers within the community and could translate this control into agreements with royal power. This was the case with Nehemiah and Ezra, and became the characteristic pattern of survival in the centuries that followed.

Under the Ptolemies, the Egyptian community became a great center in the Diaspora, and eventually Alexandria came to rival Babylon as a center of Jewish culture. The processes begun in Babylon continued to develop in Alexandria and other cities of the Diaspora. For a number of reasons Babylon remained the center of the Jewish Diaspora for a thousand years. In the beginning, the power of Babylon rested on its numerical and economic strength relative to any other concentration of Jews. Jerusalem developed as the religious center, but never rivaled Babylon in commerce or as a center of culture. Segregated communal Judaism got its support from good relations, frequently symbiotic in character, between the two centers.

Part of Babylon's power rested upon its special position with Jerusalem. Both cities used the Aramaic language, and together they had among their citizens the leading families of prophetic tradition. Jerusalem's power rested upon the command of Yahweh to worship in the Temple of Jerusalem. Jerusalem also received a tax from throughout the Diaspora. This tax freed the Diaspora communitites from the obligation to build their own temples, because through the tax, temple sacrifice was being carried out in their behalf in Jerusalem. With Jerusalem as the home of the Temple and Babylon as the center of learning and wealth, the Pharisaic or communal tradition which was dominant in both was in an ever stronger position during the period of the Second Commonwealth. But it must be remembered that in the ensuing centuries it was only one of a number of strong traditions that existed within the Jewish nation. It was a period of distinct and competing forms, a condition which is described by Weber as almost one of "caste segregation" (Weber 1952, 1917, p. 387).

## SECTS IN THE ERA OF THE SECOND COMMONWEALTH

The basic and major separation was between the Pharisees and the Sadducees. The Pharisees were of course the major sect representing the traditions developed in Babylon during exile and in Jerusalem by those returning from exile. More than a new approach to religion, it represented a new type of social organization for the descendants of Israel. It was urban and communal with strong bourgeois tendencies. The Sadducees in contrast represented the mainstream of the old tradition which derived from a religion that was king-based and which developed within the area of nationhood. In the case of Israel this originally developed from a confederation of tribes who were united in their belief in Yahweh. In this system there were priestly clans whose religious functions were inherited. The sect which we call the Sadducees in the era of the Second Commonwealth were those who affirmed the old ways in large part because their status was derived from the old system. In addition to priests, many of the Sadducees were patrician landlords or occupants of important positions in the Sanhedrin. They emphasized worship in the Temple and animal sacrifice according to the commands of Yahweh.

From the period beginning with the return of the exiles to Jerusalem and continuing all through the Second Commonwealth, there was a steady ascendancy of urban demes, the Pharisaic tradition, over priestly clans, the Sadducaic tradition. Within their communities, the Pharisees recognized the traditional rights of the inherited priesthood. They were obliged to as it was affirmed by scripture. In turn their reforms were sanctified by priestly leaders out of necessity. But with the passing of the years, the urban religious community became more and more powerful and priests came to be judged more on their inherited rights. Thus we have during this period a continuation of the development of the Pharisaic community, the idea of a congregation and its slow takeover of the temple functions occurring with the leadership and approval of members of priestly clans. However, later in the period of the Second Commonwealth the two traditions began to polarize into different sects and the differences between them became so pronounced that ultimately the separation became highly structured. Each looked to a different tradition and a different social system. The Sadducees defined their rank in terms of a national system with a central temple and a governing body, the Sanhedrin, which they controlled. The Pharisees became more and more a religion which ignored national borders. They looked outside the country to Babylon as their cultural and economic center. Although Jerusalem and the Temple was their religious center, the central idea of Pharisaism was one of urban communal obligations emphasized over the demands of a national religion. As the nation had been controlled by outside imperial powers for centuries, communal organization was highly functional even though nationhood was a reality within the framework of occupying empires.

The nature of the relationship with the empires that occupied their homeland was a fundamental point of difference between the Sadducees and the Pharisees. The Sadducees did not resist Hellenism. To the contrary they were very impressed with the great advances it represented, as was most of the eastern Mediterranean at that time. The Pharisees, as has been obvious in their development, were less interested in cultural advances than in preserving the purity of the sacred aspect of their culture. They wanted to maintain a pure, ritually correct Jewish tradition and this was their *raison d'être*. From 721 B.C. on, the people of Israel had survived intact, but with great losses, one foreign occupation after another, first the Assyrians in the north, then the Babylonians in the south. With the defeat of the Babylonians, the Persian empire dominated the land. The Persians were in turn conquered by Alexander the Great, and with this we see the beginning of Hellenic domination which continued through the competition for political control between Saleucid and Ptolemaic kingdoms. In 63 B.C., Rome took over as imperial power and ruled Palestine as an occupied nation until 70 A.D., after which the rights of Jewish nationhood were no longer recognized. Through a period of almost eight hundred years the problem of relations with occupying powers was a focal point of Jewish religious and political policy. The greatest assimilationist threat had come from Hellenic culture whose ideas were far more powerful than its military might. The social form created in the urban ecosystem of Babylon to resist an assimilationist dilution of sacred beliefs developed further, resisting the assimilationist pressure of the occupation forces of the homeland as well as the native rulers in the cities of the Diaspora.

The Sadducees, whose traditional positions of leadership were recognized by occupying empires, were eager to maintain good relations and were inclined to emulate the superior force, while continuing the traditions which provided them an inherited priestly role. They denied any tradition that did not come directly from the Torah, such as the oral tradition of the Pharisees that centered in Babylon. The Sadducees were rural oriented to a degree as their wealth came from the land. They valued the national political system; they controlled the power positions there. They emphasized temple worship, as custom demanded their presence for correct worship. In contrast, the Pharisees were urban and bourgeois and their foundations rested upon reinterpretations of the Torah that justified and venerated communal organization and ritual purity through rules of self isolation.

Although these two traditions represented the focus of division in Palestine, there were a number of other segments. Most important in the homeland were the Samaritans and the Essenes. The Samaritans, as we have seen, represented a partially assimilated Torah tradition and were defined by the urban communal tradition as outsiders. They lacked connection with most of the period of prophecy, and like the Sadducees rejected the hope of resurrection and encouraged friendly relations with Hellenism. The Samaritans like the Sadducees had a territorial and clan-based social organization.

The Essenes, in contrast, came out of the exilic tradition. They were communal and self segregating, but in a more monastic manner than the Pharisees. Monastic communities of Essenes existed in every city in Palestine and were made up primarily of male artisans who rejected wealth and family life in order to pursue an existence devoted to the spirit and communal ritual. Like the Pharisees, the Essenes protected themselves from ritual pollution from the outside world. They left their communities only to practice their crafts in the city. The majority neglected wedlock. Recruitment was through the training of children from the larger society who were treated as kindred. A chosen person conducted relations with the outside and stewards managed communal affairs. For most, monastic life began with pre-dawn prayer and consisted of communal meals, meditation, study and work in an atmosphere of sobriety and quiet (Baron and Blau 1954).

Membership could be acquired only after three years of probation. During this period the initiate learned communal life but could not partake of meals with others. At the end of the three-year period, the petitioner took an oath of piety toward God, justice toward men, humility, truthfulness, honesty, and loyalty to the commune.

The latter included vows never to conceal anything from sect members or reveal sect doctrines to outsiders. Like the Pharisees, punishment for violation of communal rules was ostracism. In the case of the Essenes this could mean death, as commensal regulations forbid partaking of any food from outsiders. The ostracized member could eat only grass and would eventually starve to death if he were not forgiven by the community court of one hundred.

The Essenes were even more strict in regard to Sabbath regulations than were the Pharisees. Like the Pharisees, Essenes could find immediate acceptance in any community of the sect. A small minority married but did so only for offspring, rejecting coitus at any time that fertilization was not possible, such as during periods of pregnancy. Essenic communities existed throughout Palestine, and much has been learned about them recently through archeological discoveries at Qumran which included the so-called Dead Sea Scrolls. As a group they seem to have carried Pharisaic policies of self-segregation to a level of fanaticism.

Communal Judaism had taken hold in many forms outside of Palestine. There were the *Therapeutae* of Alexandria who were monastic like the Essenes, and in Damascus the New Covenanters who, as dissidents of the priesthood, rejected temple worship and animal sacrifice and emphasized messianic expectations. Looking at all these sects together, Sadducees, Pharisees, Samaritans, Essenes, Therapeutae, New Covenanters, and later still, the Zealots, we find one common theological base—the Torah (Baron and Blau 1954). This was the common basis of all the sects of Israel during the period of the Second Commonwealth. In terms of social organization, two were organized by clan membership and territoriality, derived from the old agricultural tradition and its concept of nationhood. These were the Sadducees and the Samaritans. All the others were communal and offshoots of the urban, segregated, communal tradition begun in exile. Those who were communally organized rejected other countrymen outside the sect as ritual strangers. This practice served to emphasize the preciseness and visibility of sect membership.

## COMMUNALISM: PHARISAIC AND CHRISTIAN

Some have said there were as many as twenty-four sects existing at the time of the destruction of the Temple in 70 A.D., "but the only one to survive the national cataclysm was the Pharisees" (Epstein 1959). This is a key date in the history of Israel, for it is the time that the religion of Israel lost its base in the social organization of the nation-state. Those tied to a national organization, the Sadducees and the Samaritans, fell into insignificance, and all the minor sects vanished gradually from the scene. However, with the social organization developed in Babylon which had enabled Jews to settle throughout the Diaspora and comply with the law, and with the development of the institution of the synagogue which took the place of the Temple for prayer and worship, Pharisaic Judaism persisted in full strength. Even after the destruction of the Temple by Vespasian, Judaism was reorganized in the homeland in the formation of the Jabneh Sanhedrin which served as a spiritual, legal and academic center. But with the failure of the Bar Kokba revolt in 135 A.D., the last remnants of Jewish nationhood were gone, and all that remained were the communities (Epstein 1959).

At this time, Pharisaic communities existed within the Roman Empire as far west as Spain, throughout North Africa, and in the most important urban centers, including Rome itself. This new form which had evolved in Babylon was as a durable social unit immeasurably superior to the small nation-state in the competition for survival. While communal Yahwehism took in converts all over the Mediterranean, nation-based Yahwehism never converted other nations. Although dispersed communities provided the vehicle for survival, the continuity of the sect can only be explained by the zealousness of commitment to the unifying ideology formalized in the Torah, and a growing body of reinterpretations and modifications of the law coming out of Babylon. The Pharisaic communitites became functionally specialized in their economic roles in Mediterranean cities, but economic success cannot explain their survival. The preservation of the sacred tradition was the prime organizing and motivating force.

A minor sect grew alongside the Pharisaic tradition, a sect almost identical to the Pharisees except for their belief in a prophet called Joshua. This minor sect was, of course, Christianity in its earlier states.

From this point on we are concerned with the respective development of Christianity and Judaism in order to provide insight into their relationship in the city of Mallorca. In this discussion we will continue to focus on the organizational base as we did in our description of urban social change during exile. We do not limit our discussion to religious development or religious contact, as belief systems are only analytically separable from the social systems of which they are a part. The definition of what is sacred is bound to reflect the social arrangements of the society, a fact well illustrated in the inseparability of the caste system from the Hindu religion or the Hindu religion from the caste system. Thus we see the relations of Christianity and Judaism as one thing when both sanctified the communal form of social organization, and another when Christianity attached itself to the structure of the Roman Empire.

In the earliest phase of Christianity we see Christians organized into communities of the Pharisaic pattern; and Christian-Jewish relations at this period of history are seen as communal organizations of Christians relating to Jews who were also communal. Following 70 A.D., each survived *only* in the form of communal religious sects within the orbit of the Roman Empire. Christians were perceived by Romans as nothing more than a minor variation in Pharisaic belief and a duplication of the organizational form.

Christians continued to follow the law, and their acceptance of Jesus as the messiah was viewed by themselves and outsiders as an internal dispute among Jews.

It is a common belief that during the formative years St. Paul was the organizing force of Christianity, for so much of what happened seems to have resulted from his decisions. However, we really cannot say how much he led or to what degree his actions were merely responses to the changes he witnessed. In any case, what was at first a purely Jewish sect in membership, ritual, and leadership spread out to include the Gentiles and in this process the requirements of the law, especially the regulations on ritual purity which kept Jews isolated from their neighbors, were relaxed. This act more than any other began to make Christian communities something apart, something quite distinct, from other Jewish communities.

These internal disputes were of little consequence to the Romans, who, seeing little or no difference between Christian and Pharisaic communities, treated both the same. This meant that Christians had all the legal rights of Jews in the Roman Empire, and these were extensive and well established. The two communities competed for membership. The Christians hoped that all Israel would enter into the new doctrine, while the Pharisees looked forward to a resolution of difference on the messianic attributes of Jesus and a reunion of Christians and themselves. Both sects competed for members among the Gentiles, but the rules for membership in the Pharisaic community were unvarying while the Christian communities found the requirements of the law less relevant and emphasized the message of Jesus. The parting of the ways seems to be mostly attributable to Paul who, though keeping the law himself, did not require its acceptance by converts. Following the law was advisable, but faith in Jesus was, according to Paul, sufficient for finding salvation (Flannery 1965).

The period of competing communities is separable into two periods: the time from the death of Christ to the destruction of Jerusalem in 70 A.D., and the period from 70 A.D. until the Bar Kokba revolt of the year 130. In the first period the Christians were a dissident community, and as already stated, each sect sought the unification of Israel under its leadership. Following the fall of

Jerusalem the split became irreparable. The Christians, in their increasing neglect of the law, were in the eyes of the Pharisees foregoing the most sacred part of the faith. This was seen as more serious than their acceptance of a false messiah. The destruction of the Jewish homeland was interpreted by the Christians as divine disapproval of traditional Judaism, for, in the manner of the Old Testament, wars and natural disasters were seen as signs of the will of God as they pertained to the actions of his people. The Pharisees no longer saw Christians as brothers in error. They were instead heretics who were to be fought rather than tolerated. In prayer, the Pharisees remembered the Christians in a way that made their feelings clear. "May the heretics perish in an instant. May they be effaced from the book of life and not counted among the Just."

The last hopes of Jewish-Christian reunion were dashed in 130 when Bar Kokba was hailed as the messiah by the majority of Pharisaic Jews. Although Bar Kokba was not ultimately accepted as the messiah, in this period the two sects separated behind the ideologies and prophesy of two distinct messianic figures—Bar Kokba and Jesus. The severity of the competition is indicated by the fact that Bar Kokba himself had slain Christians who refused to deny Christ.

The competition of Pharisaic Judaism and Christianity became more open and severe in the second century. They could not separate and go different ways for they represented differing interpretations of the same events and revelations. Thus they were continually at odds with one another on matters of belief, interpretation and ritual. This did not mean that the followers of each were enemies. Together, they still represented a minority in an empire where the pagan beliefs of Rome predominated. Both were subject to the whims of Roman leaders and were at times the victims of persecution. From the appearance of Bar Kokba to the conversion of Constantine was a period of intense competition in proselytizing between the sects. Each sought to cleanse itself from the influence of the beliefs and customs of the other. But ultimately the competition for converts was lost by the Pharisees who due to the detailed requirements of the law were less adaptive to changing times, cultural difference, and the needs of those they would convert. As a long established religion, its social order had already been defined as sacred, even to the minutest detail. As a new religion, Christianity had not so thoroughly sacralized one social order and was able to move readily into whatever organizational matrix universal acceptance required. With the death-bed conversion of Constantine in 329, Christianity ceased being a communally organized sect based on the organizational scheme of Pharisaic Judaism and became a religion of state and empire. Thus it was the state level of organization (Steward 1955) and the imperial unification of states that eventually became the sacred social form of Christianity, this being formalized in the rule of the divine rights of kings under the universal dominion of the papacy.

The competition and variation of beliefs that developed in competing Jewish sects (Pharisaism and Christianity) during the first three centuries of the Christian calendar were important and fundamental. But more important and more fundamental in defining the relationship of the two religions in the millennia to come was that Judaism, following the fall of Jerusalem, was a religion that was exclusively communal; and that following the conversion of Constantine, Christianity began an organizational change from the communal to the nation-state and empire levels of integration. From this point on the relationship of these two belief systems would always develop in relation to these respective organizational bases.

In the fourth and fifth centuries by means of councils and decrees, the leaders of Christianity reinterpreted and reevaluated the teachings of scripture to make them valid for and supportive of nations and empires, just as the Jewish prophets of the sixth and fifth centuries B.C. had transformed an agricultural religion into one suited to the needs of urban demes. Thus the Christianity of Spain is a religion of nationhood under the organizational remnants of the Roman Empire represented by the dominion of the papacy. The Judaism of Spain was a religion of communities dispersed in a state controlled by *amme ha aratzath*. The feelings of medieval Jews towards Christian Spaniards were fundamentally no different than those of the Pharisees towards the Hellenic and Roman civilizations whose values had threatened sect purity in their native Palestine.

## COMMUNALISM IN MALLORCA

The Jewish community of medieval Mallorca was a product of nineteen hundred years of development and adaptive change. It was a direct descendent of the form created in Babylon, later refined in Jerusalem under the guidance of Nehemiah and Ezra, then put to the test before the assimilationist pressures of Hellenism, and pagan and Christian Rome. A more mutually productive relationship developed with Islam, whose rapid rise through conquest and commercial expansion provided the setting for the florescence of the community during the ninth and tenth centuries.

Under Islam, it was prepared for the highly specialized economic role it performed in a resuscitated Christendom. This is the community that Christian kings of developing nations found so valuable to the growth of cities and commerce. It is also the community that bedeviled the Spanish state by refusing to assimilate while playing a key role in the economy and involving itself in the most crucial matters of state.

A background of communal living from the sixth century B.C. until the fourteenth century produced the all encompassing milieu that made it next to impossible for those enculturated in the medieval Mallorcan community to live as private citizens apart from it, even after voluntary conversion. This is well illustrated by those Jews who converted to Christianity in Mallorca in 1391. Though some were able to assimilate into the larger society, most attached themselves to a re-formed community, the community of Jewish converts. The second community, officially separated from the Halakhic tradition, organized under the most likely structural arrangement of Christian culture, the guild order, which by this time had diffused to Mallorca from northern Europe through Barcelona. The Jews who converted in 1391 reorganized as a guild by 1404, and were sufficiently compliant to guild norms by 1410 to obtain legal and religious approval. After 1410, the second community, the community of Jewish converts, was known as the New Brotherhood of Saint Michael the Archangel (Santa María 1956).

The guild organization allowed the Jews to do publicly and with approval what they had always done by religious tradition and custom: live together communally. For example, the guilds were organized to regulate the quality of craftmanship just as aljama Jews had always had communal supervision of workmanship and quality. Each guild member contributed to a fund to handle the extraordinary and unexpected expenditures of any of the members. Each guild set up committees to visit the sick and dying and to provide bail for those who were imprisoned. If a member were kidnapped by pirates, the guild paid the ransom. The guild provided gifts at marriage, care for the aged and funeral services and burial for the deceased. All of these were social services already supported by centuries of tradition in the Jewish community.

Guilds functioned with the approval of both the church and the *state*. Once the *Decreto de Erección* was proclaimed by the state, all members of the stated profession were required to belong. When rules of quality, sharing, or price were violated, the state imposed fines which were divided equally between the royal treasury, the guild treasury and the accuser. The religious life of the guild members was focused on the guild's own altar or chapel in a parish church, as well as its own burial ground. Each guild had a patron saint whose day of honor was marked by great festivities. Together, the guild members carried a *paso* (a processional float carried on the backs of men) in the then numerous religious processions (Quetlas Gaya 1957). For those at the artisan or professional level, the primary mode of participation in the city life occurred as members of a guild.

The guild of the converted Jews appeared as just another professional organization on the surface, but in actuality it was in almost every sense a continuation of the Jewish aljama they lived in prior to conversion. Many of the functions of the guild were, as stated above, identical to those of the aljama, but the Brotherhood of St. Michael the Archangel was more than just another guild. In guild organization, social benefits accrued only to those who were members. Among the Conversos, benefits were extended to any Converso whether or not he was a member or even if he were not a Mallorcan. The Converso members had not forgotten the obligation of dispersed Jewish communities to each other. In the ordinance of the Brotherhood of St. Michael there was no mention of religious festivities, nor were there organizational arrangements for religious training as existed among other guilds. The payment of social quotas were, by guild tradition, made on Saturday. The Conversos paid theirs on Friday. Within the guild system, the leadership function of the secretaries of the aljama could be reinstated and legal disputes on any matter could be adjudicated by men of peace guided by custom and the Talmud.

The period of *two communities* lasted from 1391 until 1435. The effects of poverty, peasant rebellion and economic disorder were felt throughout it. This was a precarious period for the Jews. As the sole cultural strangers the Jews were blamed by the Christians for the bad times. Conflict and argument between Christians and Jews was the order of the day. Finally, a crisis developed in 1435, a crisis so colored by medieval interpretation that we can only approximate the events and their meaning by evaluating them in the cultural context of the period. It was alleged that on the Good Friday of that year, the rabbi of the unconverted aljama, along with accomplices, had ridiculed the crucifixion of Jesus by crucifying a Saracen slave. The story of the alleged crime spread throughout the Christian community and the public, enraged by these reports, demanded justice. The accused were found guilty by the court and sentenced to death (Isaacs 1936).

Then, the story goes, the Jewish community was so saddened by the events and so smitten by guilt, that, seeing the error of their ways, and overtaken by great religious fervor, they decided en masse to convert to Christianity. A more cynical interpretation would be that once their rabbi and his associates were condemned to death there was no hope of saving them, except by giving in to the one thing Christian leaders sought from Jews more than anything else—acceptance of the Christian messiah. This being the only recourse for saving their leader, the Jews accepted conversion.

The Jewish community went en masse to the great Cathedral of Mallorca at the edge of the sea, and there each partook in the sacrament of baptism. It was a day of great celebration among the Christians. The Jews, who had been among them so long as cultural strangers would now share with them their most cherished belief, the personal message of salvation given to them by Jesus. The wel-

**The Cathedral, Palma**

coming of the Jews into fusion with Christian society revealed the nonracial character of antipathy that had existed during the period of the aljama. Jews had never been perceived as racially inferior, even though described as diabolical or as living satans. The success of Jews not only in the economic sphere, but in their endurance of national disasters such as the plagues of the previous decades, was evidence to Christians that they were in league with satan. Conversion of the Jews was thus seen in the context of medieval cosmology as a triumph of good over evil, and this in a period of despair was a providential sign of new hope for less suffering and a better life for a depressed Mallorca.

What individual Jews were thinking as they moved through the cathedral ritual into the welcoming embrace of Christians is purely a matter of conjecture. Historical data on the assimilation of converts demonstrates that there was a continuous but slow assimilation of individual Conversos into the Christian society. But for the mass of Jews, those still involved in communal life, it was merely an undesirable but necessary step for the preservation of their faith. Since the suppression of Jewish ritual and Torah scholarship by Hadrian in 135, Jews had been permitted to violate any of the commandments except those forbidding idolatry, murder and incest in order to save their lives. Publicly accepting conversion to Christianity while privately maintaining allegiance to their traditional faith may have been perceived as duplicity by Christians, but for the Jews it was a step readily and conscientiously taken in periods of oppression by the larger society.

After the rhapsodic ceremonialism of the conversion, both Christians and converted Jews had to return to the realities of their quotidian existence. The converts returned to their workshops and worked and prayed as a communal unit as their ancestors had for so many years before. Their new designation as Christians altered their old patterns only slightly. Where before they had lived in one marked off territory in the city, they now split up into pockets throughout the center of the city, all within easy walking distance of one another. The obligations of sharing and of support for and dependence on the community changed little. The daily, monthly, and yearly cycle of prayer and ritual changed not at all, except that under their new designation what had before been private was now secret. The only thing baptism had really changed was their official status. Publicly, they now had to declare themselves and act as Christians, but insofar as their daily life was concerned—their work, custom, and religious duties—everything continued exactly as before (Santa María 1956).

# Mallorcan Conversos and the Inquisition

The years between the Christian conquest of 1229 and the conversion of the Jewish community in 1435 was a period in which Jews lived as Jews, and were recognized as Jews by the law.

In the period covered in this chapter, 1435 to 1691, Jews continued to live as Jews, both in their community life and in the role they played in the larger society; however, their legal status was now that of Christians. The community's new identity, that of guild, convinced almost no one that the Jews had truly accepted Christianity. But this was a problem neither for the officials who the converted Jews supported with bribes, nor for the man in the street to whom the local anomaly was merely a national norm. For practicing Jews occupied the legal status of Christians in all parts of Spain; it was a new class, and it was a sign of the times. However, not everyone could live with or tolerate the divided loyalties of the Converso communities, and within the church and state an old institution designed to investigate heresies of this order was reinvigorated; and in the Spain of the Catholic monarchs, it came to be known as the Holy Office of the Inquisition.

The Inquisition as an institution first appeared in the Iberian peninsula in Aragon in the year 1238. However, in the liberal climate created by the reign of King James I, it ultimately fell into insignificance, and was never of any consequence to Jews. Where it finally did become an institution of central importance was in the cultural milieu of Castile. Through the dominance of Castile, it spread as national policy to all parts of Spain. The Inquisition was an institution of unification and is best perceived in the overall context of the Christian reconquest of Spain. It was one activity among many in which the values of Christianity, nobility, and militarism became the dominant themes of a unified Spanish national culture. The Inquisition was not simply an anti-Jewish institution; it was rather an institution of cultural purity which acted to eliminate *all* and *any* foreign elements, anything which was deemed non-Spanish and non-Christian.

The ethos of the reconquest which became the national ethos of an emerging Spain is composed of many elements. One of the most basic is the concept of nobility. It is a concept which pertains to the noble class, as well as all those who would be noble or deem themselves noble, and in fifteenth-century Spain that included almost everyone. Nobility places honor above wealth, and pride over success. In contemporary Spain one hears mention of nobility frequently: it is still a valid concept. In a recent conversation with a priest in which I questioned him on his views concerning illegitimacy, he said, "The unwed mother who chooses to care for and raise the child on her own is unquestionably a person of great nobility." As unusual as this application of the term might seem, the essential ingredients are there. Ideals are more important than consequences; spiritual values supersede pragmatic values.

This world view developed in the period of reconquest in which the Christian armies of the north were little more than roving bands, sniping at Muslim military posts. The eight-hundred-year Muslim occupation within Spain was a period in which the essential Christian cultural milieu grew and developed through military conquests attained by armies of peasants led by their lords. The odds were enormous. The Muslims outnumbered the Christians and were by far their superiors in technology. The ideals of nobility were exemplified by those nobles who had fought against all odds and won because their courage and tenacity were greater than that of the enemy, and because they were fortified in this endeavor by a belief in Christ.

This was the dominant ethos in the reign of the Catholic monarchs Ferdinand and Isabella during the fifteenth century, a

time when the conquest was not yet complete. The kingdom of
Granada was still in the hands of the Muslims and Christian Spain
was unifying from what had once been the separate kingdoms of
Castile, Leon, Aragon, Catalonia and Navarre. Aragon had united
with Catalonia, and Castile with Leon, and with the marriage of
Ferdinand to Isabella, Aragon and Castile came together. The
uniting force through the reconquest was above all other things,
Christianity. The conquest of the kingdom of Granada in 1492 was
the final Christian victory over Islam and was concomitant with
the formation of one nation. In this new united Spain there could
be no distinction between religion and patriotism. They were inseparable.

The culture of reconquest was in some respects democratic, both
institutionally and philosophically. The power and wealth of the
noble class was almost total, but the peasant considered himself
"just as good." The noble had gained power through military conquest, and the peasant felt that with the same opportunities, he
would serve just as well in the same position. And he was probably
right. Those qualities that were the ideals of the noble class were
also the ideals of the peasant. The peasant felt that there was nothing qualitatively different between himself and nobility. True, the
nobles had wealth and power, but otherwise, they were the same.
The rights of peasants and townsmen were institutionalized in the
charters or *fueros* which had legal force in every part of Spain. The
ancient parliaments of Spain included townsmen in the national
political system and gave them some power and a voice in policy.
The first parliament *(Cortes)* was established in Aragon in 1162 and
Castile had its first cortes in 1250. The first British parliament met
in 1295; the beginning of institutionalized democratic government
in reconquest Spain antedates the British form by 132 years. The
oath of allegiance of the Cortes of Aragon to the king was "We, who
are as good as you, take an oath to you who are no better than we, as
prince and heir of our kingdom, on condition that you preserve our
fueros and liberties, and if you do not, we do not."

This was the condition of Spanish culture in the fifteenth century. The ethos of that era, dominated by a reverence for a nobility
attainable by all, still distinguishes Spanish culture, and for those

who lack some insight into the meaning and origin of these traits, the Spanish national character shall remain a mystery and the behavior of Spaniards appear strange and incongruous. One does not attempt to define these traits in positive or negative terms. The same traits have produced completely different results when conditions were altered. Spain has in different periods been the most democratic and the most autocratic country in Europe. "As early as medieval times, enemies of the king and common law criminals alike, conspirators and rebels, enjoyed all the judiciary guarantees that other peoples were not to know until the eighteenth and nineteenth centuries. But at the end of the sixteenth century, any Spaniard could be thrown into a church prison on the strength of a denunciation, real or faked, could be kept for an indefinite time in a dungeon, and tortured merely at the whim of the Inquisitioner, and would be given no choice by the Inquisitioner-Judge than that between confession of imaginary crimes or death by fire—inevitable reward of his obstinate denials" (La Souchere 1964, p. 81).

The Inquisition as an institution was a major force in the transformation of Spain from an exemplary national culture in which minorities knew more rights than at any prior time in history to a crusading fanaticism where total conformity was enforced by law. It is noteworthy that the Inquisition was never anywhere near so important in other countries as it was in Spain. One must distinguish between inquisition as a form, and the Spanish Inquisition, for the Inquisition in Spain was unlike any other comparable institution.

An inquisition is an inquiry into the possibility of heresy. It had in its beginning nothing to do with Jews. To be guilty of heresy one must be a member of the faith. For example, within the aljama, the Jewish court could ostracize or excommunicate a member for a violation of the norms of the community. The crime of heresy is essentially the same thing. Both Jews and Catholics in medieval times would have found each others rights to excommunicate for violations of religious codes easily comprehensible, for the practices were directly parallel. The source of the tradition of punishing those whose beliefs were not in accordance with societal religious beliefs was in both cases the Old Testament. The idolater of the Old Testament was stoned to death. The idolater was a worshipper of foreign gods, gods attached to foreign states. The emotions aroused by treason in contemporary nation-states provide a modern parallel to the feelings evoked by the betrayal of religious codes in the medieval period.

The Inquisition in Roman Catholicism came into being in 1184 with a decree by Pope Lucio III in which he ordered the bishops to seek out those suspected of heresy and send them for judgment to the curia of the diocese. If there was a sentence it was to be executed by civil authorities. This was called the Episcopal Inquisition. The insitution was reinvoked in 1227 in Narbonne and Toulouse but was ineffective because the bishops lacked the zeal to activate it (Torroba de Quiros 1967). Responding to this failure, Pope Gregory IX transferred jurisdiction from the bishops to those of the mendicant orders, the Dominicans and Franciscans. In their hands, religious zeal far outweighed judiciousness and the most reprehensible characteristics of the Inquisition became institutionalized. Information and testimony was acquired secretly. The accused was not told who his accusers were or who had testified against him, and was not allowed the right to legal counsel.

The Inquisition spread throughout Europe but was of little consequence except in France, Italy and Spain. In 1312 it was used in France in the course of a war by Philip the Handsome against the military orders of Templars, and then fell into disuse. In Italy it was used on various occasions but was of little import. It was officially introduced in Spain in 1237, but never really functioned until the fifteenth century when Ferdinand and Isabella utilized it to act against the influence of Jewish and Saracen beliefs on Spanish Catholicism. The Spanish Inquisition, beginning in 1480, did not function under the authority of the Pope. The clergy who administered it were directly appointed by the Spanish monarchs.

The first act of the Inquisition occurred in Seville, and the trials there were a direct outcome of a visit by Queen Isabella in 1477, during which she had been convinced by a Dominican named Alonso de Hojeda that Jews converted to Catholicism had converted for pragmatic reasons only and were secretly adherents to Judaism. It should be re-emphasized here that the Inquisition had no jurisdiction over Jews. However, once baptized, a former Jew was subject to

its procedures if there was suspicion that he was continuing in the
ways of his prior religion. The reports of Hojeda were supported by
the archbishop of Seville and the prior of a Dominican convent,
Tomás de Torquemada. They added that not only in Seville but
throughout south and central Spain Jews converted to Catholicism
were practicing Jewish rites in secret. By 1480 the Inqusiition was in
operation in Seville, and began its activities by burning nine of the
city's leading Conversos at the stake (Kamen 1965).

The results of the first stage of the Inquisition was a rapid exodus
from Spain of both Jews and Conversos. Those who had remained
Jews could not be brought before the Inquisitors, but they suffered
other torments at the local level. "The number of refugees fleeing
abroad was so great, that for every Judaizer burnt, tens and hundreds
were burnt in effigy as fugitives" (Kamen 1965: 55). In 1492 all Jews
remaining in Spain were given four months to either convert to
Catholicism or leave the country. At least 150,000 left; but many
stayed and accepted baptism. Only two religions were then legal in
Spain, Christianity and Islam. In 1502 a royal decree gave all Muslims the same alternative as the Jews had been given—baptism or
exile. From that time on, accusations of non-Christian behavior
were sufficient to bring one before the church tribunal. Evidence of
judaizing were any of a number of things including wearing cleaner
clothes on the Jewish Sabbath than the rest of the week, having no
fire in the house on the Sabbath, or washing a corpse in warm
water. The traditional ritual of bathing was mentioned in acts
against former Muslims, so that the taking of too many baths was
commonly given as evidence for apostasy (Crow 1963).

It should be re-emphasized that Mallorca in the fifteenth and
sixteenth centuries was one of the more remote provinces of the new
nation of Spain, geographically distant and culturally and linguisti-
cally different from the Castilian power center. The Inquisition in
Mallorca is a product of both national and local forces, sometimes
distinguishable, but frequently fused and indistinguishable. The
Inquisition which began in Mallorca back in 1232 was a church-
instituted form and was almost totally without effect or consequence. As in Aragon, Mallorca was not at that time a fertile ground
for legal inquiries into heresy. The riots of 1391 show that there did

The Star of David is seen in the principal window
at the Church of Mercy, Palma.

exist a problem in the relationship of Jews with segments of the
larger society. These riots were part of a national phenomenon, for
as we have noted there were anti-Jewish riots and massacres in every
part of Spain that year. The events had to do with culturally parallel
situations which were repeated again and again throughout Spain.
Their repetition was the product of an internal communications
network where the news of anti-Jewish activities from other areas
stimulated local uprisings.

The Inquisition that began in 1488 is something quite different.
It was a national policy imposed on Mallorca by the center of state
and church power. The Spanish Inquisition had its own bureaucracy, and could establish policy for all the provinces of Spain. For

this reason we have looked at the Inquisition as a national phenomenon, prior to examining it in Mallorca. Local conditions and
events created a situation that was somewhat at variance to what
happened nationally. Therefore, we will cover the Mallorcan Inquisition in some detail.

The Spanish Inquisition as a national institution began its activities in Mallorca in 1488, at the same time that it was initiating
similar inquiries in other Spanish cities. In its early years one segment of the population was the focal point of all inquiry, the Conversos. Jews converted to Catholicism, were, legally speaking,
violating the precepts of Roman Catholicism by continuing to practice Jewish rites and customs. They were also violating Jewish practice by publicly denying their own faith in order to gain the advan-
tages of conversion to Christianity. Those who had remained publicly loyal to Judaism had only contempt for the opportunism of the
Conversos. Jewish law and tradition permits false conversion under
threat of death, and even encouraged secret ritual or so-called
crypto-Judaism, when Jewish lives were threatened by the state for
carrying on traditional practices. But these were not the circumstances under which most Conversos had chosen Christianity. They
had become Christian because in every realm of life there were
more opportunities to one publicly identified as Christian than to
one labelled Jewish.

Looking at the situation a bit more benevolently, we might see
the Conversos as an intermediate stage in the assimilation process.
Jews who insulted their faith by pragmatic conversions to another
religion were surely not the most ardent followers of traditional law
and custom. Their commitment to Judaism was based on a lessen-
ing repulsion towards a foreign faith, which allowed for more pragmatic responses to financial and status opportunities in the emerging state.

What the Conversos did not give up were communal ties. One
wonders whether they could have, or better stated, to what degree
were retention of communal ties acts that were consciously considered. As products of a complex communal social organization,
how much could the individual undo the intense socialization of his
childhood. In this intermediate condition of assimilation com-

munal Judaism was still a primary and major element of the Converso sub-culture. Following conversion, converted Jews were welcome in all levels of Spanish life. They married into nobility in such numbers that not a single noble family in Spain could declare itself free of Jewish ancestry. They joined the clergy and were to be found at every level of service to the church. The rabbi of the Jewish community of Burgos, Salomon Ha Levi became Padre Pablo de Santa María, and thence Archbishop of Burgos (Kamen 1965). A problem in this intermediate stage of assimilation was that, even within Christian social organizations, the converts continued consciously or unconsciously to reinvoke the sense of community, and this inevitably evoked fears of plotting among the so-called Old Christians.

Within nobility, within the church, within governmental service, Conversos, lacking intense commitment to either Catholicism or Judaism, behaved as good Spaniards, and emphasized their Catholicism with Catholics and their Judaism with Jews. The sense of community among Conversos was not always noticed by Old Christians, or if noticed was given little importance. However, when the Old Christians were too naive to observe Jewish communalism among Conversos, there were inevitably those Conversos whose commitment to Catholicism was complete, who were eager to point it out. This was the case at the most important level of all, that of royal power. The influence of the Converso Tomás de Torquemada on Ferdinand and Isabella was enormous. As a man of Jewish origins who had become an intense Christian ascetic, Torquemada recognized the lack of religious commitment among Conversos, and eagerly exaggerated the dangers of the situation to the monarchs whose relations with Jews and Conversos prior to the time of the Inquisition were close, equitable and harmonious.

I take notice of the various stages of assimilation to clarify a situation that is usually dealt with badly in both Jewish and Christian versions of the Inquisition. Both versions tend to emphasize the secret communities, the Christians taking note of the duplicity involved and Jews seeing the same phenomenon in heroic terms— Jews continuing their religion in secret in the face of existing pressures to accept Christianity. Christians have responded so strongly, at that time and since, that the existence of secret communities is given as one of the major justifications for the Inqusition. How is it possible, they claim, for a country to carry out viable policies while a fifth column operates at the very centers of power? Even some Jewish writers see the Inquisition as an effective and necessary measure in the attainment of national cohesion and unity of purpose. I prefer to see the secret Jewish community as one inevitable stage in an assimilation process, and the alleged fifth column danger as mostly an illusion.

One foundation of the fear of the betrayal of Jews was the affinity between Jewish and Islamic culture. During the fifteenth century, Spain was still at war with Islam, and following the conquest of Granada, the Spaniards lived in fear of an organized invasion of the peninsula in retaliation. It was felt that in such a war, the Jews would betray the Christians to their Saracen cousins. This is a mistaken view, I think, primarily on the ground that there would have been no single Jewish response, but rather various responses in accordance with subcultural identity. Jews in aljamas would have responded one way, Conversos retaining communal organization another, and wholly converted ex-Jews another. In the case of aljama Jews, history demonstrates clearly that they would have sided with whichever society best guaranteed their rights of communal independence. The history of Jews in the Iberian peninsula is one of repeated changing of sides in the long Christian-Islamic struggle, in accordance with respective governmental policies regarding the rights of aljamas. In the case of Conversos, the conversions they had volunteered were, although not based on Christian piety, nevertheless a strong indication of the increaisng power of nationalism and national cultural values as against the decreasing attractiveness of the communal values and the culture of the aljama. Their commitment to the state was strong. The third group was of course those Conversos whose commitment to the church and state was total and unequivocal. They would respond as the most patriotic of Spaniards. Thus we see among those of Jewish origin no unified body organized to act in unison behind any policy involving betrayal or allegiance, but rather we see a diversity of groups where attitudes and policies were directly related to the state of assimilation away from aljama life in the direction of nationalism.

## MALLORCA

The focus of our study of the Conversos of Mallorca is on those organized in a community. Those whose conversion and assimilation was complete blended with the larger population in a generation or less; and their former affiliation with the community was soon forgotten. The evidence suggests that their numbers were large, probably at least as large as the number of Conversos remaining in the community. The degree of conversion or assimilation was a product, among other things, of the motives and the means by which the conversion had taken place. The first wave of conversions which occurred following the massacre of 1391 were, like the fleeing of refugees from the country, an outcome of fear and panic. This sort of situation did not readily lead to assimilation.

Another major stimulus to conversion were the proselytizing sermons of St. Vincent Ferrer, and the pressures that accompanied them. One is inclined to discount the effect of St. Vincent Ferrer as so much of what is said about the numbers that he converted are nothing less than outrageous lies. In Mallorca, it is alleged that he converted twenty thousand Jews, a number which is twenty times the maximum estimate of the total population of the Jewish community. But putting these exaggerations aside there is evidence that his movement was a powerful stimulant to conversions, as much from the influence Ferrer and others had on Christians to pressure Jews to convert, as on Jews directly. It is safe to conclude that proselytizing was one cause of conversions, and it is reasonable to assume that those who changed by persuasion assimilated into the Christian population.

Finally, there was the mass conversion of 1435, which may or may not be called a forced conversion depending on how one chooses to interpret the situation. We have seen that this occurred as a result of a local incident where Jews were accused of crucifying a Saracen during Holy Week in desecration of the commemoration of the crucifixion of Christ. One has to guess at what really happened, and since this was not an isolated incident, one can make a reasonable approximation. That the Jews regularly and consistently ridiculed Christian beliefs and practices, there is no doubt. This occurred within the community as a reaffirmation of their own beliefs. But Christian accusations of child murders and blood sacrifice were in all cases products of popular hysteria, the occurrence of any single such event never having been proven throughout the many centuries that such rumors were rampant. Nevertheless, a series of events, most importantly an escape to the mountains which was interpreted as an admission of guilt, led to conviction and sentencing to death of the accused. The decision of the entire community to convert can be seen as a strategy by the members of the community to free their leaders. If this was the case, and I am convinced that it was, then the conversion of 1435 was a hoax, and such conversions would hardly result in assimilation into the larger society. In Mallorca, as in all of Spain, there were many types of conversions and a variety of outcomes. The Conversos community, *post* 1435, was, we have seen, nothing more than the aljama continuing under a new title. But through the partaking of the ceremony of baptism, the Mallorcan Jews became subject to the legal authority of the church, and more specifically, of the office of the Inquisition.

Only the most naive could have believed that in the period between 1435 and 1488 the converted Jews had really given up the faith they were born to. Although many were convinced in the aura of the ceremony of 1435, the events of the years that followed made it perfectly clear that the Jewish community was functioning as it always had. The local act of 1436 which declared the practice of Judaism illegal on the island of Mallorca had little force. But the power of a nationwide Inquisition was of great concern to the Mallorcan Conversos. In its beginning in 1488, the Inquisition heard only four cases, all of the defendants being reconciled to the faith. One year later 337 Conversos came forth asking to be forgiven for their errors and reconciled to the church. By the following year the number grew to 424 voluntary confessions and requests for reconciliation. In all cases reconciliation was granted (Braunstein 1936).

When a person appeared before the Inquisition the assumption was that he was guilty. The tribunal could either forgive the defendant his errors and *reconcile* him to the church, or decide against forgiveness and *relax* (turn over or transfer) the defendant to the secular arm for the administration of punishment. Neither the church, nor the Inquisition as part of it, could administer punishment, but this was not necessary as the secular office did it for them.

In the early years, the Inquisition in Mallorca reconciled those asking forgiveness, but there were also large numbers who were officially relaxed, 53 in 1489 and 36 in 1490. But the vast majority of these were fugitives from the island, whose flight was considered sufficient evidence for finding them guilty. All of the fugitives were burned in effigy, and should they ever be found, their bodies would be treated in the same way their effigies had been. In one case, a female Converso burned in effigy in 1489 was discovered that same year and then burned in person. From 1488 to the end of the century, 257 persons were relaxed, the majority executed in effigy. However, relaxations in effigy were more than just ceremony, for the decision entitled the Inquisition to confiscate all the property of the condemned, including that which had passed into the hands of heirs. The amounts confiscated were considerable, so much so that the crown became extremely concerned about keeping accurate records of the amounts, to insure acquisition of its rightful share (Braunstein 1936).

The early stages of the Mallorcan Inquisition was characterized by caution in administering punishment and an eagerness to confiscate wealth by legalistic means. Two Edicts of Grace or periods of mercy resulted in the coming forth of the aforementioned 424 reconciled. In some cases, where there had been a relapse into old religious customs, the Inquisition allowed the penitents to avoid confiscation of property through the payment of a fine. Compared to later activities, these were cautious measures, with limited financial return. In the case of relaxations, the Inquisition garnered fortunes by confiscation of the wealth of those burned in effigy. This was the pattern of the activities of the Inquisition during its first twelve years, involving 770 decisions of reconciliation of relaxation.

From 1510 to 1519, 120 decisions of relaxation to the secular arm were given, five in person, and 115 in effigy. This was the end of predominantly effigy punishments by the Mallorcan Inquisition. The ceremonies served a teaching, or better stated, coercive function as regards the seriousness of the crime of heresy in a period of high illiteracy. The large numbers burned in effigy demonstrated that many Jews were fleeing from the island. Nevertheless, a sizeable community continued, and as long as they remained the inquisitional tribunal grew wealthy extracting funds from its members through repeated confiscations, which by church law were entirely legal.

From 1520 to 1536, the Inquisition relaxed only 46 persons, three in person and 43 in effigy, a marked decline from previous years. From 1536 to 1675 there were no relaxations whatsoever, 139 years of inactivity insofar as inquiry into the heresy of Conversos is concerned. During that 139-year period the Inquisition heard 887 cases, but they dealt entirely with the clergy and non-Conversos, and only seven persons were relaxed on all charges during this period (Braunstein 1936). The Inquisition had been weakened by conflicts of jurisdiction with other bodies and was limited in its activities. If former patterns hold true, the possibility that Converso merchants were sending funds directly to the crown to stymie the Mallorcan Inquisition is altogether plausible. For like modern charitable organizations which utilize large percentages of their take in administrative costs, the Inquisition had little of its acquired wealth left to share with the crown after the expenses of its ceremonies and officials had been properly deducted.

## THE COMMUNITY DURING THE INQUISITION

The anti-Converso activities of the Inquisition began in earnest in 1675. Prior to this date frequent and open attempts were made to acquire proof of heresy, involving the practice of Judaism, and the encouragement and teaching of others in these practices. In 1624 the Inquisition issued an edict of faith in which it spelled out the ways that the enemies of Christianity might be detected. It listed the rituals and customs of Jews, which when practiced by Conversos indicated a continuation of the observance of Mosaic law. It is interesting to note that not a single person came forth with information, even though the existence of distinct traditions within the Converso community was common knowledge. Again we see the common people abiding by the rule of live and let live. This does not mean they liked the Jews, but the pattern is clear that openly aggressive acts by the populace occur only under conditions of great turmoil, as in the case of near starvation in 1391. Surely those in the Inquisition realized this when they called for reports of heresy through an edict of faith. They did not need the information for they were as well-informed as the rest of the populace on the practices of the Conversos. But in publicly seeking the aid of all in rooting out heresy, they hoped to arouse the populace to action.

In 1672 the Inquisition had already received new information which clarified the degree to which the Mallorcan Conversos had remained in contact with other communities in the Mediterranean. They heard from a Mallorcan who while traveling in Italy was contacted by Jews of the city of Leghorn, inquiring about the Jews of Mallorca. The Mallorcan told them that there were no Jews in Mallorca, that everyone was Catholic. The Leghorn Jews responded that they knew the Mallorcan Jews were as faithful as themselves and proceeded to describe them, providing family names. They also knew the streets where they resided, the Street of the Silver Shops and the Street of the Pursemaker Shops. That all this was common knowledge in Leghorn would lead one to conclude that the Conversos of Mallorca maintained contacts with other communities, almost to the extent a nonconverted Jewish community would have.

In 1673 the Inquisition was told of heresies in Jewish households, by a servant girl who had worked with a Converso family. The girl reported on fasts and feasts that were foreign to her and not Catholic, such as extensive preparations for ushering in the Sabbath on Friday evening, and the slaughtering of fowl with a special knife. Although the Conversos secluded themselves while slaughtering, the simple servant girl was nevertheless able to describe the rite in great detail. The slaughtering allegedly took place on the top floor of the house and a pan full of ashes was used to catch the blood. The maid had observed an identical ceremony in another Converso household (Braunstein 1936).

In the above testimonies we see believable evidence being submitted to the Inquisition for the continuing practice of Judaism in Mallorca 240 years after it had been declared illegal. They knew and had known of the continuing community, but were restrained from doing anything about it by political motives and the willingness of the populace to leave things as they were. To the inquisitional mind, the failure of the populace to respond with information even after a public plea for it by an edict of faith must have itself seemed a sign of weakening religiosity, emphasizing the need to demonstrate to the public the seriousness of heresy and the power of the church. By 1675 it overcame the obstacles that had kept it inactive for so long, and proceeded to search out the heresies with few restraints.

The existence of a community of Jews was a fact known by all, but the degree to which this community was engaged in the practice of Judaism was not. The public assumed that the Jews continued in their old ways, but few knew what this meant exactly. In the inquisitional trials both Converso and non-Converso witnesses informed and testified and the details of Converso practices came to light. Through court records available in the *Archivo Histórico Nacional* in Madrid, and the analysis of them by Baruch Braunstein in the 1930s there is abundant data on Converso practices of this time.

### RITES OF PASSAGE

The most basic and fundamental ritual of Jews could not be performed by the Mallorcan Conversos, for circumcision was clear and incontrovertible evidence of the continuing practice of Judaism. The severing of the foreskin was a completely foreign custom to Mallorcans, and had Conversos continued this practice they would hardly have been able to deny their true religious feelings. There is a record of only one circumcision among the Conversos, and that was by a man who performed it upon himself with a piece of glass while in the prison of the Inquisition.

The major event of puberty was the revelation to the teenager of all the details of ceremony, prayer and religious organization within the community. At this same time the youth became aware of the marriage arrangements that were being made for him or her, and was instructed in the importance of continuing the practice of the Law with the children. The beginning of the menstrual cycle of the female necessitated instructions on ritual purification. The girl was instructed not to eat cooked food for eight days, and at the end of this period to bathe herself in a solution of water, salt and marjoram. She learned that as a married woman, she must remain away from her husband during menstruation.

Marriages were performed in a Catholic church, with a priest officiating. This was entirely unavoidable, for without a church wedding there would be no public record of the marriage contract. However, following the church ceremony, the party retreated to the garden of a private home or to the cemetery of their ancestors, and there they sealed the transaction with a Jewish oath. The wedding having officially taken place in the church, there were no restraints placed on public celebration of the event with festivities.

Although circumcision could not be performed on the infant, at birth the mother continued the practice of remaining away from her husband for a period of two months after parturation. At death the body of the deceased was turned so that it faced the wall. The doors and windows were closed and the corpse was washed with water and ointment in observance of the rite of *Taharah*. The body was then placed in a clean shroud. Catholic priests were not invited for last rites. A day of fasting followed interment, and members of the immediate family did not change garments for a month following the death.

## SABBATH AND CALENDAR OF HOLY DAYS

Prior to the onset of Sabbath, the house was cleaned, clean clothes replaced soiled ones and all the lamps were cleaned and fitted with new wicks to insure their burning for a full twenty-four hours. A special meal was prepared, usually fish, and when this was not possible, the Conversos ate only snacks throughout the day. As Saturday was the day that peasants came into the town to market, Sabbath was usually the busiest working day of the week. Sabbath was introduced and concluded with prayers to St. Tobit, who held an honored place among Conversos throughout Spain (Roth 1959).

On the Day of Atonement the Conversos prayed and fasted for twenty-four hours. This was the most solemn of all days, and in their prayers they asked forgiveness for their sins and pleaded with the Almighty that he should not foresake them. The prayers were communal, led by a reader and repeated by those assembled. They were in Hebrew, and the Conversos had only the vaguest knowledge of their meaning. As the service ended, each of the assembled asked forgiveness of the others, and forgiveness was granted by a symbolic kissing of the hands.

Next in importance was Purim which the Conversos called the Fast of Esther. This was celebrated on the eleventh day after the new moon of March. It was commemorated by a three-day abstention from food. The importance of the day to Conversos was attributable to the parallel they saw between the story of Esther and her secret practice of the faith, and their own condition. They ended the fast with bathing, a change to clean clothes and a meal of fish, peas and spinach. Here again they asked each other pardon amongst much kissing of hands.

Fasting was the primary means of commemorating holy days. The Conversos celebrated the Fast of Lentils in July and the Fast of the First Born on the eve of Passover, and some fasted on the day following the appearance of a new moon. Excessive fasting was a means of allaying guilt over their failure to carry out the observance of the Law in all its detail. They knew their practices were inadequate, and they feared the disfavor of God. With fasts they hoped to appease him and seek his protection from the ever present dangers that were part of their daily life.

As the Conversos struggled to maintain Judaic tradition, they were nevertheless influenced by Catholic values in ways they were not aware. The custom of asking the intercession of saints was a Catholic not a Jewish practice. Nevertheless, the Conversos prayed to St. Tobit, St. Esther and St. Rafael to mediate between themselves and God, for these were Jewish not Christian saints, and they could speak in their behalf. The Conversos also adopted the Catholic practice of seeking salvation for the individual, rather than all Israel. They believed that the individual gained salvation through belief in and practice of the Law of Moses. The Conversos knowingly repeated the prayers of the Christians in Church, but were careful to leave out references to the Trinity. They kept in mind that all their prayers, whatever they were, were to the God of Israel.

Judaic tradition was maintained not only by the passing on of prayer, ritual and other customs from generation to generation, but by continuing reinvigoration from Jewish communities in other countries. The influences for assimilation to Christianity were strong, but they were retarded by a reaffirmation of traditional values from places where these values were still primary. Just as we see the Spanish-speaking people of the American southwest retaining their Mexican culture in full force over the centuries by continuing contact with Mexico, while other ethnic groups lacking these contacts assimilate, so did the Converso persistence benefit from contact with other Jews while each other foreign group in Mallorca was totally absorbed. Their contacts extended from Marseilles to Alexandria. Traveling merchants witnessed ceremonies, heard discussions of the Law, and were able to return with books and ritual paraphernalia. Jewish books reinspired Jewish beliefs and enabled Conversos to intelligently criticize Christian practices while affirming the theological bases of their own faith.

In the late seventeenth century, and almost certainly for the years prior to that, the Conversos had a religious leader who performed the ceremonial and educational functions of a rabbi. He was the first to study new books from foreign sources, and he explained the complexities of the Law to the confused. Those who became skeptical of Jewish practices were sent to him to reaffirm their faith. In his teaching he declared that Christ was a man like any other man, born of a woman; that he was a mortal, not God, and that no one could be both mortal and God. He taught that the Messiah had not come, nor would he until the Hebrew people had made penance for their sins. Christians were pitied for their alleged worship of idols, a practice expressly forbidden in Deuteronomy. The power of priests to forgive sin was criticized, for no mere mortal, only God, could do that. There could be no Trinity, he said, if there was but one God, and finally in the matter of the crucifixion, it was taught that the Jews did not deserve punishment as the crucifiers of Christ, for they themselves were the suffering and crucified people. With sources of reinspiration for the Jewish faith arriving from foreign communities in various forms and the influences of local Christianity surrounding them in their daily lives, we see a push-pull situation among the Conversos that resulted in little change in their community over the years.

Apart from religious practices, the sense of community among the Conversos was supported by a strong sense of interdependence and rigidly enforced social boundaries between themselves and outsiders. Although they contributed to church charity, they did not utilize its service, preferring to collect alms among themselves on holy days to care for their own needs. They developed an argot which allowed identification of one another in the midst of outsiders. As with the residents of the aljama, the informer was the most dreaded enemy, so precautions were taken against weak or dishonest members. But most fundamental of all was the strict enforcement of the rule of endogamy. The rabbi taught that only those with untainted blood could find salvation through the God of Israel (Braunstein 1936). Intermarriage between Conversos and Old Christians was expressly forbidden, and the person who broke this rule was ostracized and denounced as *Malshen*, or slanderer. The family of the participant in an exogamous union disowned the renegade, and mourned him as if he were dead. There was contempt toward the offspring of exogamous marriages, expressed in terms such as mulatto and half-breed.

In the arrangement of marriages the same values prevailed. Dedication to Judaism was the most important consideration; everything else was secondary. A youth whose family demonstrated a strong and unswerving dedication to the Law was much sought after in the marriage market, commanding the interest of parents who offered the largest dowries. Internal divisions existed, and these too were in line with Jewish customs. The seemingly absurd segmentation on the basis of "tribe" was enforced, and it was considered a serious breach when a member of a "higher tribe" of priests or levites married into an "inferior tribe" of ordinary Israelites. Class distinction within the community only serves to emphasize the viability of the community as a whole. It responded as a whole, however, on most occasions, most notably upon the news of death of any member, when the entire community went into mourning for a day. For each death was an example, a demonstration of a life completed in which submission to the Law had won out over an impinging and foreign faith. The dedication of the Conversos could only be matched by the jurists of the Inquisition in their meticulous and efficient work in discovering and proving the existence of heresy in the Christian State.

Well-informed on the practices, traditions, and beliefs of the Conversos, the Inquisition set out to change the ways of the heretics, while collecting enormous rewards in the form of confiscations, apparently received as a bounty from heaven in payment for their dedication and work. From 1675 to 1692 the Inquisition was extremely busy, and as before the activities were easily separable into phases, a first phase of reconciliation and a second phase of relaxation and severe punishment. This is explained by the complexities of legal procedures and the practical problems involved in extracting wealth from the community.

## INQUISITION SPECTACLE: THE FINAL PHASE

The high point of the Inquisition began with an *auto de fé* and public burning of a Portuguese Converso who persisted in his heresy and died a martyr. A crowd of thirty thousand witnessed the execution, and the ceremony served to solidify the respective beliefs of both the Conversos and the Christians. Seeing the Portuguese sacrifice his life for Judaism provided inspiration to the Conversos, who saw new meaning in their rituals which they practiced with even greater fervor. The first general arrest of Conversos occurred in October of 1677 with the detention of the rabbi Pedro Onofre Cortés, his wife, son and three others. In the following year the arrests continued until October when the total reached 237. The Inquisition referred to these arrests as "the conspiracy of 1678."

Testimony was heard over a period of a year and a half. Some denied heresy, but led by their rabbi who confessed that he had finally seen the light, the whole group proclaimed Christianity as their religion and asked for forgiveness. The sentences were pronounced in five separate *autos de fé* in the year 1679 during the months of April and May. The *autos* were held a week apart as they involved considerable preparation. They were great ceremonial occasions whose impact continues to be felt in modern times. For this reason we shall briefly review the ritual.

The commonsense view of an *auto de fé* is that it involved the public burning at the stake of heretics. This is not the case: in fact, when executions did occur, they were carried out by secular authorities after the conclusion of the *auto*. The *auto de fé* is instead a public ceremony, comparable in some ways to a bull fight or a chariot race in which all the ritualistic elements of a spectacle are engaged to heighten the impact of penitent heretics publicly acquiescing to the faith. Literally translated, it is an "act of faith," and the testimonies of accused heretics repenting was not unlike the act of coming forward and being saved that we see in contemporary fundamentalist revival meetings. The impact of the transformation and religious zeal of penitent heretics would at times influence the non-repentant, and the *auto* was frequently the scene of last-minute conversions.

The *autos* of 1679 in Mallorca were held on Sundays, some beginning early in the morning and lasting until just before sundown. The ceremony began with a mass, and was followed by a procession of the guilty to a platform where they stood bareheaded with lighted candles wearing *sanbenitos*, a penitential garment which symbolized their heresy. The penitents publicly abjured or renounced their heretical beliefs and practices and their sentences were read to the public. There were no sentences of death and all were reconciled to the faith.

In the five *autos*, 219 Conversos were reconciled and the punishments announced were prison terms of various lengths and confiscation of wealth. Prison sentences ranged from six months to life, but in fact almost all the prisoners were released within a short time. The prison was run by public officials and through bribes the prisoners managed to have almost all the comforts that can be brought into a prison, including food and beverage from home and entertainment from wandering minstrels. The real punishment was the confiscation of wealth. Many students of this period feel that money was the underlying motive behind the actions of the Inquisition. There is abundant evidence to support this. For example, the amount of confiscated wealth in Mallorca alone, over two million dollars by today's standards, made the Inquisition competitive with the government in its acqusitions of funds.

Following the reconciliations of 1679, the Conversos struggled to make a living, but bad crops and ensuing economic decline made survival difficult. As part of their punishment many were compelled to wear the penitent garment, the *sanbenito*, for years afterwards. Burdened by this stigma, it was almost impossible to conduct business with a Christian public. Under conditions of relative poverty, public stigma and close supervision by public authorities, many of the Conversos decided to leave the island and start a new life in some place where they could practice their religion freely. A number of them tried to leave the island on an English ship but were driven back by a storm. Upon their return they were arrested. These arrests, ensuing confessions and information provided by a Converso informer who had married a Christian led to wholesale arrests in 1688. Three years of trials resulted in four *autos de fé* held in 1691.

The year 1691 is the most infamous of the whole Inquisition period in Mallorca, for it represented the inquisitional process at its worst—suffering, torture and death by garroting and fire. The most serious penalty of the first *auto* was seven years as a galley slave, permanent wearing of the *sanbenito* and two hundred lashes. In the second, sentences of death by garroting followed by burning of the corpse were given to twenty-one Conversos. In the third *auto*, eleven were sentenced to be garroted before being burned, and three were sentenced to be burned alive. In the final *auto*, there were no death sentences. The difference between the *autos* of 1691 and those of 1679 were that the later *autos* involved accusations of heresy for the second time. Death sentences were administered to those who had once confessed their heresy, abjured, were reconciled to the church, and then had *relapsed* into heresy again. The *autos* of 1691 were the final stage of a confrontation between the adamant leaders of differing beliefs. The leaders of the Conversos were unswerving in their commitment to Judaism, and as this became clear to the tribunal of the Inquisition, the sentence of death was imposed to prevent continuing heresy. The *autos* of 1691 finally broke the will of the Conversos, and organized crypto-Judaism became little more than an awareness of Jewishness among a stigmatized ethnic community. Thus we move into the period of the Xuetas (Braunstein 1936).

# The Period of the Xuetas  6

The persistence of the Xueta community in the eighteenth and nineteenth centuries derives from quite different conditions than community persistence prior to 1700. At about the turn of the century, post-inquisition assimilation should have begun, if it were going to take place at all. It did not. To explain this, we will look at conditions before and after 1700.

The ability of a Jewish community to persist, even in the most hostile environment, was due above all to the strength of commitment its members had to religious ideals and values. The religious message provided meaning for suffering and degradation, and as we have seen in Mallorca the community persisted against all odds. Supporting the religious beliefs and strengthening community cohesion were practices of economic cooperation, specialized economic function and traditions of mutual aid. The community in Mallorca had been tested under the hostile domination of the Almoravides and the Almohades. Under the supportive policies of James I and II it thrived and continued to flourish even as the island economy declined. As we have seen, the forced conversion of 1435 changed little in the Jewish community apart from outward appearances. It was still supported by the same religious ideals, although at this time they were reiterated in secret rather than public ritual. It could even be said the secret practice of Judaism and the attendant risks of exposure made the religious values all the more meaningful, and made assimilation an even more intolerable violation of order than it had been in an openly practicing Jewish community. But whether secret or open, commitment to ideology was the mainstay

137

of community survival. Following the *autos* of 1691, this was no longer the case.

By 1700 the community no longer practiced Judaism, even in secret. The Inquisition had succeeded through the severity of its punishments and the coercive power of public degradation and confessions in the *autos de fé* to break the will of the Conversos. The conquest had been total, for it resulted not only in physical domination, but the obliteration of the will to resist. Where the forced conversions of 1435 had succeeded in nothing more than the extraction of a public commitment to Christianity, which in the end meant little, the *autos* of 1691 had finally attained the goal of complete submission to the Catholic faith.

The Xuetas of the ensuing eighteenth and nineteenth centuries were undoubtedly practicing Catholics who no longer adhered to the Jewish ideal of endogamy. From 1700 on, resistance to assimilation was no longer an internal concern, but in its place new anti-assimilationist pressures developed in the larger society. The Mallorcans were advised by church officials to limit their contacts with Xuetas. In the widely dispersed book, *La Fe Triunfante* by Father Francisco Garau (1931, 1691), they were provided with details of the wickedness of these shameless heretics. The garments which the accused had worn in the *autos*, the *sanbenitos*, were hung from the walls of the Church of the Dominicans as a reminder of their crime. In an age where posted proclamations and town criers were the principal urban media, the display of hanging *sanbenitos* bearing the names of the heretics was an even more effective means of spreading public dishonor than Garau's book. The Xuetas were officially denied public office and honors, and they were denied the right to enter military service. The stigma attached to them by the Inquisition made the Xuetas more a pariah people than Jews had ever been before, and this stigma proved as effective as internal community values had before in keeping the community endogamous. As before, specialized economic function and traditions of mutual aid, now reinforced by the increased hostility of the larger society, provided the organizational base of the community. But more than 275 years of persistence after the final *auto* of the Inquisition in 1691 was for the most part a product of public exclusion by the larger society.

As practicing Catholics, the Xuetas continued to play the *role* of Jews. In this role, they had a special relationship to the Mallorcan economy and society. The changes which occurred in their status were very much linked to changes in the larger society, so in looking at the Xuetas in the eighteenth and nineteenth centuries, we shall examine them against a backdrop of the island economy and urban social organization. Finally, we shall look at the major historical events that affected the Xuetas prior to the beginning of the twentieth century.

## THE JEWISH ROLE: LAND, WEALTH AND SOCIAL RELATIONSHIPS

The economy of Mallorca is historically characterized by shifts in emphasis between foreign trade and internal agricultural production. When trade flourished there was little interest in the land, and when trade declined capital shifted to land investment and agricultural production. Following the conquest of 1229, the king had great difficulty in getting people to settle the interior. This was essentially frontier land, already exploited, but by foreign methods, and not likely to yield a return in the near future. Those who participated in the conquest were rewarded with estates, but most of the recipients returned to Aragon willing to settle for whatever rents the land might produce. The estates were moderate in size, 83 percent being less than 150 hectares and 50 percent less than 70. The Jews, "Los Judios de la Almudaina" in the Repartimiento, received 897 hectares, the award being given to the community as a whole rather than to individuals. Other community awards were 159 hectares to the Templars and 920 hectares to the Hospitallers (Bisson 1969).

The rate of settlement was slow during the reign of the Conqueror, and his son, Jaime II, offered peasants advantageous terms to settle farms. Each settler was offered 15 cuarteradas (10.7 hectares) of land in emphyteusis, which entitled him to rights of usufruct for an indeterminant length of time in exchange for a moderate payment *(censo)* to the owner. This plan was part of a larger program of town formation throughout the island. The towns were placed at reasonable intervals in the agricultural areas, and small estates were awarded at the outskirts of each to insure an initial population. This was a successful program as long as the port was busy with trade, for the city bought whatever the peasant could sell and apart from this the urban traders left the peasants unmolested. The program was successful and more and more families settled land, and those with small holdings bought additional land for expansion. Those urbanites with rural holdings were eager to sell or "lease" them to peasants, as they had no interest in exploiting the land themselves.

However, when the economy declined at the end of the fourteenth century because of the fall off in foreign trade and the effects of the bubonic plague, the urbanites shifted their interest to the land and began exploiting the obligations of censo which peasant farmers were required to pay. City aristocrats and merchants controlled the island legislative body *(Consell)* and through legal means were able to raise the censo. When peasants could not pay, they reclaimed the land through the right of *retiment* (Salvador 1965). The city dweller bought and sold censo rights like stocks in an exchange. They contracted with absentee landlords on the peninsula to administer their holdings, offering their skills for attaining the maximum return from the land. In time the aristocrats and merchants of the city became in effect the colonial administrators of the rural peasants. The Jewish community was a participant in this domination, as landowner, as collector of censos for absentee landlords and as moneylender to those who could not pay the censo obligations. The retaliation of the peasants has already been covered—the sacking of the *call* (or aljama), and the murder of three hundred Jews remaining in it by the peasant army formed in the countryside to attack the city. It has been emphasized that the peasants attacked the Jewish quarter only after failing to reach Christian aristocrats and merchants secluded in Bellver castle.

The process of takeover of rural holdings by city dwellers and the ensuing subjugation of the peasants continued into the fifteenth century, in spite of the open conflict it had caused. In a document listing recently acquired properties in the fifteenth century, José María Quadrado (1939, 1895) shows that 90.4 percent of the land exchanged at that time had shifted from rural to urban control. Throughout the fifteenth and sixteenth centuries there was an ongoing civil war in Mallorca, the rural peasants on one side and the merchants and aristocrats of the city on the other. In this battle the peasants perceived the Jews as part of the urban colonists, and of course they were right. But beyond that the Jews were seen in a mystically diabolical role because of their rejection of Christianity, their dubious allegiance to the state, and the foreignness of their commercial practices and cultural values. Thus the peasant attitude toward the Jews was based on religious and cultural as well as economic antipathy.

The loss of foreign trade in the fourteenth century not only turned the attention of urban investors to the land, it began a process of continuing isolation and traditionalism which lasted up until the twentieth century. With the decline in trade, Mallorca became of even less interest to the national government, and in some periods was almost forgotten apart from the collection of taxes. Piracy from the Barbary coast continued up until the nineteenth century and at times almost isolated the island. It became with isolation poorer and more tradition bound. The values and provincialism of the countryside dominated the city. What had been a cosmopolitan society in periods of international trade became in the absence of it what Harold Innis (1946) calls a "time bound" society, a society focused on its ancestors rather than progress and change. Medieval Catholicism in its most primitive form dominated the countryside and allowed the Inquisition to flourish. With continuing civil war, plagues, piracy and crop failures, the populace became more and more fatalistic, rigid and inward looking.

In their dealings with the peasants, urban Jews and aristocrats frequently worked together. The Mallorcan aristocrats were atypical of Spanish aristocracy as regards their interest in commerce; and in time they acquired a guarded respect for their Jewish compatriots. In the early stages of development in Mallorca, some aristocrats had even become involved in cooperative or exchange ventures with

Jews, but with a decline in commerce and a return to the land there was a strong tendency for Mallorcan aristocracy to become more and more like its estate-rich counterparts on the mainland—presumptuous, indolent and ostentatious. With the influx of French nobility in the eighteenth century, Mallorcan society became obsessed with noble status and values. We have seen in the case of the *perucas* that the pressures were so great that even well-to-do Xuetas wanted to become nobles too. We also saw that when the *perucas* discarded the work values of the Xueta community and took up the ostentation and indolence of nobility that their large fortunes declined with each passing generation. This happened to the Mallorcan nobility as a whole in the nineteenth century, and those Xuetas who remained active in commerce are alleged to have profited greatly from aristocratic decline. In the short essay "Another Street" by Santiago Rusinol (1905) we have seen how the ambition and acquisitiveness of the Xuetas were considered inappropriate on an island which had through centuries of slow decline learned to exalt the peace and quite of noble life on the "Isla de la Calma."

The loss of family fortunes among the nobles from which the Xuetas are alleged to have profited, came about for a variety of reasons. During an early nineteenth-century war many nobles sold holdings in order to pay the fee which would exclude their sons from military service. In the ongoing contests for control of the Spanish government, the nobles of Mallorca were inclined to back the losing side. But the most basic problem was that the land did not provide sufficient monetary return to pay for the sumptuous life that nobles found necessary to maintain their status in court society. A correct marriage or a coming out party for a daughter involved enormous expenditures which had to be paid for with the sale of land. Many nobles presumed to socialize in the court life of Madrid where even larger expenditures for the maintenance of status were required. While they did this, their properties were being managed by overseers who operated the estates more to their own advantage than to that of the absentee landlords. Some nobles who sold their lands attempted business ventures. These were from the beginning so destined for failure that jokes about nobles in business became common. In spite of the refinement suggested by their ownership of heirlooms and fine works of art, many nobles could barely read and write, let alone keep account books.

The period of noble decline is well documented in a book by a famous visitor who came to Mallorca in 1838, the Baroness Aurore de Dudevant, bettern known as George Sand. Her account, *Winter in Mallorca* (1956, 1855), is a treasure of detail on Mallorcan life in the nineteenth century. George Sand saw the role of the Xuetas as very important in the declining fortunes of nobles. Even at this late date she does not refer to them as Xuetas, but simply as Jews.

Although rich in capital, the aristocracy are poor in income, and ruined by the loans that they have been obliged to raise. The Jews, who are numerous and rich in ready money, hold all the Cavallers' lands in their wallets, and are the real owners of the island; thus the Cavallers are no more than aristocratic representatives commissioned to the honours of their domains and palaces, one for the other, as well as for the occasional foreigners who visit the island. To fulfill these exalted functions in proper style, they must annually borrow from the Jews, and every year the snowball grows bigger. In the first part of this book I explained that Majorcan economic life is paralysed by a lack of openings for industry; but the indigent Cavallers make it a point of honour to achieve ruin in their own good time, peacefully and quietly, without abandoning the luxury, or rather the spend-thrift liberality, of their ancestors. The interests of the speculators are therefore closely linked with those of the farmers, a part of whose rents they collect by virtue of the title-deeds made over to them by the Cavallers.

Thus the peasant, who perhaps profits by this division of his debts, pays as little as possible to his lord, and as much as possible to the banker. The lord is resigned to his position of helpless dependence, the Jew is relentless but patient. He makes concessions, feigns great tolerance, allows time to pay, but pursues his end with devilish genius: once he has his clutches on an estate, sooner or later it must all come to him; and his interest is to prove indispensable until the debt reaches the value of the security. In twenty years' time no landed aristocracy will be left in Majorca. The Jews will establish themselves in power, as they have done in France, and arise their heads which are now still bowed in feigned humility beneath the ill-disguised scorn of the nobility and the childish hatred of the common people. Meanwhile the peasant quakes before them. [Sand 1956: 145]

George Sand's comments are those of a perceptive nineteenth-century observer, but hardly an unbiased one. Her prediction that the Xuetas would take over the estates was not borne out by history. However, what is more interesting is the aggressive economic role the Xuetas continued to play in spite of the degradation heaped upon them by the larger society. With a decline in the fortune of the nobles, and their increasing dependence on Xuetas to lend them money and buy their heirlooms, the antipathy of the nobles towards the Xuetas increased. The peasants, dominated for centuries by urban power which included both aristocrats and Jews, envied and emulated the nobles and despised the Xuetas. Their position relative to both groups is apparent in the quote above from George Sand. Her opinion of the peasants as a group is summarized in the following statements.

The Majorcan peasant is a gentle, kind creature, with peaceful habits and a tranquil, patient nature. He has no love of evil, and no knowledge of good. He goes to confession, prays, and thinks incessantly of how to earn an entry to Paradise, yet is ignorant of the true obligations of human kind. You can no more hate him than you could an ox or a sheep, for he is close to the savage, whose soul is lulled in animal innocence. He recites his prayers like the superstitious savage; but he would eat his fellow-man without a qualm, were that the custom of his country, and were he unable to satisfy himself fully with pork. He cheats, extorts, lies, abuses and plunders without the least scruple, where foreigners are concerned not regarding these as fellow-men. [Sand 1956: 146]

George Sand's book, though rich in cultural data from the island's nineteenth century, is nevertheless from beginning to end an attack on the traditionalism of Mallorca. She is an urban sophisticate from the cultural center of Europe and she sees Mallorca as deformed, backward and primitive. Her feelings are in part due to the crude living conditions she had to contend with while caring for her tubercular companion, Frédéric Chopin, who almost died in the chill and dampness of the Mallorcan winter. Granting her bias, the book is no great exaggeration. Mallorca was, up until the twentieth century, one of the most technologically retarded places in Europe. Agriculture was less developed in many ways than it had been during Islamic domination in the twelfth century. Communications were almost nonexistent. The ship *El Mallorquin*, which Sand and Chopin traveled on, was the first to provide regular weekly service to the island, and the famous couple traveled with a boatload of pigs. The roads that tied the towns of the island together were little more than footpaths and cart tracks, and bridges were nonexistent. Internal horse and carriage travel on the island in 1838 is described by George Sand as follows: "What they call a road is a string of impassible precipices, and the unfortunate traveller journeying from Palma to the hills of Galatzo is confronted with death in every step" (1956: 97).

Whether one reads George Sand or another nineteenth-century Mallorcan resident, the Archduke Luis Salvador who wrote a twelve-volume work on the island, it is clear that Mallorca was as isolated as a Mediterranean island could be in the nineteenth century, and frozen in an unchanging social mold in which the values of the church and nobility predominated in a simple and technologically retarded agricultural economy. These conditions not only prevented a community of Catholics descended from Jews called Xuetas from assimilating, they prevented assimilation by any group whatsoever. Social change was miniscule in the larger society and among the Xuetas themselves. Apart from their humilating acceptance of Catholicism, they continued in the simplest mode of the market-place culture, each generation re-enculturated in the traditions their forbears had brought from the Mediterranean southeast. In Mallorca especially, they fit the designation of pariah capitalist assigned to the Jewish merchant class by Max Weber. They entered new markets as they developed in the countryside, long before they were deemed profitable by esteemed merchants, and seemed able to find a profit wherever one was to be had. The scorn of their clients, noble or peasant, was an everyday affair, counteracted by the loyalty and solidarity which awaited them in their home community.

Although those who have written on the Xuetas, for example Lionel Isaacs (1936), have stressed their suffering, their degradation and their inability to attain status in proportion to their wealth, their actual suffering was not really great when compared to the life of the peasant. In the relationship between the two, the peasant was the inferior. In times of plague, crop failure or the high taxation of war—and these occurred throughout the nineteenth century—it was the peasant who lived at the borderline of starvation, even while working from sunup to sunset. It was the peasant who in his ignorance was always the victim of changing circumstances, seeming to have no control whatsoever over his own destiny.

In reading the works of George Sand we see the peasants through the eyes of a person devoted to cosmopolitanism and progress. Her sympathy for the Xuetas is derived from whatever empathy urban-based people feel for each other. In the works of the Archduke Luis Salvador, we are presented with an alternative view, the peasant as perceived by a rural-based foreign aristocrat who is fascinated by the richness of their folklore and the contrast they provide to the changing societies of Europe. Seen as traditional people, the Mallorcan peasants were not extraordinary. They were an isolated and homogeneous group living in an oral tradition of superstition and profound faith in their formal religion. All outsiders were feared and distrusted, reports George Sand, and were perceived as no different than Muslims or Jews. Within the society there existed among the peasants a trust and honesty incomprehensible to anyone socialized in a technologically advanced society. Even today in the towns of the Mallorcan foothills of the Tormentana one finds keys in the front doors of houses whose dwellers are out for the evening. The key symbolizes the faith all have in each other and in the high value on honesty existing within the community. The honor among peasants was matched by the concern Xuetas felt for each other, and even the aristocrats did not treat each other badly. But in the relations between groups, each was in its own way ruthless and unscrupulous.

## THE INTRANSIGENT CITY

The walled city of Palma de Mallorca (its name was changed from Ciutat de Mallorca to Palma in 1721) had changed between 1200 and 1840 only in the growing number of churches and convents within its perimeter. The population during its peak in the Islamic era was 45,000 inside the walls, making it the eighth largest city in western Europe in the twelfth century. In 1840, it was still 45,000, still contained within the walled framework set up by the Saracens, still organized in a pattern of meandering streets so typical of Muslim cities. The urban plans of Saracen-controlled Medina Mayurka, Ciutat de Mallorca in 1641, and Palma in 1831 show little in the way of visible structural change (Borras Rexach 1966). Periods of rapid expansion were characterized by the development of satellite towns called *arrabals*. In the Saracen period there were a number of arrabals outside the walls, giving the urban area at its peak a maximum population of 80,000. In the apogee of trade in the fourteenth century, the arrabal of seamen between the walls and Porto Pi is estimated to have contained 30,000 persons. In the nineteenth century this arrabal was at times only a few thousand. Reaching a peak population of 6,000 by 1870. Thus, by the nineteenth century, Palma was, measured by the indices of population and space, a declining city. In all stages we see a pre-industrial city, built as a fortress, port and agricultural market center, almost completely unchanged through more than six hundred years from the twelfth to the nineteenth century.

In 1800 André Grasset de Saint Sauver arrived in Mallorca as the French representative for commercial relations in the Balearic Islands. In his book *Travels Through the Balearic and Pithiusan Islands* (1952, 1808), he describes a city which is rundown and isolated. He is of the opinion that these Mallorcans, isolated by miles of sea, are unable to comprehend or imagine what exists in the outside world. He describes the harbor as shallow and suitable only for the docking of a few small ships along a narrow, paved pier. Although he finds the cathedral and the city hall beautiful, he is unfavorably impressed by the large number of monks, their dubious morals, and the large sums they extract from the populace. He finds scarcely any books in the library, only a few religious volumes. He reports that the hospitals are clean and well attended, but finds great numbers of the poor living in what he calls urban caves, with no light whatsoever except that from the entrance. He observes in the cloister of the Monks of St. Dominic "pictures that recall the barbarianism of other ages." The pictures he saw were those of the victims of the *autos* of 1691 and under each painting he read the name of the victim, his or her age, and the date of execution. He observed afterward that the "Jews live today in peace...."

From Salvador (1880), Rusiñol (1905), Blasco-Ibáñez (1919), Infante (1866) as well as Grasset de Saint Sauver (1808) and George Sand (1855), we have a picture of eighteenth- and nineteenth-century Palma as a quiet city, overly conscious of class distinction, a city in which the family was the focus of all social activity, with each family associating with only a small circle of friends. The walled city was on the inside, crisscrossed by social barriers of every conceivable type. The guilds, so powerful in the sixteenth century, had declined, but their forms continued in the division of the city into occupational barrios. Craftsmen still worked on the streets which designated their trade, and the values of the neighborhood regulated product quality, membership and comportment the way the guild organization had before. Imposed on this, and sometimes coterminous, were parish boundaries, dominated by forty-six churches. A man was known by his neighborhood and parish. The tanners from the barrio of Calatrava were called *Calatravins*. Those from *Puig des St. Pere* were known as *d'es Puig*. It is in this system that the Xuetas got the vague designation *d'es carre*, "those of the street."

The rigidity of social forms in the city made guilds superfluous. No young man could hope to enter a profession or trade unless his father or the father of his bride was already established in it. The Xuetas were not unusual in the exclusiveness of their occupational control over the metals trade. No one dared compete in this area without kin contact with a master. At all levels, boundaries were approached with elaborate rituals of courtesy, but in this regulated interaction between sectors there was almost no mingling of family lines. The nobles were endogamous, as were respectively the classes of merchants, artisans and day laborers. Within the merchant and artisan level, arranged marriages regulated entrance into specific occupations, creating further divisions whose boundaries were in many cases as rigid as the boundaries of class, all this serving to keep the populace segmented into small endogamous units.

The best description of class in nineteenth-century Palma comes from a novel by Blasco-Ibáñez (1919). He points out that the nobles were divided into two groups, the *butifarras* and the *cavallers*. Butifarra is a Catalonian sausage, and as a name for the nobles is a corruption of *botifler*, the name for French nobles who as supporters of the Bourbons used the emblem of the *fleur de lis*. Although refugees from the political disorders in France, the Butifarras looked down on the land-owning nobles of indigenous title (cavallers) and intermarried only among themselves. Beneath both was a class called *mossons*. One still encounters this designation in Mallorca as a title of honor for wise old men, but in the nineteenth century it referred to the intellectuals, artists, doctors and lawyers who loaned their service to the illustrious families. The *mossons* were not acceptable for marriage alliances with either noble group, and given the precariousness of their status they refused to marry with artisans or merchants. At the bottom were those who lacked special skills and hired out for so much a day for whatever labor was available. Although the day laborers *(jornaleros)* were at the bottom within the city, lower still were the *pagés*, the peasant from the countryside. There were periods in Mallorcan history when laws were in effect which forbade the peasant to enter the city except for specific purposes, and threatened him with imprisonment should he dare to stay overnight. The Xuetas were in a sense outside this system, as a class apart. Blasco-Ibañez says they lived ostracized with no allies in any social class. There was segmentation within the Xueta community at different times, as we have seen in our discussion of the *perucas* and the *orella d'alt* and *orella baix*, but the population was for the most part at the merchant and artisan level.

One has to mention, finally, another group that was, in a sense, also outside the system. They were the residents of the arrabal of Santa Catalina, outside the city walls, spread out around the port area. The *Catalineres* as they were called were dock workers, fishermen, merchant seamen, and of various other occupations associated with the waterfront. In the world view of Palma, the *Catalineres* were considered a peculiar but harmless people noted for their exhuberance and lack of pretension. To be from Santa Catalina was to be of a particular type of personality, something quite different from those who resided within the walls. Although the arrabal was made up of neat little whitewashed bungalows at the edge of the sea, while the interior of the city was cramped, old and possessing only the most primitive and inadequate water supply and sewage system, it was nevertheless much more prestigious to live within the walls.

The consciousness of class extended into every aspect of urban life. One traversed only in designated sections of the city: in one's own barrio, at the city gates, at the market, in the barrio of vice, in the public promenade, or on the walls of the city looking out over the sea. Even the strolling places were dominated by values of class, with the *Borne*, near the sea, designated as an upper-class promenade, and the *Ramblas*, back into the city, assigned to the lower classes. Cafes, bodegas, churches, clubs and bath houses by the sea all admitted the traffic of some classes and deemed inappropriate the entrance of others (Salvador 1965, 1880).

In its social organization and physical structure Palma was very typical of pre-industrial cities. Eight roads of seasonally variable passability led out from the urban hub into all parts of the island. As the only port, the city was the gateway to the outside. The power of church, state and nobility superseded the influence of commerce. In contrast to the monument to commerce that dominate contemporary sky lines, the great buildings of this period were churches, palaces, government fortresses and bureaucratic centers. Commerce was carried out in small shops away from the center. The titled aristocrats lived in palaces located near the architectural monuments of the church and state. The buildings that houses rich and poor were invariably old. In this respect, pre-industrial cities vary, either as changing and growing forms, or as time-biased structures dominated by the past. The nineteenth-century urban dweller in Mallorca lived with history all around him. The physical plan was ancient Saracen, with streets so narrow that the passing of a single horse-drawn carriage forced foot traffic into doorways. The city hall *(Casa de Cort)* dated from the sixteenth century, the sea trade center *(La Longa)* from the fifteenth century, the castles of Bellver and Almudaina and the cathedral from the fourteenth, and the churches of Santa Eulalia and Montesión from the conquest (1229) or before. Inside the city walls in the mid-nineteenth century the approximately 45,000 residents lived in 3,046 dwellings. With approximately the same population within the walled perimeter, the Saracens occupied 3,493 dwellings, a difference of 450 dwellings. The sites of the former dwellings were occupied by churches and public buildings, so in actual dwelling space we see greater congestion in the nineteenth century than in the twelfth (Barcelo Pons 1964).

One cannot overstress the role of formal religion in Mallorca at this time. It pervaded every aspect of life. Education was religious at all levels, from the child's first lessons to the university. Noble families had a resident priest in the home to teach the children and say daily mass in the family chapel. The less well-off sent their children to schools in monasteries and convents. Every kind of status was certified by the church in formal blessings and benedictions. All charity for the poor passed through the church channels. Daily and yearly cycles were ritualized in prayer, ceremony and festival. Attendance at daily mass was common, the rich accompanied by servants carrying their chairs, the poor carrying their own. All knelt on the cold stone floors of the churches and the cathedral, and citizens of every class festooned the sacred statues with rich embroidery and even bejeweled shawls, treating the symbols of the divine with the greatest respect they knew, with a deference due royalty. In the evening the moaning and chanting of the rosary could be heard in the streets of every neighborhood, as families joined together in parlor vesper services. Ever fearful of sin, the populace attended confession weekly and by custom the young returned home to kiss the hands of their parents while asking forgiveness of sins, this the final act of penance. On the street, the normal greeting was *"Deus vos guard de perill,* may God protect you from danger."

The customs of prayer, rosary, regular church attendance, glorification of holy objects, religious education, piety, humility, in

all a total submission to the credo of Rome, were even more infused
into the life of the Xuetas than in other sectors. The traditions of
Jewish piety were given full vent in the Christian realm and sub-
scription to regulations and restrictions was strong in tradition. The
religiosity of the Xuetas was manifest in over-conformity, reflecting
a strong desire to assimilate, to be thought of as just another barrio
of artisans and merchants. It also represented a concern for improved status, available through and apportioned by the church.

But what did the pious Xueta think, leaving the church after mass
or confession encountering possibly an insult on the way home
which challenged his religiosity or accused him of killing the
Savior. One has to wonder why the Xuetas did not migrate to nearby
Barcelona or Valencia, for the minute they left the island their
pariah status disappeared. One has to measure the effects of public
insult, the pain of stigma, exclusion from prestigious and offical
positions, and weigh them against a relatively secure and comfortable economic position, the rewards of rich communal life and the
generally satisfying traditional culture in the larger society. It must
not be forgotten that the Xuetas were fiercely loyal Mallorcans, who
in typical island fashion distrusted and even feared foreigners. One
must see them at two levels, communal and societal, realizing that
socialization has taken place at both. The strong sense of *we* as
against *they* existed within the community in their relation with the
larger society, but this was repeated in their feelings as *we* Mallorcans in their relations with the outside world. As Mallorcans, the
Xuetas were not inclined to travel to the mainland where their
accent was strange or their language incomprehensible. The Xuetas
were never forced to migrate as were many peasants and laborers
following crop failures, plagues and economic depression. Secure in
their economic position, the paths of migration to Algeria and Latin
America were relatively unattractive. At home they could try to get
even richer and fight for their rights step by step through the years.
Overall, the history of the Xuetas through the eighteenth and
nineteenth centuries was dominated by an ongoing struggle by the
community to attain the rights of other Mallorcans and discard the
stigma of the past.

## MAJOR HISTORICAL EVENTS AFFECTING THE XUETAS

The principal steps forward as well as the crises affecting the status of the Xuetas in the eighteenth and nineteenth centuries were closely linked with changes going on at the national level. In the late eighteenth century many of the Xueta leaders decided that the time was right for seeking relief from the penalties of the Inquisition, which by this time, eighty years later, had become crystallized in local tradition. The legal status of these prohibitions was dubious, but there was little hope for change on a tradition-bound island. So the Xuetas, like their predecessors in the aljama of the thirteenth and fourteenth centuries, sought redress from local infringements through direct appeal to the power of the throne. The appeal went to Carlos III, one of the most liberal kings in Spanish history. Carlos was of the Bourbon line and nurtured in Naples, and his liberalness was in many ways related to his foreignness. Having matured outside of Spain he was free of the fear and passionate distrust that many Spaniards felt towards Muslims and Jews.

By 1770, Carlos had been king for eleven years, and his record of enlightened leadership convinced the Xuetas that the chances for royal assistance were good. Their problem was that local authorities refused to allow the Xuetas the status of full citizenship that had become rightfully theirs when the punishments decreed by the Inquisition had expired. Those condemned by the Inquisition were not only deprived of their property, but were declared unfit to receive or obtain ecclesiastical or secular distinctions and honors. They were also denied the right to hold public office and were forbidden to carry on their person precious stone, gold, or silver. They were also forbidden to travel on horseback or to carry arms. The punishment was extended to the wives of the condemned and their descendants on the male line for two generations. By 1770 the grandchildren of the victims of the Inquisiton were elderly, and the great and great-great-grandchildren were adults, yet they were still subject to those rulings. It is doubtful that the regulations on carrying jewelry had been enforced, or the prohibition of riding on horseback. The Xuetas had to do both to conduct their business, and in Mallorca custom always outweighed written regulations. However, custom also decreed that Xuetas should not hold public offices nor receive public honors, and this was a tradition the Xuetas wanted to eliminate.

Among themselves the Xuetas elected six representatives who the group thought could best represent them at the royal court. They did not pick the wisest nor the most eloquent, but rather the richest and most powerful. The selected men traveled to the capital in great luxury, wearing the finest clothes available, to impress the king that they were indeed *grand Señors* (Forteza 1966). With them they had a letter from the Bishop of Mallorca certifying that they were "good Christians, as are all Mallorcans." On February 12, 1773, they submitted their petition to the king and explained their plight. The king read their petition and the letter from the bishop, which said the Xuetas "were of good custom and pious in life and death." He sought further information from the local government and the university and members of the clergy. Representatives of all three sent statements arguing against the appeals of the Xuetas.

In 1782, nine years after the petition had been submitted, King Carlos pronounced the first of three Xueta *pragmáticos* (royal legal decisions) dealing with the Mallorcan problem. The results were all that the Xuetas had hoped for. The pragmático stated "individuals called those of the street" not only cannot be denied the right to live wherever they choose, but they are conceded the "right of protection to carry out this choice." The pragmático also freed them from any emblem or symbol which distinguished them from others, instructing that not even a vestige should remain. It prohibited the use of the designations Jew, Hebrew, Xueta or offensive nicknames for those "of the street." The second pragmático, issued in 1785, granted to "those called of the street" the right to enter the military service or occupy any other office of the state. The third pragmático, 1788, entitled "those called of the street" the right to practice any occupation or profession. Miguel Forteza (1966) says that the pragmáticos of Carlos III were to the Xuetas what the civil rights laws in the United States were for American blacks. But analogously, state intervention did not resolve the problem.

Shortly thereafter, around the beginning of the nineteenth cen-

tury, Mallorca entered a period of serious political turmoil. Refugees from the French Revolution were flooding the island and
Mallorcans were choosing sides on the issues of liberalism and
monarchy. Spain was enduring the reign of a weak monarch, and
Napoleon responded to the situation by sending his troops in to
occupy the country. He placed his brother, Joseph Bonaparte, on
the throne and the Spanish War of Independence began on May 2,
1808, with a spontaneous uprising against the French and continuing guerrilla warfare. In Mallorca, soldiers were drafted, but were
not overly eager to join the fighting on the mainland. Also at this
same time there was a public scandal that had to do with the murder
of a militiaman by a Xueta, and the accusation of a pay-off of six
judges by Xuetas. The feelings of resentment were strong, especially
from militiamen who, not wanting to leave their homes, were predisposed to believe a spate of rumors that the Xuetas were the real
cause of the war. Worked into a frenzy, three hundred soldiers
attacked the Plateria with stones and left the neighborhood in deso-
lation. The government then had to set up a guard for eight days to
protect the neighborhood. It should be noted that this attack, like
the sacking of 1391, occurred during a period of great political
unrest, and was only one of various incidents of violence. Another
incident occurred in the same year, 1808, when tax collectors trying
to collect a new and unpopular excise on wine were attacked by
peasants in the villages of Muro, Llubi, Sineu, Sa Pobla and Vall-
demosa. War and piracy had left the island in an economic slump,
and the tax increases came as an intolerable shock. In periods such
as this, the Xuetas were destined to suffer the role of scapegoat.

With the beginning of the War of Independence against Napoleon the number of refugees to the island was greater than its capacity to house them. By 1810, twenty thousand people of every class,
merchants, aristocrats, clergy, all with servants, crowded into Palma
to occupy every empty room and porch. By 1812, the number
reached thirty thousand (Barcelo Pons 1961). The war lasted until
1814, and with the defeat of Napoleon, the Spanish people returned
their own monarch to power, welcoming him back to Spain with
"Down with the Cortes [Parliament]. Long live our absolute king"
(Crow 1963). During the war, the Spanish Cortes, previously under

the thumb of the king, fled from Madrid to Cadiz and set up a
liberal constitution. Their supporters were primarily urban and
commercial people, and on Mallorca this included the Xuetas.
With the return of Ferdinand VII at the end of the war, the old
traditions of absolutism were reinvoked with the support of the vast
majority of the people. Ferdinand abolished the changes made by
the liberals, and ordered the reinstituion of the Inquisition and
seignorial privilege. Those who opposed him were imprisoned, and
free discussion was suppressed. During the reign of Joseph
Bonaparte the American colonies had declared their independence,
and Spain was no longer an empire, only a poor country in a state of
postwar anarchy.

Mallorca, suffering from the national political insecurity, was in
a state of economic paralysis. The situation reached tragic propor-
tions with another scourge of bubonic plague in 1820. Twenty-four
hundred died the first year, and in 1822 it struck again with five
thousand victims in Palma alone, the count in the interior being
unknown (Barcelo Pons 1961). Poverty was so bad that even the
convents had to sell their property just to survive. The quarantine
on vessels prevented a much anticipated return of trade with the
mainland, and even impeded internal commerce. Chaos and poverty throughout the island resulted in another attack on the Xueta
quarter in 1823.

This second sacking, only fifteen years after the first, resulted
from conditions of poverty and disorder and also from political
rivalry between liberals and monarchists. Merchants and jewelers
were accused at the national level of being the authors of the liberal
constitution, and on the island the Xuetas were the living symbol of
the liberal bourgeoisie. As supporters of the national reforms, which
were much in their interest, the Xuetas were viewed by the tra-
ditionalists as revolutionaries and traitors. No one was killed in the
sacking of 1823, but the furniture and account books of the Xuetas
were burned in a huge bonfire in the middle of the street, accompanied by cheers of "long live the king." The day following the
attack, a band of poor women dressed in rags passed through the
neighborhood scoffing at the Xuetas, "Poor folks, they didn't leave
you anything. Poor people!" It is clear that at this time the urban

and rural poor saw their suffering as caused by the acquisitiveness of the bourgeoisie, rather than the indolence and absolutism of the aristocrats.

The fourth major historical event in the lives of the Xuetas during this period came in the form of a book published by one of their own, a priest, who openly attacked the traditional and illegal prejudices which continued on the island. *Comments on the Religious and Social Situation on the Island of Mallorca* was published in 1877 by José Taronji y Cortés, a Xueta priest who was later to reach the status of Canon of the Sacromonte of Granada. Taronji points out that, in spite of the pragmáticos of Carlos III and of the reforms of the Cortes in 1860, Xuetas were still the victims of prejudicial exclusion from full participation in the society. He said that this prejudice infiltrated every level of the social order and that the only means of combating it effectively was through the power of the church. He gave examples from his own experience as to how the church in Mallorca continued to support the exclusion of Xuetas. He told of how a rural priest did everything possible to prevent his sister from marrying a Xueta, for example suggesting to the relatives on the day of the wedding that they should attend instead a funeral for the bride. He cited a case where the Sisters of Charity of Saint Cayetano had refused the admission of a Xueta child, even though her family was of high social status. He spoke of his own difficulties in his priestly training, pointing out that at a certain point it was necessary for him to leave the island to continue his career. He spoke of a *"mano oculta,"* a hidden hand, that continued these prejudices, especially in the ecclesiastical sector of society. He said that Mallorcan clergy supported this provincial hate for a class apart as if it were "a schismatic and disobedient church" (Taronji 1967). Citing the laws of Spain in which all were declared equal regardless of origin, he pointed out that they were of no use in Mallorca where the prejudices submit to no law whatsoever, but continue on and on.

Taronji tarnishes his plea for fairness by claiming that the Jewish origin of the Xuetas is dubious. He goes through genealogies to point out the unauthenticated Jewishness of names such as Pomar and Taronji. He then maintains that the Jews of Spain were not those responsible for the crucifixion of Christ, for they were at that time already settled in communities in Spain. They had even sent deputies to Jerusalem to protest the execution of Jesus, he said, and these were the Jew-Christians who were the ancestors of the Xuetas.

Taronji's book is a landmark for it was an open attack on official and ecclesiastical support of the pariah status of the Xuetas. He represents as a priest the authority of the church in speaking on the issue, and as an individual a spokesman for new ideas on the rights of free-men that were then gaining force in Spain. One can say that by the end of the nineteenth century most urban people in Mallorca did not believe that Xuetas were secretly practicing Judaism or that they were against the nation, nor did they deny that Xuetas were being deprived of their rights as Spanish citizens. Yet no individual or group seemed capable of removing traditional fears and attitudes that were so ingrained in the Mallorcan culture.

In the course of the eighteenth and nineteenth centuries, the Xuetas had removed almost all of the legal sanctions that had previously been used against them and had openly attacked the prejudice. But even though the Xuetas and the urbanites of Palma were thinking and talking about "the rights of man" and scoffing at traditions which asserted that some classes were more noble than others, the authority of tradition still weighed heavily at the beginning of the twentieth century. Apart from occasional Xuetas who mixed at the intellectual and commercial levels of society, they were at the beginning of the twentieth century still a pariah society, over 95 percent endogamous, occupationally distinctive and the bearers of many traditions of Jewish community life, integrated into the forms of an urban Mallorcan neighborhood.

# The Modern Era  7

Throughout the twentieth century there has been a slow but continuous decline in the exclusionist attitudes Mallorcans have held toward the Xuetas. In the early decades change occurred slowly, so slowly that it was not readily apparent to outside observers or even those who had been a part of it. By the mid-1930s, when Baruch Braunstein carried out his study of the Inquisition records, he saw almost no change in the status of the Xuetas who had been stigmatized since the *autos* of 1691.

> Up to our day the Chuetas remain a pariah-folk in the Mediterranean region, isolated in a Catholic land, among people whose faith they share. . . . This anomalous situation is in large part a relic of the Spanish zeal for unity of faith, inspiring the establishment of the Spanish Inquisition, and which beginning in the fifteenth century, has not altogether spent its force in our times, a century after its extinction. [Braunstein 1936].

Although change was not readily visible to Braunstein in the thirties, historical data show that significant social alteration had already begun to emerge. By the sixties, attitudes towards Xuetas had improved enormously. Nevertheless, one still encountered informants who acted as if things were as they had always been. They were right insofar as there was still a very clear distinction made between Xuetas and other Mallorcans, but the consequences of these distinctions were not so severe for the Xuetas of the sixties as they had been in earlier decades.

As we search back into Mallorcan history for the first signs of progressive change, for the beginnings of a break from a pertinacious past, we find amidst the earliest evidence the emergence of a dialogue initiated by social critics in the first half of the nineteenth century. It is from this marker that we begin our analysis of Mallorcan modernization and its affect on the Xuetas. The early progressives, though few in number, launched vigorous attacks on traditions which from their view appeared increasingly anachronistic with every passing year, especially when compared to the rapid social changes taking place in the rest of Europe. The reformers gathered in associations, held discussions in clubs and cafes, and wrote articles and pamphlets. Their ties to the island were intense, but this motivated rather than restrained their ridicule of quaint and provincial custom. Among the customs they found intolerable were the restrictions that kept the Xuetas in a pariah status.

For the large majority of Mallorcans the exhortations of the new intelligentsia made little sense and were disparaged as strange ideas from foreign countries. What did make sense to them were the social distinctions they had grown up with, distinctions which were continuously reinforced in their day-to-day encounters. The activities carried out by the spokesmen for tolerance, their pleas, their essays, their arguments with the old guard, were by themselves almost entirely futile. Their words were heard and tolerance became an acceptable position in the cultural dialogue, but it is doubtful that they changed many minds. Where the early activists were effective was in joining with others in the initiation of economic reform. Once this had taken hold, the groundwork was laid for desired social changes. But the changes they sought were far in the future, and when they did arrive they took shape in ways that the nineteenth-century reformers could not have foreseen.

In our examination of the changing status of the Xuetas we see an interplay between economic, social structural and attitudinal variables. Analyzing change in this manner, one encounters a recurring dilemma, that being whether people actually change their societies, or whether individuals merely respond to overwhelming social forces. The history of twentieth-century change in Mallorca would tend to support the latter view, but certainly the will and acts of individuals cannot be discounted. Reviewing the economic developments of the twentieth century and their origins in the nineteenth, it seems apparent that economic alterations produced changes in the social order, which in turn changed people's attitudes about themselves and their relations with others. It is interesting to note that this was not generally the view of Mallorcan informants. They tended to see change as the diffusion of new attitudes and values from higher levels (church, state, etc.) and their eventual acceptance at lower levels (Mallorcan society). We will keep these two views of change separate, presenting a survey of economic developments first, and then including the Xueta view of their changing status in the final chapter.

The major economic and social changes of twentieth-century Mallorca are clearly linked to the growth of tourism on the island. With tourism Mallorca was able to extirpate itself from an enduring poverty which had been the inescapable and dominant factor of Mallorcan life from the late middle ages until the beginning of this century. Tourism, though in a sense imposed from the outside, did not simply happen. It was, that is to say, not an entirely fortunate development presented to Mallorca by changing circumstances. Before a tourist economy could take hold, many smaller changes had to occur to lay the groundwork. To understand the development of twentieth-century tourism, we must again return briefly to the nineteenth century when the stage was set.

The poverty of medieval Mallorca was, as we have seen, characterized not only by a below subsistence survival, but also by desperate out migrations to developing areas. Piracy, plagues, national political disorder, crop failures as well as internal tensions made Mallorca more inward, immobile, isolated and technologically retarded at the same time that other parts of Europe were experiencing dramatic growth. Somewhere around 1830 the period of decline began to come to an end and a period of stabilization began. Many factors made this possible. Relative political stability returned to the nation of Spain and this resulted in the suppression of guilds and the selling off of large land holdings by religious orders. Around the same time piracy was eliminated from the western Mediterranean as a result of the conquest of Algeria by France. This enabled the maritime trade of Mallorca to develop and grow, and this growth was reinforced by technological advances, most importantly the

El Mallorquin, an early (1837) ship that linked Mallorca with the mainland

utilization of the steam engine on the ships that were Mallorca's only communication with the outside world (Pou Muntaner 1970, Barcelo Pons 1968).

On the island itself, as we pointed out, one of the earliest signs of progress was a dialogue on reform initiated by early nineteenth-century social critics. We said their pleas for tolerance did nothing to help the Xuetas or to change other social unjustices, but those in that era who worked for economic reform laid the groundwork for social reform that would not arrive until many years later. One organized group of economic reformers who called themselves *La Societat d'Amics del Pais* (the Society of Friends of the Land) set out to improve the island's agricultural economy by replacing inapt traditional practices with imported innovations of demonstrable or proven merit. The island lacked the environmental resources for industrial development, but the agricultural economy could benefit immensely from the recommendations of a group devoted to the rational analysis of agricultural potential. The changes they intro-duced were of enormous consequence, but not to be overlooked is the fact that the idea of planned change found acceptance. For Mallorca, this may have been the most important change of all.

An example of the kinds of changes the society advocated was a shift in agricultural production to crops more suitable to the island (such as almonds, oranges and grapes). These were crops that Muslim agriculturalists had cultivated successfully in the twelfth century, but which had been displaced by the crops Christian conquerors brought with them from the mainland. Over the centuries of the Christian era agricultural production had consisted mostly of cereals, along with vegetables and olives, all cultivated in the most antiquated manner. The almond, since its introduction by the *Amics*, has proven to be the most successful cash crop ever produced on the island. In contrast, grain production had never been high, as the island was not suited for its cultivation on a large scale. Because inadequate trade facilities compelled Mallorcans to grow their own grain in order to supply the needs of traditional preferences, vast amounts of land were used for low-yield grain production, and as a result periods of hunger were common in the rural areas. Barcelo Pons (1968) points this out as a clear-cut case where isolation contributed directly to poverty.

Ensuing contributions of organization and technology to the rural area emanating from the work of the *Amics* included the drying out of the *Albufera*, an enormous swamp in the north of the island. The reclaimed land was fertile, and with irrigation it became the most productive agricultural area of the island. This project not only contributed first-rate crop land to the economy, but it did away with the breeding ground of epidemics that had caused suffering and economic loss to previous generations. In addition to agricultural innovations, the nineteenth century saw the beginnings of small industry in manufacturing and mining, and an attendant increase in sea trade. Small trading companies exchanged the newly available export items in a triangular trade that went from Mallorca to the Antilles, to European ports, and then back to Mallorca.

Agricultural productivity, trade, national stability, the suppression of guilds, the breakup of monastic estates and the end of piracy all contributed to a newly found stability that characterized the last two-thirds of the nineteenth century. There were periodic dips, and

the situation was at times precarious, but the suffering and hunger
of the first third of the century had been overcome. The precariousness of the new agricultural era is emphasized by a series of setbacks
which included a sudden falloff in sea trade with the Antilles in
1868 due to competition from the United States, the destruction of
the orange crop by plant disease in 1870, and a plant epidemic in
grapes producing major losses in the wine industry in the 1890s. As
oranges and wine were export items, losses in these sectors were felt
throughout the island economy. Added to all this were dislocations
in the Spanish nation resulting from a war with the United States in
1898. The net result was that Mallorca ended the nineteenth century in severe economic decline. Many islanders, seeing little hope
in their struggle with poverty, migrated to Algeria and Latin
America. The setbacks of the late nineteenth century merely emphasize the seriousness and scope of the struggle, but in spite of
them the period from 1830 to 1900 was, overall, a time in which
*relative* stability attained through innovation replaced long-term
poverty caused by isolation, rigidity and the retention of antiquated
technology and social forms.

## TWENTIETH-CENTURY CHANGE

Moderate changes in the nineteenth century made possible the
radical changes which came in the twentieth. Activities such as
those of the *Amics* opened the island to newer and more profitable
ventures. The most important of these was of course tourism.
Where nineteenth-century visitors such as George Sand (1855) and
Grasset de Saint Sauveur (1808) were appalled at the primitiveness,
ignorance, and poverty they found in Mallorca, twentieth-century
visitors could, as a result of agricultural revitalization, extol the
simple virtues of a prosperous country life, as well as the climate of
the island. Thus, the beginning of modernization in Mallorca occurred in the agricultural sphere, and progress in this area provided
the base for the development of tourism.

In planning the research of the Xuetas, as a cultural historical
study of the persistence of an ethnic group, only minor consideration was given to tourism. It was viewed, along with other economic

data, as important background material, but nothing more. As the study developed, it became abundantly clear that the changing status of the Xuetas was merely one facet of a process generated primarily by an increasing flow of tourists to the island. *Entrepreneurial tourism*, which began in the first decade of the twentieth century, opened the island to international traffic and made it prosperous. *Industrial tourism*, which began in the 1950s, literally tore apart the social order of the old city and set the ghetto Xuetas free. We will first examine the phenomenon of tourism, and then evalute its influence on Mallorcan life.

\*   \*   \*   \*   \*

The development of tourism in the twentieth century was instigated and encouraged in much the same way that change had been induced in agriculture in the previous century. An organization called the *Sociedad Fomento del Turismo*, formed in 1905, was in many ways a replication of the earlier *Amics del Pais*. Like the earlier organization, the Society for the Encouragement of Tourism was composed mostly of representatives of the business and professional stratum. Added to their efforts were those of journalists such as Bartomeu Amengual and Miguel de los Santos Oliver who wrote prescient articles about the possibilities of touristic development on the island. Their fondest dreams for touristic development have long since been exceeded.

The first decade of tourism witnessed two major changes in the quiet urban scene, the tearing down of the centuries-old city walls and the construction of two major luxury hotels. The first tourists were met by businessmen who welcomed any opportunity to make money. Their enthusiasm is reflected in an absurdly large guide book which pointed out the location of scenic points on the island, and listed all the merchants and services available in all the towns. The itineraries it suggested were more for the hardy adventurer than the leisurely tourist. Though a fourteen-mile railroad had been constructed from the capital to the island center, the rest of the island was accessible only on horseback or at best in a carriage over the most primitive thoroughfares. However, from these early efforts, tourism grew yearly until it reached an annual volume of 12,000

FIGURE 3
Tourism and Population

| | Number of Tourists | | Population of Palma de Mallorca |
|---|---|---|---|
| 1900 | 10–12,000 | | 63,000 |
| 1918 | 40,000* | | 94,000 |
| 1936 | Civil War | | 114,000 |
| 1939 | 55,000 | WW II | 126,000 |
| 1945 | 98,000 | | 136,000 |
| 1951 | 188,000 | | (New Resorts Open) |
| 1955 | 400,000 | | — |
| 1960 | 1,000,000 | | — |
| 1965 | 1,400,000 | | — |
| 1968 | | | |

\* Plus an additional 50,000 cruise ship passengers.

visitors by World War I. Following the war, the increase was even greater, reaching a high point of 40,000 visitors annually, in the best years, between 1918 and 1936. These figures include only those visitors who spent at least one night in a hotel. In addition to this, Mallorca had built up a reputation as a cruise ship port, and passenger visitors reached 50,000 a year. (See figure 3.)

During the Spanish Civil War tourists could not come to Mallorca, but tourist facilities were utilized by members of the right-wing forces of Spain and Italy. The economy of Mallorca thrived during this period, at least in comparison with the war-ravaged mainland. Where mainland informants recall hunger and violence from this era, Mallorcans endured little more than a shortage of rice. It was a period when many new facilities were built on the island by the Italians, who in the role of soldiers were not averse to enjoying the touristic features of the island.

With the end of the Civil War in 1939, tourism increased to a maximum of 55,000 persons a year. This number was made up almost entirely of Spaniards. Only 700 were Europeans from other nations. With Spain a nonparticipant in World War II, tourism continued from the mainland throughout the European conflict. Growth was stabilized in this period of internal tourism, but then in the early fifties an isolated Spain was opened to the world with the lifting of trade and travel restrictions by the United Nations and the negotiation of a military pact with the United States. These events opened a new era for Spain, and particularly for Mallorca. The period of industrial tourism began in the 1950s and continues until the present. Its impact was felt throughout the nation in a number of ways. For example, the peseta moved from an almost worthless currency to one of the strongest in Europe. The economy was stabilized through a favorable balance of trade and as a result areas that never saw a tourist were able to benefit in some measure. However, in particular areas such as the Canary Islands, Mallorca and various coastal regions, the effects of industrial tourism were felt directly, and the resulting changes were large-scale, basic and in some respects enduring (Moore 1969, 1970).

The industrial age of tourism is best understood by contrasting and comparing it with entrepreneurial tourism which preceded it, and out of which it grew. The first half of the twentieth century, the era of entrepreneurial tourism, was a period in which hotels, pensions, restaurants and transportation facilities in Mallorca were run almost entirely by individuals or families. The employees of service facilities were in many if not most businesses members of the owner's family, personal friends or neighbors, or at the very least Mallorcans of long residence. Those who traveled to Mallorca came as individual purchasers in a service market. Typically, the trip commenced with the purchase of a train ticket from the travelers home to Barcelona, and not until arriving in Barcelona did the traveler book ship passage to Mallorca, as it was next to impossible to arrange passenger space from outside the country. Once on the island, the traveler selected a hotel or dealt face-to-face with a hotel owner he had corresponded with in reserving the accommodations. For his day-to-day needs of food, transportation, recreation and accessories, he dealt entirely in a market of small entrepreneurs whose individuals decisions as to the marketability of their goods

and services was often based on little more than the experience of
the year before.

The rate of growth, slow but continuous, was directly limited by
the capacity of available shipping between Barcelona and the island.
Passenger travel was primarily seasonal and supplemental to the
normal shipping operation: thus the frequency of trips increased
only with the overall increase in the size of the urban economy, and
only indirectly with the demand for passenger service. The steady
pace of growth during the era of entrepreneurial tourism is illustrated in figure 3, where one sees the rate of touristic growth accompanied by a proportionately steady increase in the size of Palma
where most of the facilities were located. Then in the 1950s growth
was such that new resorts in various coastal regions of the island
were opened. In the 1950s the number of annual visitors doubled
and between 1960 and 1970 they quintupled. These dramatic increases mark the introduction of the industrial age to the island of
Mallorca.

It is interesting to note that the stage which we call *industrial
tourism* was not at its inception perceived as industrialization by the
residents, but as a boom phase in a traditional business. Many
expected it to peak, and looked for things to return to normal.
However, it was more than a mere boom, for the industrializing
process in Mallorca resulted in a whole new way of doing business,
an entirely new technology, and an enormous concentration of
capital goods. Associated with this was a massive immigration of
technicians, managers and workers, resulting in a rapid population
increase, especially in urban areas.

In industrial tourism the capital goods exist as mile after mile of
resort facilities, as fleets of jet planes, ships, buses, cars, as dispersed
booking offices and transportation centers. The managers and
specialists needed to run this were recruited from every country in
Europe. The great corporate enterprises that operate this system are
organized to move hundreds of thousands of travelers at any one
time, the timing being so critical that hotel facilities are frequently
unused for little more than an hour as one group moves in to
replace a departing group of equal size. In the industrial phase, the
scope and volume of tourism is far beyond what anyone in the past

**Part of the waterfront and modern marina of Palma**

could have foreseen. Although Mallorca is an island only 35 miles wide and 75 miles long, in the months of heaviest tourism the airport which serves it is the fourth busiest in Europe.

The industrializing process in Mallorca manifests features of industrialization witnessed in other parts of the world, such as those apparent in the manufacture of goods or the extraction of resources. What is observed is a reorganization of economic life based on standardization, specialization and an advanced technology dependent on energy from fossil fuels. In industrial tourism, hotel rooms, meals, bus and plane seats, and indeed, the travelers themselves become interchangeable units in patterns of carefully times movement. Specialists function at key points to maintain an ongoing system, which above all else is dependent on the technology of air travel, and more specifically on the jet engine, an absolutely essential input for the development of industrial tourism in Mallorca.

The development of industrial tourism can be measured by various criteria. A sudden increase in the number of annual visitors, as we have seen, is one measure. (See figure 3.) However, equally important is the quality of the visitor's experience or the interaction between traveler and residents during the holiday period. As we have seen, the essence of entrepreneurial tourism was a series of person-to-person contacts for the contractual arrangements of the visit. In contrast, in the industrial age something as seemingly simple as an outdoor barbecue in the Mallorcan countryside may be arranged and booked in Frankfurt, and involve company representatives in two countries arranging purchasing, transporation, food preparation and entertainment for five hundred guests per seating. In industrial tourism there is only the illusion of personalism and informality, and this is created by managers operating on assembly-line time schedules.

The consequences of industrial tourism were nothing less than a total reordering of Mallorcan society. An islander born in the forties or before has lived in two worlds. Those living in the capital have seen their city change from a slowly improving port town to a busy industrial center. The new city operates by new rules that are overtaking and displacing a doggedly persistent traditional life. Should industrial tourism continue to dominate the island's economy, and there are good arguments both for and against this projection, traditional values and categories will become completely irrelevant.

## PALMA IN THE INDUSTRIAL AGE

One of the most important effects of tourism was a turn-of-the century reversal of a perennial pattern of out-migration by Mallorcans seeking a better life elsewhere. In the last decade of the nineteenth century, 5,500 Mallorcans migrated to other lands. In the first decade of tourism, in the twentieth century, the population stabilized and there has never been a decline since. The population of Palma in 1900 was 64,000. It is now more than 200,000. More than 50 percent of its growth is the result of in-migration from other parts of Spain. (See figure 4.) These were the people who came to work in the tourist industry, and housing for these migrants had to be built concurrent with hotels, restaurants and other tourist facilities. With two distinct kinds of growth we see the city expanding in two directions (figure 5). New barrios serving tourists developed along the shoreline of the Bay of Palma with construction extending inland only two, three or four blocks. Another kind of expansion took place from the land perimeters of the city inland toward the center of the island. This is composed almost entirely of new apartment buildings arranged in a grid-pattern between spoke-like roads which emanate from within the city. Here live migrants from the mainland and from the island's center along with former residents of barrios from the old city. (See figure 5.) The semi-circular outline around the old city marks the perimeter where the walls once stood, and the present course of a major traffic artery. Over this boundary between the old and the new, many Xuetas have moved from residence in a clearly demarcated ethnic barrio to their present, less-visible status.

In the old city, the Xuetas were locked into their old neighborhood by an unchanging urban order, as much as by persisting negative attitudes. In a system where occupation was closely linked to kin ties, Xuetas tended either to dominate an occupation or trade or to be entirely absent from membership in it. With the transformation of the city to the needs of industrial tourism, not only the

172

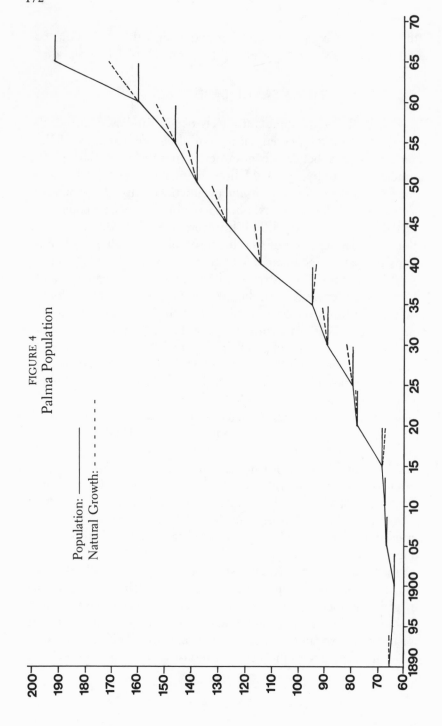

FIGURE 4
Palma Population

Population: ———
Natural Growth: - - - - - -

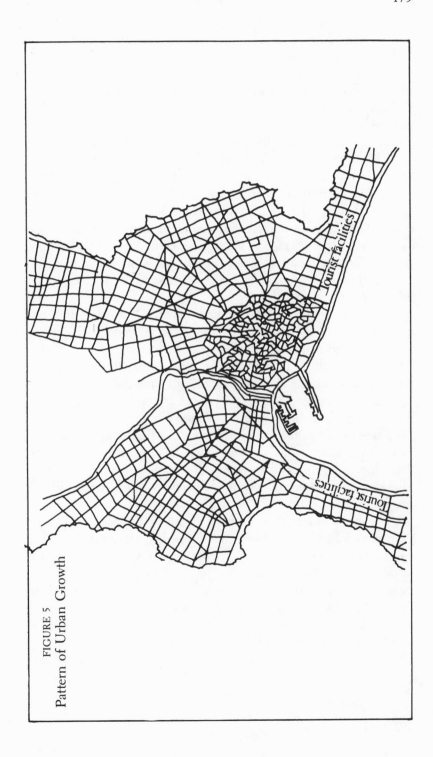

FIGURE 5
Pattern of Urban Growth

Xuetas but all occupational groups and classes tended to diminish in visibilty and importance.

In the new neighborhoods residents are not so readily identified as either Xueta or non-Xueta, and even the Mallorcan-mainlander distinction tends to lose its potency after a generation. What the residents of the new neighborhood have in common are similarities in income, life style, and life goals. The non-Xueta Mallorcans who moved to these new neighborhoods are still acutely aware of distinctions from the past, but the migrants from the mainland, like any casual observer from the outside, find it difficult to be moved by this local distinction. Hence large numbers of mainlanders have married both Xuetas and non-Xuetas, identifying both as simply Mallorcan. In the new Mallorca, life style, income, personal attraction and religion are important factors in selecting a mate, and by these criteria there was no reason for Xuetas and migrants from the peninsula not to intermarry.

The most basic trend in twentieth-century Xueta life emerges from the demographic data on rates of intermarriage. Figure 6 shows that the percentage of endogamous marriages was between 85 and 90 percent in the first decade of the twentieth century. The author researched the marriage records of Palma and found that by the late sixties endogamous marriages were down to 20 percent. This change is directly linked to a modernizing process that has been generated by touristic growth since the beginning of the century. There seems to be an even more direct connection between declining endogamy and the increasing immigration of mainland migrants. This future, of course, is directly proportional to the expansion of the tourist sector of the economy.

Though endogamous marriage is declining the results of many years of endogamy are still very much a part of Mallorcan life. The double Xueta names which one encounters on numerous occasions throughout the day still reinforce the awareness of in-group marriage. My survey of the 1965 telephone directory, which revealed 70 percent endogamous surnames reflected the unions of half a century. When one considers that the telephone directory includes family names which are the outcome of marriages that took place when endogamy was as high as 90 percent, and that telephone

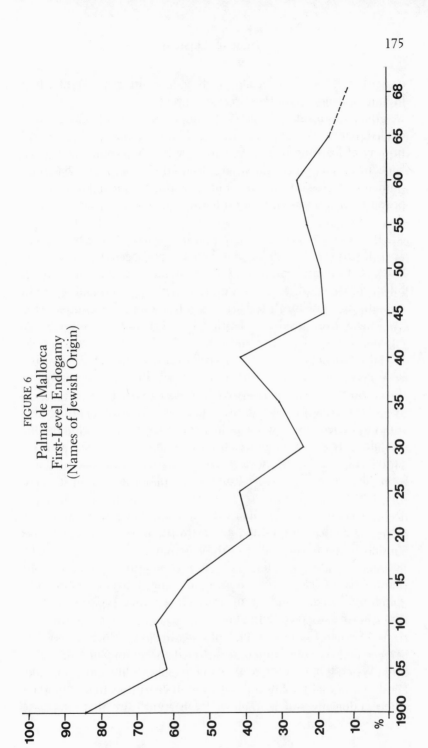

FIGURE 6
Palma de Mallorca
First-Level Endogamy
(Names of Jewish Origin)

ownership is closely associated with age, wealth and stability, then
the rate of endogamy the directory reveals is not surprising. After
weighing the results of the 1965 telephone directory data, I concluded that the actual endogamy would be much less, but there was
no way of learning in that first inquiry how rapid the decline had
been in recent years. However, it should be repeated that those
numerous endogamous unions in existence tend to have an inward
pressure for communal continuity for fifty to seventy-five years after
they are established.

The consequences of being Xueta in the industrial city of Palma
are still strong in the 1970s, but the basis of it becomes less and less
that of community and more a matter of *identity*. The Street of the
Silver Shops is still an almost entirely Xueta barrio, and the sense
of community within the barrio is still strong. However, most of
the Xuetas live outside the barrio. The Street of the Silver Shops
remains a symbol of bygone eras when Xuetas lived territorially
locked into a ghetto, and the survival of this symbol affects the lives
of Xuetas living in every part of the island. But those living within
the barrio still value the rewards of intimate contact and interdependence that have been so much a part of Xueta life over the centuries. The jewelry business holds them together, but added to this
are other types of close relationships that are more than just
neighborliness. Each Xueta within the barrio, and without to a
lesser degree, still feels a strong sense of responsibility for, and
interdependence with, those who share the same background. This
feeling manifests itself in loans for new families and business ventures within the community, and a strong feeling that no member
should be allowed to fall to a level of poverty that results in his
becoming a public charge. A destitute or criminal Xueta is still
considered a negative reflection on all, and to avoid this, families
will come together and act in whatever way necessary at whatever
cost to avoid disgrace to the group.

As stated in the beginning, the very people who are most concerned with Xueta identity, with the image other Xuetas project,
and its reflection on the group, are at the same time eager to tell one
that the designation Xueta doesn't mean anything any more. What
they are in fact telling you is that it is no longer the painful stigma it

once was, that the public insults have disappeared completely, that marriage with outsiders is the rule rather than the exception, and that Xuetas now live in all parts of the city. However, the awareness of Xueta identity is vivid, and is still of enormous consequence in day-to-day interaction in the city and throughout the island.

In discussing the role of Xuetas in modern times, we should be careful to distinguish between community and category. The Xueta community of Palma today consists of only a small portion of the total Xueta population. For the community really exists only on the Street of the Silver Shops. When speaking of all the Xuetas of Mallorca who are today dispersed throughout the city and island, we must speak of them as a category, a category with a vivid awareness of its distinctiveness and visibility in the social system. If industrial tourism and economic growth can be sustained, one can project that in decades to come Xueta identity will become an anach-ronism. If influential Xuetas have their way, the Street of the Silver Shops will fall victim to urban renewal, and this will effec-tively end the Jewish community which has had a continuous exis-tence on the island for over a thousand years, seven hundred and forty of these under Christian domination, and five hundred and thirty-five of which the members of this Pharisaic social form were themselves Christian.

# Xueta Experience and Persisting Identity

We have said that being a Xueta is still important but becoming less important, that projecting current trends we can foresee the eventual assimilation of the Xuetas in the next century. In this ambiguous state, a condition that many American ethnics understand quite well, an awareness of Xueta identity varies somewhat from person to person. There is of course a marked difference between the young and the old, and the experience and conception of self of those living or working on "the street" are notably different from Xuetas living mixed throughout the city. Mindful of these and other differences, we can nevertheless still recognize basic commonalities characteristic of Xuetas in general.

Examing our data to separate the essential elements of Xueta identity, we should first give recognition to the all-too-obvious fact that the vast majority of Xuetas are to begin with simply bourgeois Mallorcans. Their thoughts and feelings on most matters are indistinguishable from other Mallorcans with whom they share the same island, regional culture and dialect, and with whom they recall many of the same events of recent local history. Yet as a Mallorcan, the Xueta even now lives his life as a variation on a theme. The reasons for this are various, for there are many ways in which an awareness of one's "Xuetaness" are transmitted to the individual. However, in contemporary life, kinship ties more than anything else provide the individual with a distinctly Xueta experience and out-

179

look. The long-range effects of endogamy and the Mallorcan custom of married children purchasing apartments in the same building as a parent makes it highly likely that any particular Xueta will be in close contact with kinsmen who are primarily Xueta, and from whom he will learn of life on "the street," Xueta views on the Civil War, Vatican II, the state of Israel, and so on. In this chapter, we will examine the Xueta as a Mallorcan, and then consider the ways the Xueta distinction continues to have relevance to the Xuetas themselves, and to those they relate to on and off the island.

## THE XUETA AS MALLORCAN

As a Mallorcan, the Xueta, like his middle-class contemporaries, struggles to increase his worth in a flourishing touristic economy, but also, typical of his time, he views this current horn of plenty with distrust and apprehension. While Mallorcans reap the harvest of modernization, and it has been bountiful for many, they share intense fears as to where they are going. Mallorca is a small and powerless island, and with its newly developed economic interdepence, many fear that it has gotten itself into something it cannot control. Like all Mallorcans, the Xeutas are devoted to their island and have a deep, characteristically Spanish, reverence of *pueblo* and *patria chica*. Their ties are first to region and then to nation, and in the current situation they are partners in a shared resentment of the increasing power of Madrid. Though not unaware that corporate-controlled business, much of it international, must be regulated by the central government, they are nevertheless disturbed at seeing their island become more Spanish and less Mallorcan. As this process accelerates they have a feeling of being stripped of their values, their local language and their cherished sense of peoplehood.

Mallorcans in general, Xueta and non-Xueta, are characteristically possessed with an inferiority complex as a local trait. Throughout their history they have been an isolated and abandoned piece of Spain. A day's trip from the coastline, they were easily forgotten. Lacking communication with the outside world, they tended to dwell upon themselves. Except for the most educated, they have always distrusted outsiders while at the same time envying them.

Most were unprepared for the sudden intrusion of the industrial world which, while having resolved their problems of poverty, disease and illiteracy, has at the same time begun to incorporate them into a larger order which they are less and less sure they want to be part of. So the Mallorcan, Xueta and non-Xueta, is torn between a past he recalls with both reverence and loathing and a future filled with promise and anxiety. In this sense they are merely joining the rest of the modern world, but as the past is so recent, and change has come so rapidly, the contrast is perhaps here a bit more vivid.

In the current instability the urban Mallorcan has acquired a new view of Mallorcan rural life. Where the citizens of Palma dominated the countryside in centuries past, using it only as a larder and treating its inhabitants with disdain, the encroaching power of Madrid has produced a new reverence for the once-scorned peasant life. The contemporary urbanite thinks in terms of a polarity, with Madrid to the west as a symbol of statism, corporateness and the moneyed life, while the countryside to the east and immediately accessible has more and more become the repository of morality, personalism and authenticity. In this situation, the newly prosperous Mallorcan, Xueta and non-Xueta, will use a large portion of his earnings to buy a small farm, a plot of land, or an old house in the countryside as a weekend retreat where his children can learn in village life the values their parents acquired in urban barrios not too long ago.

The Mallorcan, like other modernizing Mediterranean people, finds himself torn between progress and traditional fatalism, democracy and privilege, anonymity and identity, corporate power and God. He admires the tourist, welcomes the opportunity to make money from him, but with the profits from this exchange the Mallorcan seeks to secure himself a better life in ways defined by traditional culture. It is with this same inconstancy that Mallorcans look at the boundary that has separated them into Xueta and non-Xueta. They are not proud of it, they are pleased to see it diminish, but at the same time they are not terribly ashamed. It is seen as one of the less fortunate aspects of a past which serves as an anchor in a period of dubious change, (Schneider, Schneider and Hansen, 1972).

## THE XUETA AS XUETA

If the Xueta *as Mallorcan* is apprehensive about the passing of traditional culture, the Xueta *as Xueta*, a stigmatized member of the old order, views the changes of the modern era as part of a process of amelioration. He has heard from still-living relatives of their experiences as a scorned minority in the early decades of the century. He sees the improvement in the Xueta's role in society as due more to political than economic factors. He identifies his former role as one defined in an order controlled by church and state. With surprising uniformity Xuetas date contemporary processes of change from the era of the Spanish Republic, a period in which a new government challenged the church's power. They speak of it as a time when everything opened up. The Republican government itself is not seen as the specific initiator of change, but more precisely, the period of its power is seen as the beginning of change for the Xueta community, a time after which things have improved continuously.

Given that the Xuetas were strong supporters of the Republic, there was intense anxiety among them with the outbreak of the Spanish Civil War. With the collapse of Republican authority on the island, the Xuetas, who had always been supporters of liberal causes, had reason to fear for their well being. However, in the Civil War period they were never in jeopardy, and in retrospect they tend to view it as other Mallorcans do, as a time when they were fortunate to be far removed from the bloody warfare that raged on the mainland. With the advent of World War II, and with Spain, though neutral, ideologically tied to the Axis powers, the Xuetas retreated to a defensive posture. It was a time in which a small number of anti-Semitic extremists, appealing to the authority of German rather than Spanish national policy, were openly critical of suspected Jewish elements in the society. We will comment on this briefly in the next section.

With the end of World War II, the Xuetas were never again in any jeopardy from political authority. They have had good relations with the Franco government, and many members of the community have been ardent supporters of the "Movement." In the post-

Arch of Almudaina on Almudaina Street

Apartment dwellings in the new sector of Palma

Mallorcan fisherman relaxing in the Palma harbor

Main street of a Mallorcan village

war period the Xuetas, like all Spaniards, shared an anxiety about their nation's precarious role in the world, and among themselves they were particularly responsive to the plight of displaced European Jews. The revelations of the mass murder of Jews by Nazis were particularly alarming to a people of Jewish identity who had encountered Nazi propaganda first hand. In the years that followed they were moved by the news of the creation of the state of Israel, for though the Xuetas are not and do not see themselves as Jews in a religious sense, they are acutely aware of the problems of the survivial of the Jewish people on a world-wide scale.

If the Xuetas are concerned about the problems of Jews as people, they are even more concerned with the Vatican and its policies toward Jews. They are of the opinion that changes in the Vatican's relations with Jews have improved their image in Mallorcan society. They say this, mindful that from the perspective of the Vatican the Xuetas were never more or less Catholic than other Mallorcans, and that the local church has for centuries recognized the full Catholic status of Xuetas. Yet in a local taxonomy, the Xuetas have been perceived as Jews, and as the church's relations with Jews improved on an international level, they feel their status in Mallorcan society has improved. One rarely meets an educated Xueta who is not knowledgeable on the statements of Pope John XXIII or the work of Cardinal Bea as regards the redefined status of Jews by the Vatican. The Xueta is Mallorcan to the core, and he shares the islander's concerns and perspective, but the special identity Mallorcan society has provided him leads him to perceive events selectively on a world-wide scale in a way that is distinctively Xueta.

Discussing the Xueta as a *Mallorcan* and a *Xueta Mallorcan* an apparent contradiction emerges in that the Xueta *as Mallorcan* reveres the past and is apprehensive about modern change, while the Xueta *as Xueta* disparages the past and approves of twentieth-century change. If there are contradictions within persons who support both views at the same time, they are merely the natural creations of a complex modern experience. Similarly, if the Xueta is intensely Catholic, but with a strong awareness of being Jewish, it is simply because history has made him thus. The Xueta lives with this conflict as part of his inescapable essence, and it is for this reason that the individual Xueta is vitally concerned about relations between the two religious traditions; for as they improve, the internal personal conflict that is part of his social heritage diminishes proportionately.

## THE XUETA INFORMANT

In our interviews with Xuetas, it was not unusual for an informant to speak of both Catholic and Jewish aspects of his identity. There were some informants who denied a connection or association with anything Jewish and these interviews tended to be short and unreflective. However, most informants were quite outspoken about their ethnic identity, and some had a well-developed awareness of it. With the latter we arranged extended taped interviews. We have summarized three of these in the following pages so that the reader can sample some of the ways that Xuetas in a personal discussion might talk about themselves as a particular kind of people.

The first summary is from an interview with an older man who is intensely religious and participates regularly in the activities of his small neighborhood church. When we asked him what it meant to be a Xueta in modern Mallorca, he moved easily to a conception expressed in religious terms. The last portion of the interview consisted of a very eloquent lecture on Christian theology.

> Oh yes, we are Jewish, but as you know the Xuetas are totally ignorant of Judaism. They couldn't establish a synagogue here if they wanted to. They wouldn't know how. I suppose it is true that we have an inclination to commerce, and we are Jewish in other ways. Also, there will always be a prejudice against us by the vulgar for being what we are. But there is a lot of friendship between the Jews and the Vatican now, so there is no serious problem.
>
> You know St. Paul was a Jew, so we all come from the same tree. I am a Catholic, but I have an intense sympathy for Jews. They are the people of God. We feel strongly about the idea of Judaism. I personally believe strongly in prophesy, in the coming of a glorious Messiah who will defend everyone, and the Jews will be included. We know that God is the father, and that his love is infinite. To communicate

his felicity and to interpret, he sent Christ to all of us. The infinite love of the Son for the Father, and the Father for the Son—that is the Holy Spirit. That mutual love is the Holy Spirit, and together they are the Holy Trinity.

Another informant, college educated and much involved in the day-to-day activities, did not describe what it meant to be a Xueta in religious terms. Rather he tended to see himself as a member of an urban ethnic category.

The middle class in Mallorca is very large now, and among them there are those who are very traditional and some who want to be super modern. The most distinctive people from the past are probably the Xuetas and the nobility. The friendship between the Xuetas and the nobility is based on an understanding that each has its own path, his own way. We can have a friendship of proximity, but of complete social separation.

People from the outside are completely confused by this situation. The highest nobles will not speak ill of the Xuetas. They know better than anyone else that the Xuetas are purely Catholic. The nobles have their sector and their own names just as the Xuetas do. I can name noble names the way others can identify Xueta names. But in this new life what does Xueta mean and what does noble mean? You know you can still buy a title in Mallorca, and nobility, though always interesting to everyone, is only respected when titles are supported by wealth. It is better to be of "good family" without a noble title than to be noble and poor. But as you have seen Mallorca is mostly middle class. There are also distinctive groups, the Xuetas, the nobles, the poor, the loud fishermen in Santa Catalina and so on. In this modern situation people can be very friendly in school or on the street, but still maintain old family prejudices. I am always suprised at how much some of the old ways continue.

A third informant presents a position that introduces other elements. We have said that Xuetas tended to view the old order as one dominated by an alliance of church and state. The informant, who grew up both Xueta and poor sees himself as having been a victim of that system.

I went to a Catholic school for poor children and there I was taught only to read and write. Rich Xueta families offered my mother support to educate me for the priesthood, but she did not accept it. I remember being insulted as a child, being called a Xueta fool by playmates, and once someone spit in my face.

There has always existed a sense of community among Xuetas and from my grandparents I learned pride in being a Xueta, a descendent of Jews. My grandparents told me about the Inquisition and what it did to Xuetas.

There is more freedom now than there used to be. I think it is because people are better educated. The distinction doesn't have the same force as before, and with freedom and better education there is less Jewishness among the Xuetas. Some Xuetas are fanatic Catholics, and others are only officially Catholic. There are some who deny any connnection with other Xuetas. They always say, "We are all equal under God." The most actively Catholic Xuetas behave publicly in a very Catholic way, but among them there is a strong Xueta feeling. They try to hide this and give the exact opposite impression. There are Xuetas living on the *Street of the Silver Shops* who are extreme Catholics, but they live a Jewish life. I think they are afraid of non-Xueta Catholics. But you know on that street two silversmiths are not just two silversmiths. They are two Xuetas.

Xuetas have always helped each other. I remember rich Xuetas dying and leaving money to be distributed among poor Xueta families. The more freedom and liberty there is, the less necessity there is for us to help each other. We do not share one belief, but many think we are all one race. Foreign Jews who come to Mallorca tell stories of secret ritual practiced by the Xuetas. This is completely untrue. If this were to happen, it would be something entirely new. What we have is a common feeling that comes from the same problems and the same history.

In these days when someone calls a person a Xueta it is not an insult. It is just a description. There is no intention to offend when someone says, "Go down to the Xueta grocery store." That is not meant as an insult.

## XUETA IDENTITY AND "JEWISH BLOOD"

The Xueta is a middle-class Mallorcan Catholic with a sense of Jewishness that makes him acutely sensitive to the affairs of Jews in the world. Though he does not practice Jewish rituals and does not understand Jewish theology, he nevertheless "feels" Jewish. The foundations of this awareness are various, but for large numbers of Mallorcans the Xueta's Jewishness is a physical fact demonstrable by readily observable physical features. As our last informants noted, "Many people think we are a race." He himself was not sure. Earlier in the text we saw that Xuetas could describe themselves in terms of specific physical attributes. These traits, it is said, are characteristic of a Jewish race and the product of "Jewish blood."

"Jewish blood" it was alleged not only produced certain physical types but was also responsible for Jewish behavior. Xuetas behaved differently, according to many non-Xuetas, and for some the distinctive behavior was characteristic of a Jewish "race," that is to say, a people with the same "blood" running through their veins. Many anthropologists treat "race" as a folk taxonomy, the position being that superficial morphological features that are the criteria for distinguishing race are important only insofar as they are attributed importance in a particular culture. Though they may be seen as evidence of the climate or region of a person's ancestors, they are irrelevant in the explanation of behavioral differences among individuals or groups. Many Mallorcans would support that position but a racial conception of the Xuetas persists on the island, among Xueta and non-Xueta alike. For the most part this is a rather inconsequential and colloquial understanding of ethnic difference, functioning at the level of gossip; however at certain points in recent history the matter of Jewish ancestry became a public and therefore serious concern. The first of these was in World War II.

Miguel Forteza (1966) reports that in 1942, through the efforts of the German government, or possibly the German citizens then forming a colony on the island, there was an official inquiry into the status of descendants of converted Jews. The reason for the inquiry was alleged to have been the investigation of a possible connection between local descendants of Jews and the representatives of international Jewish organizations, as well as the possibility of subversive acts by local Jewish sympathizers. Historical data was available on the family identity of those condemned by the Inquisition, and the investigators demanded a report from a local historian who was referred to them by the archbishop of Mallorca. The list of Jewish

surnames provided by the historian included not only the 15 surnames of Xuetas, but 101 other well-known Mallorcan surnames.
The historian reported to the 1942 investigators that 35 percent of
the inhabitants of the island were descendants of Jews or of those
accused of judaizing by the Inquisition. Forteza says this figure is
high, and that 18 percent would represent a more accurate estimate.

It is very possible that the historian doubled the figure, to confuse
the inquirers. By making the numbers absurdly large he diminished
the possibility of any policy or program being carried out which
specifically dealt with descendants of Jews. Thirty-five percent of the
total populace included many from the most prestigious and powerful families in commerce, government and the church. In any case,
nothing official ever developed from the inquiry and beyond a few
threatening letters, the Xuetas and other descendants of Jews survived the period of the second World War connection with Nazi
Germany unscathed. Although the reasons for the failure of this
specific inquiry will probably remain unknown, it has been well
established by historians that during the second World War the
Spanish government consistently ignored recommendations from
the German government that the Spaniards do something about
their "Jewish problem." Spanish officials answered the inquiries,
but in platitudes undiscernible to German. In the end, the
Spaniards did nothing.

Concern with "Jewish blood" and descent have a long history in
Spain. The expulsion of Jews and the activities of the Inquisition
resulted in a mania over contamination by things Jewish. A series of
laws and rulings dealing with the *"limpieza de sangre,"* or *purity of
blood*, were an outcome of an obsession with Christian purity,
linked to ties of descent. As the heirs of Jewish mercantile fortunes
who had converted to Christianity were the most mutually advantageous marriage partners for the impoverished heirs of family titles,
there was hardly a noble family in Spain that could not count Jews
among its ancestors. The only "pure" descendants of Christians
were peasants from the most isolated rural areas, the only place
where Jewish communities never flourished. The mania of *limpieza
de sangre* subsided, but not entirely. Most Spaniards are aware that
the assimilation of Jews has resulted in some Jewish ancestry for

almost any Spaniard. Nevertheless, some consider the charge unworthy, and are willing to dispute any claim that they are of Jewish origin.

A more recent concern with genealogical purity developed with the publication of *Els Descendents dels Jueus Conversos de Mallorca*, by Forteza, in 1966. It provoked a public debate in the newspapers of Palma over who was and was not the descendant of Jews. As an amateur historian and Xueta leader, Forteza was concerned with eliminating anti-Xueta sentiments, and one way of doing this was to demonstrate that the Xuetas were not the only descendants of Jews. In his book he showed the Jewish origin of many common Mallorcan surnames and the possible Jewish origins of noble families. It would seem that these revelations would inspire nothing more than idle curiosity on the part of Mallorcans, to the extent that anyone might be curious about their family origins. This was the response of most Mallorcans, but many were disturbed by Forteza's assertion that they might be of Jewish ancestry.

Those who challenged Forteza's conclusions pointed out that some of the names he said were included in the Inquisition records were not, and names that were, were those adopted by converts from their Christian sponsors during the conversions of 1391 and 1435. That is to say, those converts who were later charged for judaizing by the Inquisition were the Jewish bearers of Christian names and were not related to Christians of the same name. Hence many persons in contemporary Mallorca who carried the surnames were not the descendants of Jews, but rather the descendants of those old Christians from whom the Jews took their names. Forteza was charged with lack of rigor in his research, and for assuming that anyone was the descendant of Jews who could not prove otherwise. The debate involved various persons including an official director of educational programs who in four newspaper articles reiterated the national and religious policies regarding racial equality in Spain. The polemic ended when one of the participants, a leading Xueta attorney, died suddenly of a heart attack, said by some to have been brought on by the excitement of the furor over Forteza's book.

The positions taken in the debate are of relatively less interest than the fact that the discussion could arouse so much public

interest. From the discussion it is apparent that some Mallorcans are
still concerned with the purity of their ancestry, especially with
respect to the presence or absence of Jews in the family lineage.
Most Mallorcans accept the possibility of Jewish ancestry and think
little of it, and purity of blood is not their concern. Mallorcan
writers emphasize that Mallorcan heritage includes Phoenician,
Iberian, Greek, Celtic, Nordic, Semitic, Roman Carthaginian and
Latin infusion. Mallorcans are proud of their mixed heritage, including the Jewish part of the mixture, but concern with Jewish
origin still remains strong with some elements of the populations,
principally the Xuetas and the nobility.

Forteza's inquiries into family names to point out who are really
the descendants of Mallorcan Jews has placed an undo emphasis on
genealogies. His inference that others are as Jewish as the Xuetas
because they too are the descendants of Jews is unfounded. Although the Xuetas are of unmixed Jewish descent, it is not their
genes which makes them Jewish. It is rather their conservation over
the years of Jewish customs as members of an urban ethnic community which has survived from the period of the Inquisition. This
community has served to protect its members and was able to continue both by the traditionalism of its social system and the
exclusivistic pressures of the larger society. Forteza's inference that
other Mallorcans are just as Jewish as the Xuetas is not supported by
the cultural data. As the presence of so-called Jewish genes or Jewish
blood in no way determines or influences behavior, the argument
about Jewish descent is frivolous. The preservation of Jewish cultural patterns among the Xuetas long after their conversion to Christianity is on the other hand an observable cultural phenomenon,
and to the degree that individual Xuetas are products of the community, they are bearers of Jewish traditions. This is a matter of
pride among some Xuetas, and of shame among others.

## XUETA IDENTITY AND ISRAEL

In 1948, a letter addressed to David Ben Gurion, and the Minis-
ter of Religion in Israel, appealed to the new nation of Israel for
assistance in guiding the descendants of Jews in Mallorca back to the

religion of their forefathers. The letter was sent by Cayetano Martí Valls, a Mallorcan Xueta with a passionate desire to learn about and return to what he sees as his religious and cultural roots. Cayetano was one of my closest associates and most helpful informants during more than two years of fieldwork in Mallorca. Employed as a wage-earning artisan, Cayetano spends his evenings with his hobby of painting, and the study of books of Jewish prayer and history. His quest is to be what he says he is by birth, a Jew.

The 1948 letter read, in part:

> We have heard that God has remembered his people and that after two thousand years the Jewish state has been recreated. We are several thousand men, women and children, the remnants of Spanish Jewry. The cruel Inquisition forced our ancestors to deny their religion and accept the Catholic faith. We appeal to you as head of the Israeli government to help us return to the faith of our fathers, to our people, and to our homeland. Regretfully, we know very little of Jewishness, and therefore urge you to supply us with books on Judaism written in the Spanish language. We Marranos yearn to return to our people.

Cayetano spoke only for himself but in some sense his reasons for writing the letter reflect feelings then current among the Xuetas, particularly their pride in the creation of a Jewish state. All during Cayetano's early life he had been ashamed of his ethnic identity. During the war years he was reminded of the perils of Jewish ties of any sort by resident Nazi sympathizers, whose anti-Semitism was publicly proclaimed, and did not exclude the Xuetas. With the creation of the state of Israel, a long-humilated man was able to share from a distance in the accomplishments of a people whose shame he had borne all his life. At this time, Cayetano had an authentic religious experience at the site of an ancient church which he had learned as a child was once a synagogue. There he was overcome by a new comprehension, a recognition of the ideals of his own ancestors and the hope of Israel as one. At that moment he decided that he wanted to become a Jew. Cayetano then wrote a letter to Israel asking for books on Judaism. It is important to note that he did not write to Barcelona to purchase Jewish books in Spanish or go there to study Judaism. This would have been the most practical procedure, but practicality is irrelevant in this case, for Cayetano was acting out of inspiration, and it was Israel that inspired him.

Those on the outside world who read Cayetano's plea on behalf of "the remnants of Spanish Jewry" in Mallorca could easily be lead to believe that there existed a group of secret Jews in Spain who had been waiting to reveal themselves and return to their people, and that the creation of the state of Israel as a refuge for homeless Jews was the opportunity for which they had been waiting. The fact is that many did conclude this, basing their conclusions on the assumption that Jews in Spain had found it necessary to hide their identity and beliefs. But this is not the case, for there has been no anti-Jewish policy in modern Spain. In fact quite the opposite was true, and there was abundant evidence of this in those post-war years.

For example, during the years of World War II, 50,000 Jewish refugees passed through Spain on the way to the port of Lisbon, and thence to various parts of the world, especially Palestine. Following the war, Spanish aid to refugees was recognized through a resolution of gratitude to Spain by the World Jewish Congress. In Spain's principal cities, Jewish communities grew with an influx of refugees, and with the passing years the relationship with the Spanish government has been marked by cordiality, and ever increasing rights and privileges for the communities. This is not an entirely new situation, for it has been the law of the land since 1920 that Spanish citizenship has been available to the descendents of Jews expelled in 1492. A more recent action, the liberal passing out of Spanish passports to Jewish refugees in various Mediterranean countries, is but an aspect of a long-held official policy, which continuing through three different governments, has been of enormous value to Mediterranean Jews whose lives have been endangered by unfavorable political conditions in their country of residence.

The Spanish policy being what it was, Cayetano or any other Mallorcan could have moved to a large Spanish city and joined a congregation, or they could have formed one of their own in Palma. As Spaniards they could also have migrated to Israel, and as we shall see briefly, some from Mallorca have in recent years, with little or no difficulty. The Spanish national religious policy, simply put, is that Spain is officially a Catholic country, but that members of other religions may follow their faith freely. Although in practice the Spanish government has acted unfavorably to various evangelical religions in pursuit of converts, this reflects a policy that is little different than those of other religious states such as Israel and the various Islamic countries. In practice, no other non-Catholic faith has been treated with greater concern and deference than has Judaism.

We have elaborated on the Spanish government's policy towards Jews because the belief persists that because of oppression the Xuetas are something other than what they say they are. If one insists that the Xuetas are secretely Jewish, then one would have to explain why they hide their alleged true feelings under a government that is exceedingly friendly to Jewish communities. Cayetano's letter contained the honest feelings of one person, but it was taken by many to be an indicator that there were many other Xuetas who wanted to become Jews. No one knew for sure until in 1966 an Israeli mission came to Mallorca to invite Xuetas to migrate to Israel.

*     *     *     *     *

In 1968, in the early stages of this research, we were told by informants that twenty-four Xuetas had left to settle in Israel in the spring of 1966, and that all but one had returned to Palma. Working jointly with Stefan Taussig, who had traveled extensively in Israel, we set out to locate the migrants and interview them. We first learned that the twenty-four were grouped into four or five entire families, and that many of those who migrated were children. We began with but one name, but that informant led us to another, and so on, until we had accounted for all the migrants. The survey ended with a body of data quite unlike anything we had anticipated at the inception.

Our inquiry led us first to a family living on a farm located in the center of the island. The family had three members, a husband, wife and infant child. Neither spouse it turned out had a Xueta surname. The father had first learned about the offer of a free trip to Israel through relatives in early 1966. He took advantage of the opportunity, hoping to improve the family's economic situation. The three traveled to Israel by jet, and upon arriving there were provided the extensive services that the nation customarily makes available to immigrants during their period of adjustment. The couple said that they stayed long enough to find out what Israeli life was like, and what opportunities existed. They ultimately returned to Mallorca, citing the strangeness of kibbutz life, language problems and homesickness as the reasons for their decision.

The second family consisted of two parents and nine children. They too went to Israel to improve their economic position. They were not only not Xueta or Jewish, but were almost entirely ignorant of what Jews were or believed. They were migrants to Mallorca from the South of Spain, and in Mallorca they learned that they would be provided transportation to Israel, should they desire to migrate. They were told they were descended from Jews because their name was Garcia. They reported that once in Israel they were well taken care of and, having a large family, they were particularly appreciative of the extensive social services. They returned because of language difficulties, too few friends, and the imminent conscription of their eldest son for military service.

The third family was a couple in their sixties. Unlike the first two, they professed a strong commitment to Judaism which the husband said he had felt even in his teen years while growing up in Mallorca. His grandmother had told him that he had Jewish ancestors. He did not have one of the fifteen surnames, and hence was not classified as Xueta. The informant was enthusiastic about his stay in Israel. He had been circumcised while there and repeated his marriage vows in a Jewish ritual. He and his wife returned to Mallorca because of an illness which he thought could be cured only by Mallorcan herbs. Another family, the fourth, was accounted for but not interviewed. The other informants refused to give us their address. They described the father as shameless, unkempt and long-haired. They said this family had gone for economic reasons also, and returned when everyone else did.

There remained only one man unaccounted for. He had remained in Israel. I traveled to Israel and found him living in a run-down section of Tel Aviv. He was married to a young French girl and they had an infant child. His involvement with her was his primary reason for staying. He said life was more difficult in Israel than in Mallorca, but he had no intention of returning to his native island.     While in Israel I talked with Dr. Israel Ben Zeev who had organized the migration from Mallorca in his role as president of the International Organization for the Propagation of Judaism. He said the whole venture had caused him a great deal of trouble. His moral and political position was that anyone who professed a desire to be a Jew should be able to come to Israel. He pointed out that there was considerable internal opposition to this view. I asserted that Mallorcans were unsure of his motives and that many had interpreted his activities as proselytizing. He replied that he did not proselytize, but merely provided the opportunity to come to Israel for those who wanted to migrate.

After talking with all the parties involved both in Mallorca and Israel, one concluded that Dr. Ben Zeev, though an apt and thoughtful man, had like many others been led to believe that there were Xuetas who were sincerely desirous of becoming Jews. He and members of his organization came to Mallorca to locate these people and arrange their transport to Israel. They spoke with numerous Xuetas, and were surprised to find that no one other than Marti Valls was interested in conversion, and that even he preferred to continue his studies in Mallorca. A number of Xuetas accused Dr. Ben Zeev of damaging their reputations by implying that they were Jewish simply because their ancestors were. There were stories about Palma that Xuetas had asked a "rabbi" intent on converting them to leave their premises.

Though Dr. Ben Zeev did not find any Xuetas who wanted to become Jews, he did locate one person who though not a Xueta had retained a Jewish consciousness through family lines. This person as we have seen was the elderly husband of the third-mentioned family. Like Xueta children, he as a child had been told of the cruelties inflicted on Jews by the Inquisition. The clear Jewish provenance of his surname supported his claim to being the descendant of Jews. The informant expressed an intense hostility towards the Spanish church for what it had done to Jews, but amazingly his feelings towards Xuetas were equally hostile. He declared that they were from an inferior lineage, and asserted that his own lineage was superior both physically and mentally to the Xuetas.

In addition to the couple who were desirous of becoming Jews, Dr. Ben Zeev found other families who were eager to try another country, provided there was hope of improving one's living standards there. None of the adults in these famlies had strong religious convictions with respect to either Judaism or Catholicism. The most amazing migrants however were the Garcías who were persuaded to go by the argument that their surname showed them to be the descendents of Jews. Apart from the many flaws in this argument, its soundness overall is challenged by the well-known fact that García is used by 20 percent of the people and is the commonest surname in Spain. Using surnames like García, Fernández or Rodríguez as evidence of Jewish ancestry, the Society for the Propagation of Judaism could have invited 80 percent of Spain's thirty-plus million residents to return to Israel as Jews. Accusations of proselytizing has been the major focus of discussion on the Society's activities in both Mallorca and Israel, but what the data of migration reveal about the Xuetas, their Jewish identity and their Mallorcan Catholic affiliation is a much more important concern to all involved. For example, going back to our initial awareness of the migration, we were reminded by our notes that we were first told that the 24 Mallorcans that went to Israel were Xuetas. We presumed that this was the case until our interviews revealed otherwise. Dr. Ben Zeev and his associates came to Mallorca, believing reports from inside and outside of Mallorca that Xuetas were eager to return to the religion of their ancestors. It was only when Dr. Ben Zeev talked to the Xuetas himself that he learned that the Xuetas had no desire to change their religious or national affiliation. What the data reveal is a persisting confusion as to what the Xuetas are, that is, the way they are Jewish and the way they are not.

We have reported and analyzed this event to demonstrate with data that the Xuetas are exactly what they say they are. Those involved in this study, including Jews and non-Jews, agreed that the monograph should make this abundantly clear. The Xuetas are distinctive, and therefore, not easily understood, but there is nothing secretive about them. They have long been linked to alleged secret activities, and this presumption has been a continuing source of anti-Semitic fear. To deny there is anything Jewish about the Xuetas, as some do, is a bit preposterous. They retain a sense of Jewishness from their past, and on the whole tend to be sympathetic to the problems of Jews on a world-wide scale. Their empathy for the Israelis in their military struggle is obvious. It would be a flight of fancy to assume from this that they wanted to convert to Judaism, or leave their homeland and move to Israel. The confusion in Xueta identity has never come from the question as to whether they were Jewish, but rather the way in which they are Jewish. To be Xueta in Mallorca means a sense.of Jewishness that is inseparable from an ardent, and even passionate, attachment to the values, and traditions of the regional culture.

## THE DIASPORA, MALLORCA AND THE XUETAS

An attendant development of large-scale tourism in Mallorca has been the emergence of a Jewish community in the touristic sector of the city of Palma. Jews have come to live in Mallorca as employees of the tourist industry, as entrepreneurs, and as investors in touristic development. There has also been a significant influx of Jewish tourists from western Europe and the United States. In response to the opportunities provided by growing Jewish tourism, a large hotel at the edge of the city maintains a kitchen and dining room operated in compliance with traditional dietary regulations. This, of course, allows Orthodox Jews to vacation in Mallorca. Although most Jews visiting Mallorca do not subscribe to these rules, the hotel is important to all as the only real Jewish institution on the island.

There have been recent newspaper accounts, given world-wide distribution by news agencies, of particular Jewish rituals, e.g., a wedding, a Bar Mitzvah, being conducted on this island for the first time in five centuries. These events took place in hotels in the tourist sector of the city. These have been the most public but not the only activities of an embryonic Jewish community. For example, both resident Jews and those visiting the island have pursued the possibility of organizing a congregation and constructing a synagogue in Palma. A local journalist of a tourist daily sought

financial support from Jews in London, hoping to initiate the construction of a Mallorcan synagogue. The support was not forthcom-
ing, but the idea has by no means been discarded, and many are
confident a synagogue will some day be built. Meetings of Jewish
groups have been held for many years (even before the appearance
of the Jewish hotel) in the local Episcopal church, an institution
which came into being to serve English residents but ultimately
became the religious center for the entire tourist sector.

Mallorcans find nothing unusual about the increasing number of
Jewish activities on the island, especially their occurrence in the
cosmopolitan atmosphere of the touristic part of the city. Jewish
ethnic activities represent only one of numerous ethnic or national
traditions that have come into being locally in recent decades. Every
day one reads newspaper accounts of British, French, Scandina-
vian, German, Italian, American, North African and Mexican social events connected with organizations, societies or language
schools. Most of these traditions have a number of restaurants
specializing in their distinctive cuisine, and many of these have
become ethnic gathering centers. There are also, as we have said, a
number of Protestant churches on the island, reflecting a range of
religious-ethnic as well as national-ethnic variety.

Xueta informants view the creation of a new Jewish community
from an entirely Mallorcan perspective. That is to say, they see it
happening in a social milieu which is not necessarily Mallorcan,
the tourist sector, and hence somewhat distant from their own way
of life. The social boundary which separates Xuetas from West
European and American Jews residing on the island has nothing to
do with religious identities past or present. The dividing line is
simply a natural segment boundary of insider-outsider. Mallorcans
tend to reinforce it in order to separate themselves from the dubious
innovations of the tourist sector, and those in the tourist sector use it
to protect themselves from local sumptuary regulations.

The perspective of non-Mallorcan Jews participating in the life of
the tourist sector varies in accordance with their length of stay on
the island. Jewish tourists on short visits to the island are likely to
learn during their stay that Jews have played an important role in the
island's history, but having heard similar accounts while visiting

Toledo, Barcelona, Cordoba and other stopoffs in Spain, it is unlikely that Mallorca presents anything special. Those Jews, however, who take up residence on the island may learn that Mallorca is
the only place in Spain where the descendents of Jews have persisted
as an endogamous community for more than five hundred years
after their conversion to Christianity, and continue to exist today as a
clearly definable ethnic group. Witnessing the various signs of the
Xueta's Jewish past, particularly the Street of the Silver Shops,
many non-Mallorcan Jews find it difficult to believe that the Xuetas
are not really Jewish and are predisposed to believe the ever-present
tales of secret Xueta rituals. Their inclination to accept relic anec-
dotes surviving from Inquisition times is not at all difficult to understand. Accounts of sustained belief surviving through centuries
against all obstacles are the kind of tales that most believers like to
hear in support of their particular faith. A longer residence and
more intimate acquaintance with Mallorcan life reveals to interested non-Mallorcans the total irrelevance of such accounts in
current Xueta Mallorcan life.

In general, the presence of a gestating Jewish community brings
to the fore, in a curious rather than hostile way, discussions of Xueta
Diaspora contact that have played a role in Xueta identity for many
years. Motivated by fear as well as curiosity, Mallorcans in years past
have speculated on the possibility that Xuetas had ties with Jewish
communities in other lands. It has been suggested that they have
been involved in wholesale trade in precious stones and metals, or
that they have shared investments with Jews of the Diaspora.
Though the Xuetas had the same rights as any Spaniard to trade
where they would, the truth is simply that they were not engaged in
the kind of ethnic-based trade characteristic of Indian, overseas
Chinese, Armenian or Jewish Diasporas. Xueta contact with the
Diaspora has been nonexistent, and Mallorcan Jewish contact with
the Mediterranean Diaspora ended in the Inquisition era. It is a
not-surprising consequence of Xueta identity that any contact whatsoever between Xuetas and non-Mallorcan Jews will be used as
proof of the truth of these long-proven untrue suspicions. However,
thinking of this type is irrelevent, for the real tie between Xuetas and
the New Jewish community is not inter-ethnic: it is historical. Many

of the Xuetas that live today may be the last products of a Jewish community which has had continuous existence on the island for at least a thousand years, or more; for some say it goes back to Roman times. That community is today disappearing, just as another, the Jewish community of the touristic sector, is moving toward a mature form. Our data on exogamous marriages indicate that the Xuetas could disappear, even as an ethnic group, in the years to come. Current trends suggest that while this happens, the new Jewish community will reach its florescence; and displacing the Xuetas provide continuation of a longstanding Jewish presence on the island, a presence which dates back to before the beginnings of recorded history in this region.

## SUMMARY

We have examined the Jewish community of Mallorca over a period of approximately 750 years, noting its transition from a Diaspora community stage, to a Converso stage, to a Xueta stage, and finally, in the modern era, to an assimilating stage. Persistence and change in this community is better understood when seen in relation to the changing value of the City of Mallorca in both Mediteranean commerce and successive national domains. Using this approach, the following stages emerge from the data.

I. *Jews living as Jews in a developing Christian City.* In a period lasting from 1229 until 1435, the Mallorcan Jewish community was an unalloyed replication of the Mediterranean Diaspora model. The City of Mallorca at this same time was coming into being as a Christian city, displacing the Saracen urban order of Medina Mayurka. In the transition of conquest, the Jewish community was the most clearly defined and stable of any urban category. In the Christian realm, category boundaries were blurred and even the transported Aragonese status system was vaguely defined in a city that had an almost frontier classless quality. Saracens who were left behind after the conquest constituted another category; but they existed as merely a fluid population, deserted by the former rulers, and lacked a specialized role and internal order. The Jews who had played an active role in commerce in the Saracen era continued intact, and participated even more vigorously in trade and exchange after the Christian takeover. Their internal governance and boundary maintenance was such they were seen even legally as a state within a state. The community was characterized by a unifying religious ideology, rules of self segregation and customary contacts with equivalent groups in other lands. As the strongest, most stable sector in a developing system, and with a strong tradition of Mediterranean commerce they were the natural allies of an expansion-minded king. The period of "Jews as Jews" was a time of growth, security and accomplishment for the community, and was the high point of Jewish life in the island's history.

II. *"Crypto-Jews" in a declining Christian city.* This period extends from 1435, the year that the Jews converted as a group to Roman Catholicism, until 1691, the high point of the Mallorcan Inquisition. The Jews of this period were legally Christian, but the community continued with few modifications in the framework of guild organization. Functioning as the guild of St. Michael the Archangel was a step towards assimilation in a highly assimilationist environment, but the long-standing institutional arrangements of Diaspora life and intense commitment to religious ideals kept the group intact as a full-fledged but secret Jewish community. Though it continued its contacts with other communities in the region, trade and exchange were much diminished from the previous era. As the island of Mallorca became further removed from the concerns of the Spanish nation, the city diminished in importance, and Jews and nobles looked inward to local agriculture for a new economic base.

Throughout this period there were almost no obstacles to a marriage between a converted Jew and an Old Christian. Conversos as individuals participated easily in the Christian realm and many were assimilated during this period. Those who retained strong Jewish communal attachments in the guild of St. Michael were unlikely to assimilate; and even though they were legally Christian, they were perceived as Jews by the ordinary city dweller. The community continued to carry out economic roles which Jews had traditionally performed. It continued religious ritual in somewhat modified form, and rules of endogamy were enforced with notable success. It is conceivable that Mallorcan society could have continued to accept the Conversos of the St. Michael guild in their ambiguous status for many more decades if not centuries. However, an agent of Spanish national political power, the Holy Office of the Inquisition, intervened in the island's affairs, and inquired into the religious practices of the Conversos.

III. *The period of the Xuetas.* One examines the beginning of the Xueta period, noting the incredible efficaciousness of the Mallorcan Inquisition. Its goal of confiscating Converso wealth was carried out with ease. Its success in attaining Converso compliance with Christianity was total, an amazing accomplishment considering that crypto-Judaism had survived in full vigor for 250 years. Its third goal, making examples of the heretics, was so effectively realized that descendents of the crypto-Jews remained a stigmatized and pariah people for more than two centuries. In this status the Xuetas continued to rely on customary modes of interdependence and cooperation characteristic of Jewish communities. The Xuetas gave up their Jewish religion, but they did not give up their "Jewishness." For being Jewish between 70 A.D. and 1948 meant before anything else membership in a community whose order derived from traditional law. This the Xuetas retained.

The Xuetas were both Catholic and Jewish. They were Catholic in their belief in the Savior, Jesus Christ, the authority of Rome based on apostolic succession, and their participation in the sacraments of the church. They were, however, Jewish in the customary practices of their community life and in their role in the economic order. The persistence of Jewish custom was so complete that George Sand visiting Mallorca in the 1830s perceived and described them as Jews, and compared them to the Jews of France. She did not see them as merely the Catholic descendents of Jews retaining some Jewish customs.

In this period, lasting from 1691 until the twentieth century, the island of Mallorca endured continuous poverty caused by isolation, crop failures, piracy and plagues. It was an age of crystallized traditionalism, and the Xuetas were locked into a highly categorized, severely bounded and unchanging social order. There was little intermarriage between any of the social categories, but given the stigma attached to the Xuetas, their chance of marrying outside of their group was almost nonexistent. Thus the period of the Xuetas is one in which a community based on the traditional Diaspora form persisted little changed over centuries even though its members were fully Catholic, both in practice and belief.

IV. *The assimilationist period.* The assimilation of the Xuetas began very slowly at the turn of the century, was further stimulated by the "opening up" of the Republican era, and became the dominant fact of Xueta life with the advent of industrial tourism in the 1950s. Some have termed the "acceptance" of the Xuetas a product of changing attitudes in church and state and of a new open-mindedness among the populace. However, the compelling fact of Xueta assimilation is that marriages have occurred primarily with migrants from the mainland, not Mallorcans, and that these migrants came to Mallorca seeking employment and profit in a tourist industry that expanded each decade from the turn of the century until the present. Intermarriage increased as in-migration increased, and in-migration increased as tourism grew in numbers and scope. As the city expanded and new middle-class barrios incorporated migrants and Xueta and non-Xueta Mallorcans, the old distinctions were diluted and being Xueta diminished in importance in the new environment. In the sixties and seventies the Xueta community persists on the Street of the Silver Shops, but only a minority of the Xueta population lives there. The street remains a symbol of Xueta distinctiveness, but for most being Xueta in the modern era is an ethnic identity. The Xuetas are vividly aware of their Jewish provenance and continue to retain a conception of self as Jews by both morphological and cultural criteria. They are also empathetic to the problems of Jews on a world-wide scale. However, the Xuetas of Mallorca as a group are passionately bound to the island culture, and being Mallorcan and Spanish comprehends a Roman Catholic commitment. Every current trend indicates an assimilation of the Xuetas in the years to come, and it is conceivable that the label Xueta will in the future mean little in Mallorcan society. It is also possible that this will not happen, for the process of assimilation is directly linked to continued growth and expansion and this could slow down at any time. Whatever the future, all that we have said and discussed is at this moment of the utmost relevance to living Mallorcans who daily walk the streets where the events of their history transpired.

# Postscript

A return visit to Mallorca in the summer of 1976 provided significant
new data on themes developed in this volume. Thus, a short ad-
dendum to the book in press seemed in order. The current crisis of
Mallorcan life is a touristic recession which creates problems for all,
from prosperous investor to unemployed kitchen helper. For the
Jews of Mallorca the organization of an orthodox synagogue has
given a new focus to Jewish life, even for those who are not members.
The most significant development, however, is the spirit of reasoned
moderation and idealism that has characterized the Spanish people's
response to the death of Franco and the ensuing problems of national
reorganization. Considering these and attendant changes, it appears
that the early seventies have introduced Mallorca to a new era of
change.

It seems that the touristic recession of the seventies had to happen;
if not this year then sometime soon. The growth rates of industrial
tourism over the two prior decades could not have continued un-
interrupted. There were too many obstacles to continuous growth,
the most basic being that industrial tourism tends to impair the
attractions of natural beauty and rural culture that bring tourists in
the first place. Beyond that, tourism is intrinsically a very fragile
enterprise, sensitive to minor economic fluctuations, technological
changes (particularly in transportation), and even fad and fashion.
All of these have affected Mallorca: a worldwide recession, devalua-
tion of sterling, new and competitive tourist facilities in distant
places, and the fad news in Europe in the summer of 1976 that
Greece was the "in place to visit this year."

Interestingly, the Mallorcan touristic recession does not constitute a serious fall-off in numbers of tourists or revenues, but only a leveling off. The current crisis reveals how much the economy has been tied to continuous growth. Building plans have been cut back, and construction, a major industry, is depressed. Unemployment in construction has created a labor surplus which has resulted in widespread unemployment in diverse sectors of the economy. Most established tourist enterprises are surviving without losses. A very few are making profits and some are struggling to survive. Scattered empty buildings and stores in the tourist sector are evidence of the failure of marginal enterprises. In spite of this, the prognosis is optimistic with almost everyone expecting an upturn in the not-too-distant future.

We have suggested that Xueta exogamy and assimilation is correlated to growth and change linked to an expanding industrial tourism. This continues to be 'our hypothesis based on data of the past. It can be measured objectively by, for example, the marriage records of the seventies. However, equally important is the subjective evaluation of trends such as those which move the society toward statism and bureaucratic and bourgeois values or, to the contrary, encourage the conservation of familiar and traditional local values. Most Mallorcans in the mid-seventies are of the impression that not only has the growth of industrial tourism been attenuated, but regional conservatism has been given great impetus by the resultant economic problems and by recent political developments as well.

The Mallorcan synagogue which we anticipated in the final chapter has now been formally organized and lists 100 permanent members. Though it lacks a rabbi, a supervisor of kashruth leads the community and assumes many rabbinic functions. The new synagogue provides Hebrew lessons for the young, kosher meat from animals killed by the kashruth supervisor, and kosher wine made from Mallorcan grapes. The group has also purchased land for a Jewish cemetery. The synagogue and kosher kitchen are located in a designated wing of a seaside hotel.

What is most significant about the synagogue is not its tradition of strict orthodoxy but the cultural background of its membership. It is made up entirely of Jews from the northern and eastern European Yiddish-speaking tradition. It is, in short, an Ashkenazi institution located in the tourist sector, and is to be distinguished from the Sephardic or Spanish-speaking tradition which is the background of the centuries-old Mallorcan community. These cultural distinctions are of the utmost importance as regards the possibility of ties to native Mallorcans with Jewish background or interests.

It is not surprising that members of the new orthodox community are interested in the Xueta tradition of Mallorca. The supervisor of kashruth (or sub-rabbi) has announced to the press that he is looking for Xuetas who practice Jewish rituals. He states that so far he has found not one. Although the inquiry has provoked particular Xuetas, overall the reception by Mallorcans to the synagogue has ranged from good to excellent. One gets the impression that contemporary Mallorcans are particularly proud to have a synagogue as part of their religious and cultural diversity.

The problems that the orthodox community encounters are primarily with individual Xueta Mallorcans. Some say that the sub-rabbi's researches are a cover for proselytizing. At least one Xueta has already converted and shortly thereafter made derogatory statements in the press, charging the sub-rabbi with denying Mallorcans a vote in the synagogue and, in her case, refusing permission for the burial of her father in the Jewish cemetery, even though she had contributed to the purchase of the land. The Xueta response to the publicized conversion and to the convert's charges against the synagogue is that each step must be viewed as idiosyncratic behavior and not as reflective of a Xueta *pattern* of conversion or hostility. Though this may be true, the conflict between the individuals involved stem in large part from cultural barriers that impede interactions. The barrier between Xuetas and the orthodox community derive not only from the Ashkenazi-Sephardic distinction but more immediately from the insider-outsider distinction that exists between natives and foreign residents. It is generally believed that Xuetas are unlikely to join the synagogue in significant numbers for the same reasons Mallorcans in general have never been attracted to the Anglican church, i.e., cultural boundaries. Or as many Xuetas have observed, the synagogue might just as well attract non-Xuetas. "It is very popular to be Jewish these days." As one Xueta informant commented, there is one tie that binds Xuetas to the Jews of the world and that is the opportunity Israel provides for refuge should the Xuetas ever face persecution again.

Finally, the post-Franco era has produced a new spirit and a new outlook on the island of Mallorca. Palma in 1976 is the site of street demonstrations, political meetings, occasional strikes and a questioning press. Forty years of fascism ends with few fascists left to defend the cause. Among college students anarchism and socialism are the more appealing doctrines, but the political ideals which bind together the largest number of Mallorcans are those of democratic reform and the rights of regions. With respect to the latter, Mallorcans more than ever are asserting their right to use their dialect of Catalan in business, art, journalism, and in everyday conversation as a boundary maintenance mechanism separating themselves from mainlanders and Europeans. The granting of linguistic rights to regions was one of the first reforms of the new king, Juan Carlos I, and the Catalan-speaking region responded immediately with a Catalan daily, AVUI. In addition, Spanish-language Mallorcan dailies now devote one or two pages to news in Mallorquin.

Though the emotional response of Mallorcans to the post-Franco era has been a new independence in thought and action, such that they are even now accused of unfriendliness to non-Mallorcans, they like other Spaniards are facing the problems of national reorganization with the utmost seriousness and restraint. They look to Europe and the U.S.A. for models on which to build the new Spanish democracy, evaluating the judicial, executive and legislative institutions of England and the U.S.A., in particular, for their pertinence to Spanish problems and character. The new governmental order will surely be distinctively Spanish, but in their caution Spaniards are looking carefully at tried and tested institutions operative in other lands.

With regard to the focus of this volume, Jews in Mallorca, the transition to social democracy is of little direct consequence apart from new overall appreciation for cultural pluralism and the rights of minorities. Though many foreigners have believed, and with good reason, that the government of a former ally of Hitler and Mussolini must surely have been suppressive to the Jewish minority, this has not, as we have stated earlier, been the case in Spain. Constructive relations with a Jewish minority were instituted early in this century and have been maintained through a monarchy, a dictatorship, a republic, a dictatorship and will continue in a liberal and democratic monarchy. The Spanish nation's rejection of anti-Semitism is too deeply rooted to be modified by the short-range decisions of successive governments. As regards Mallorca, the formation of a synagogue there is in no way tied to democratic reforms. The synagogue was anticipated by myself and others seven and eight years before the death of Franco and its development was seen in the context of the then existing political order. Likewise, the change in government will have little direct effect on the Xuetas.

Trends apparent in Mallorca in the seventies reveal an economic leveling off, a new cultural conservatism tied to political liberalism, increasing cultural diversity and caution in governmental reform. The first phase of industrial tourism has passed and overall the trends of the mid-seventies do not provide a context that is as encouraging to assimilation as were the first years of the decade and the sixties. One would therefore expect Xueta ethnic identity to continue as a fundamental and important element in the Mallorcan social order, at least for the foreseeable future.

# Works Cited

Anonymous. 1946. *Inquisición de Mallorca: Reconciliados y Relajados, 1488–1691*. Barcelona.

Barcelo Pons, Bartolomé. 1961. La Vida Económica de Mallorca en el Siglo XIX. *Un Segle de Vida Catalana*. Barcelona: Alcides.

Barcelo Pons, Bartomeu. 1964. *El Segle XIX a Mallorca*. Ciutat de Mallorca: Obra Cultural Balear.

Barcelo, Bartolomé. Realidad y Mito de la Albufera. *Boletín de la Camara de Comercio*, no. 648: 189–197.

Barcelo, Bartomeu. 1968. *Les Illes Balears*. Barcelona: Editorial Taber.

Baron, Salo W., and Blau, Joseph L. 1954. *Judaism, Post Biblical and Talmudic Period*. New York: The Liberal Arts Press.

Bisson, Jean. 1969. Origen y Decadencia de la Gran Propiedad en Mallorca. *Boletín de la Camara de Comercio*, no. 665: 71–76.

Blasco Ibañez, Vicente. 1919. *Los Muertos Mandan*. Valencia.

Borras Rexach, Cristobal. 1966. *Breve Historia de la Ciudad de Palma*. Palma de Mallorca: Editorial Tous.

Braunstein, Baruch. 1936. *The Chuetas of Majorca*. New York: Columbia University Oriental Studies.

Crow, John A. 1963. *Spain: The Root and the Flower*. New York: Harper & Row.

Donoghue, John D. 1957. Eta Community in Japan, the social persistence of outcast groups. *American Anthropologist* 59: 1000–1017.

Emery, Richard W. 1959. *The Jews of Perpignan in the Thirteenth Century*. New York: Columbia University Press.

Epstein, Isidore. 1959. *Judaism, A Historical Presentation*. London: Wyman and Sons.

211

Fabregas y Cuxart, Luis. 1965. *Ca-Nostra: Cinquenta Años de Vida Palmesana*. Palma de Mallorca: Ediciones Cort.

Flannery, Edward H. 1965. *The Anguish of the Jews*. New York: Macmillan.

Forteza, Miguel. 1966. *Els Descendents dels Jueus Conversos de Mallorca*. Palma de Mallorca: Gráficas Miramar.

Garau, Francisco. 1931, 1691. *La Fe Triunfante*. Palma de Mallorca: Editorial Tous.

Goitein, S. D. 1971. *A Mediterranean Society*. Berkeley: University of California Press.

Grasset de Saint Sauveur, André. 1952, 1808. *Viaje a las Islas Baleares y Pythiusas*. Palma de Mallorca: Ediciones R.O.D.A.

Graves, Robert. 1958. *STEPS*. London: Cassell.

Infante, D. Eduardo. 1866. *Jorge Aguiló o Misterios de Palma*. Palma de Mallorca.

Innis, Harold Adams. 1950. *Empire and Communication*. Oxford: Clarendon Press.

Isaacs, Lionel. 1936. *The Jews of Mallorca*. London.

Kamen, Henry. 1965. *The Spanish Inquisition*. New York: New American Library.

La Souchere, Elena de. 1964. *An Explanation of Spain*. New York: Vintage Books.

Lewin, Dr. 1883. Die Neuchristen auf der Insel Mallorca. *Judisches Litteratur-Blatt*, Jahrg. XIII, no. 27. Magdeburg.

Mannheim, Karl. 1936. *Ideology and Utopia*. New York: Harcourt & Brace.

Melia, Josep. 1967. *Els Mallorquins*. Palma de Mallorca: Editorial Daedalus.

Moore, Kenneth. 1969. Tourism, a Special Kind of Modernization. Paper delivered at the annual meeting of the American Anthropological Association.

Moore, Kenneth. 1970. Modernization in a Canary Island Village: An Indicator of Social Change in Spain. *Journal of the Steward Anthropological Society*, vol. 2, no. 1:19–34.

Moore, Kenneth. 1975. The City as Context: Context as Process. *Urban Anthropology* 4: 17–25.

Neumann, Abraham A. 1948. *The Jews in Spain*. Philadelphia: The Jewish Publication Society of America.

Park, Robert. 1928. Human Migration and the Marginal Man. *American Journal of Sociology,* vol, 23.

Pascual y González. 1956. *Derecho Foral de Baleares.* Palma de Mallorca: Mossen Alcover.

Perdigo, Manuel. 1945. *Judíos De Mallorca (Informe Del Año 1773).* Barcelona: Imprenta Tobella.

Piferrer, P., and Quadrado, José María. 1968, 1888. *Islas Baleares.* Palma de Mallorca: Mossen Alcover.

Pons, Antonio. 1968. *Historia de Mallorca.* Palma de Mallorca: Gráficas Miramar.

Pons, Antonio, 1957, 1960. *Los Judíos de Mallorca durante los Siglos XIII y XIV.*

Pou Muntaner, Juan. 1970. *La Marina en Mallorca.* Palma de Mallorca: Editorial Tous.

Quadrado, José María. 1939, 1895. *Forenses y Ciudadanos.* Palma de Mallorca: Editorial Tous.

Quadrado, José María. 1967, 1887. *La Judería en Mallorca.* Palma de Mallorca: Mossen Alcover.

Quetlas Gaya, Bartolomé. 1957. *Cofradías Gremiales en Mallorca.* Palma de Mallorca: Mossen Alcover.

Redfield, Robert, and Singer, Milton. 1957. The Cultural Role of Cities. *Economic Development and Cultural Change,* vol. 3. Chicago: University of Chicago Press.

Roth, Cecil. 1959. *A History of the Marranos.* New York: Meridian Books.

Rusiñol, Santiago. 1958, 1905. *The Island of Calm.* Barcelona: Pulide.

Salvador, El Archiduque Luis. 1965, 1880. *Las Baleares.* Vols. 1–12. Palma de Mallorca: Mossen Alcover.

Sand, George, 1956, 1855. *Winter in Mallorca.* Mallorca: Valdemosa Edition.

Santa María, Álvaro. 1956. Los Conversos en el Siglo XV. *Boletíin de la Sociedad Arqueológica Lluliana.*

Schneider, Peter; Schneider, Jane; and Hansen, Edward. 1972. Modernization and Development: The Role of Regional Elites and Non-Corporate Groups in the European Mediterranean. *Comparative Studies in Society and History,* vol. 14, no. 3

Sevillano Colom, Francisco. 1968. De Venecia a Flandes (via Mallorca y Portugal, Siglo XIV). *Boletín de la Sociedad Arqueológica Lluliana.*

Steward, Julian. 1955. Levels of Sociocultural Integration. In *Theory of Culture Change*. Urbana: University of Illinois Press.

Taronji y Cortés, José. 1967, 1877. *Una Mala Causa a Todo Trance Defendida*. Palma de Mallorca: Gráficas Miramar.

Torroba de Quiros, Felipe. 1967. *Los Judíos Españoles*. Madrid: Rivadeneyera.

Wallace, Anthony. 1956. Revitalization Movements. *American Anthropologist*. 58: 264–281.

Weber, Max. 1952, 1917. *Ancient Judaism*. New York: The Free Press.

Weber, Max. 1963. *The Sociology of Religion*. Boston: Beacon Press.

Weisberg, David B. 1967. *Guild Structure and Political Allegiance in Achaemenid Mesopotamia*. New Haven: Yale University Press.

Xamena Fiol, Pedro. 1965. *Resumen de la Historia de Mallorca*. Mallorca: Felanitx.

# Index

# LA CIVTAT DE MALLO

*MAIORICA CIVITAS olim Palma, amæ-*
*nitate soli, aeris salubritate, frugum omnigenarum*
*copia felix Ædificiorum vero pulchritudine speciosa.*
*Moenium, et Propugnaculorum situ, et circumualla-*
*tione trium milliarium Italicorum cum semisse mu-*
*nitissima, Maioricæ Insulæ, atq adeo totius Bale-*
*arici Regni caput, habens Episcopalem sedem, Re-*
*gium Senatum: cui Prorex, pro Chatolico Hispa-*
*niarum Monarcha præ est. Sita est in principio quin-*
*ti Climatis sub eleuatione Poli, partium 39. minut 36.*
*et longitudine part. 25. minut. 2. A meridie altuinæ*
*mari sida nauigiorum statione celebri. Ab Antonio*
*GARAV Presbytero, et Mathematico accuratissi-*
*me delineata, nunc primum lucem videt. ANNO*
*Domini. 1 6 4 4*

Porta de Iti

Porta de S
    atina

DATE DUE

Destres de Mallor
10  20  30  40  50  60

Dimidium Pedis Ita

100          200          30

Passus Italici ex Quinque